The Complete and Essential
Jack the Ripper

Paul Begg and John Bennett are researchers and authors, widely recognized as authorities on Jack the Ripper. Paul Begg's books include *Jack the Ripper: The Facts*, *Jack the Ripper: The Definitive History*, and he is a co-author of *The Jack the Ripper A-Z*.

John Bennett has written numerous articles and lectured frequently on Jack the Ripper and the East End of London. He has acted as adviser to and participated in documentaries made by television channels worldwide and was the co-writer for the successful Channel 5 programme *Jack the Ripper: The Definitive Story*. He is author of *E1: A Journey Through Whitechapel and Spitalfields* and co-author of *Jack the Ripper: CSI Whitechapel*.

The Complete and Essential Jack the Ripper

PAUL BEGG
AND JOHN BENNETT

PENGUIN BOOKS

PENGUIN BOOKS

Published by the Penguin Group
Penguin Books Ltd, 80 Strand, London WC2R ORL, England
Penguin Group (USA) Inc., 375 Hudson Street, New York, New York 10014, USA
Penguin Group (Canada), 90 Eglinton Avenue East, Suite 700, Toronto, Ontario, Canada M4P 2Y3
(a division of Pearson Penguin Canada Inc.)
Penguin Ireland, 25 St Stephen's Green, Dublin 2, Ireland (a division of Penguin Books Ltd)
Penguin Group (Australia), 707 Collins Street, Melbourne, Victoria 3008, Australia
(a division of Pearson Australia Group Pty Ltd)
Penguin Books India Pvt Ltd, 11 Community Centre, Panchsheel Park, New Delhi – 110 017, India
Penguin Group (NZ), 67 Apollo Drive, Rosedale, Auckland 0632, New Zealand
(a division of Pearson New Zealand Ltd)
Penguin Books (South Africa) (Pty) Ltd, Block D, Rosebank Office Park,
181 Jan Smuts Avenue, Parktown North, Gauteng 2193, South Africa

Penguin Books Ltd, Registered Offices: 80 Strand, London WC2R ORL, England

www.penguin.com

First published 2013
003

Copyright © Paul Begg and John Bennett, 2013
All rights reserved

The moral right of the authors has been asserted

All photographs copyright © the Evans Skinner Crime Archive

Set in 11/13pt Dante MT Std
Typeset by Jouve (UK), Milton Keynes
Printed in Great Britain by Clays Ltd, St Ives plc

ISBN: 978-0-718-17824-6

www.greenpenguin.co.uk

For
Elwyn Thomas,
who has helped in so many ways.
And for
Judy, Siobhan and Cameron
and
Laura.

Contents

Contents

Introduction

London, 25 September 1888

The red ink flows freely and elegantly across the fresh sheet of paper as the writer trembles slightly in anticipation of the deed about to be committed. On the edge of the desk sit several well-thumbed newspapers, their tightly packed columns filled with descriptions of the terrible murders in the East End of London that have held that most maligned of districts in a state of fear since the summer. Grinning mischievously, the writer puts himself into the mind of the murderer, recalling the events of the previous few weeks with relish and reinterpreting them in the first person. With one eye on the stalled police efforts to apprehend the killer of several Whitechapel prostitutes, he takes a mocking tone and laughs at their apparent inadequacies. Turning to the unfortunate victims, the writer declares a hatred of 'whores' and, relishing the growing aggression of his penmanship, delights in the skill with which the previous victim was dispatched. There will be more to come. The spirit is willing, the knife is 'nice and sharp'.

With an overtaking sense of theatricality, the writer shifts a gear and explains the red ink, employed to replace the clotted blood of the last victim, which had been saved in a ginger beer bottle. The next victim will have her ears cut off and sent to the police, just for a laugh, you understand. Should the opportunity arise. Sensing an arrogance and 'daring-do' possessed by the murderer, the writer wishes the poor, confused police officers 'good luck', but, as if to prove that the miscreant is still one of us, he signs off politely and formally, giving the pretend author a name – 'yours truly, Jack the Ripper'.

A quick afterword in pencil, and the job is done. Folded twice, the letter is slipped into a small envelope addressed to 'The Boss, Central News Office, London City'. The following day the letter will be taken to a post office, where an unwitting staff member will furnish it with a one-penny stamp and send it on its way. Having completed this little piece of fun, the letter-writer will live out the rest of his life slowly realizing that he has created one of the most notorious names of all time. Long after his death, that name will outgrow the murders which inspired it to become legend.

In all probability we will never be certain who wrote the famous 'Dear Boss' letter which created the name 'Jack the Ripper'. But this small, unremarkable-looking missive, now hidden from the world in a plastic file at the National Archives in Kew, south London, is perhaps one of the most noteworthy elements of a murder case which has many facets. It replaced the murderer's original appellation, 'Leather Apron', with something infinitely more durable, persisting into the twenty-first century as the retold story of the Whitechapel murders and the ideas behind the culprit's identity orbited around it. It would become a brand name for fear, a trademark for an unknown killer whose horrific crimes still grimly resonate over 100 years later. The murders were shocking enough in their own time and inspired great outrage; however it could be argued that the notoriety of Jack the Ripper, and thus his longevity in the scheme of things, was a result of the creation of that name.

Millions of words have been written and spoken about the Whitechapel murders, in print, online, in film and on television.

The quest to determine the killer's identity, despite taking on different methodologies over the years, is still a popular project for armchair detectives, true-crime enthusiasts and historians and shows no sign of abating. Every night, hundreds of people walk the streets of the East End to hear the chilling story and see for themselves the places fixed into history by the Ripper's knife. These uniquely chilling crimes have seared themselves into the public consciousness the world over.

In what some may deem as 'yet *another* book about Jack the Ripper' we have endeavoured to explore as many facets of the Whitechapel murders as we can. To do so, this book has taken on a tripartite structure. Part 1 deals exclusively with the crimes themselves, from the confusing events surrounding the death of Emma Smith in April 1888 to the demise of Frances Coles in February 1891; the backgrounds of the victims are detailed and the last hours of their sad lives are recounted against a backdrop of the social conditions of the East End of London, which helped lead these women to their fates; we follow the reactions of the public and the police investigation in all their histrionic highs and worrying lows, as well as the press interest, which helped and hindered in equal measure.

Part 2 is reserved for theories surrounding the murderer's identity, and here we have chosen to reflect on the methods and reasoning that led to certain individuals being named as the Ripper, starting from the autumn of 1888 itself, right up to the time of writing. In doing so, we have come up to date, analysing the effect of modern investigative techniques and the power of the internet, the latter having probably the most significant influence on Ripper studies of all.

Finally, in Part 3, we have chosen to look upon the mythology of Jack the Ripper: how an icon was created, how the media (most notably the movies) have shaped that iconography, and how public opinion has swung between fascination and abhorrence. We have also, perhaps for the first time in a book of this kind, acknowledged the phenomenon of the guided walks and how they have become the most tangible demonstration of the power of the Ripper legend today.

The Jack the Ripper mystery is a colossal subject, and a totally exhaustive overview of the case would need a publication comparable in size with the *Encyclopaedia Britannica* to contain it. We have sought to give as complete an overview of the essential facts as we know them today and the mythologies that surround them, no mean task when considering that it must all fit into one volume. To that effect we must thank the following individuals: our agent Robert Smith and our editor Daniel Bunyard for their unending support and patience; Judy and Siobhan Begg (and Cameron); Laura Prieto; Alfred and Brenda Bennett; Stewart Evans and Keith Skinner (Evans Skinner Crime Archive); Neal Shelden; Stephen Ryder's *Casebook: Jack the Ripper* and Howard Brown's *JTRForums*; Richard and Joanne Jones at Discovery Tours; Lindsay Siviter; *Ripperologist* magazine; Whitechapel Society 1888; National Archives, London Metropolitan Archives, Bishopsgate Institute and Tower Hamlets Library and Archives; special mention must go to Adam Wood for his support and help over and above the call of duty; Neil Bell; Debra Arif; Chris Scott; Rob Clack; Eduardo Zinna; and Robin Odell. Naturally, there are many others – too numerous to mention – who might not be aware of their influence. Their names may not be here, but their input is very much understood and appreciated.

Paul Begg and John Bennett, 2013

PART ONE

The Whitechapel Murders

I.

'Wilful murder against some person unknown'

The Easter bank holiday weekend of 1888 would turn out to be one which Margaret Hayes, a fifty-four-year-old resident of a common lodging house at 18 George Street, Spitalfields, would perhaps prefer to forget, for it did not end well. No doubt she would have spent much of that day carousing in the East End pubs and generally getting into the spirit of what, for many people, would have been a well-earned respite from the daily toil. Although it has never really been determined, Hayes was in all likelihood a prostitute, one of over a thousand[1] such women who plied their trade on the streets of Whitechapel and neighbouring districts at that time in an attempt to earn money for food and lodgings. The fact that the holiday would have attracted many revellers to the local hostelries meant that a woman disposed to this lifestyle could expect to make something from it. That night found Hayes in Poplar, a quarter of the East End close to the London docks, which she described as a 'fearfully rough' neighbourhood.

On nights such as this, the people of the East End were not unused to allowing their bank holiday Monday to drift effortlessly into the early hours of the following day, and as Tuesday 3 April began, Margaret Hayes was to get a sudden reminder of the unpredictability of Poplar when she was approached by a pair of young men; one asked her for the time, and then, for reasons unknown, his companion punched Hayes in the mouth, at which point both men ran off.[2] Hayes later admitted to having been badly beaten just before Christmas the previous year, an assault that had resulted in time at the infirmary,[3] and perhaps with that also in mind and no doubt shaken, she appeared to cut her losses, call it a night and make her way on foot back to the George Street lodging house a little over two miles away.

It was as she passed the corner of Burdett Road and Farrance Street that she caught sight of a fellow George Street lodger, Emma Smith, who was talking to a man. Hayes satisfied herself that this individual – who was wearing dark clothes and a white neckerchief – was not one of those who had attacked her a little while earlier and hurried on her way. The time was 12.15 a.m.

Emma Smith was a typical 'unfortunate' of the East End. As 1888 would progress, the public, courtesy of the press, would hear many more stories like hers as the issue of poverty and the problems it generated in the east London slums were brought into sharp focus by the shocking events that quickly followed that Easter bank holiday. Admittedly, what is known about her is scarce and basically comes from a police report made at the time,[4] but it does allow us to build a perhaps vague, yet not wholly unexpected, picture of her.

Emma Elizabeth Smith was apparently forty-five years of age, about 5 feet 2 inches in height with fair hair and a small scar on her temple. She was apparently 'from the country', and one would imagine that, for some time at least, hers was a respectable, maybe ordinary life. She claimed to have been married and subsequently widowed, although some reports said that she and her husband had separated and that he was still alive.[5] Two children were also mentioned, a boy and a girl, who by 1888 were supposedly living in the Finsbury Park area of north London. As with many women in her position, there obviously came a time of crisis, and thus Emma Smith found herself in the common lodging houses of Spitalfields. By 1888 she had apparently not seen any of her friends for ten years.

The lodging house or 'doss house' at 18 George Street was one of many in the small neighbourhood of Spitalfields which also included those in Flower and Dean Street, Thrawl Street and Fashion Street. Owned by Daniel Lewis since 1886, it was registered to accommodate around fifty lodgers, sharing a kitchen with a neighbouring premises, and it was perhaps a typical example of the houses available to those with no fixed abode of their own.[6] As a result of the transient population of these lodging houses, many had mean reputations, offering shelter on a short- or long-term basis to all manner of people. Sure, there were the journeymen traders and their professional ilk, but also the dispossessed, the chronically homeless, criminals lying low and, naturally, prostitutes. The George Street area was particularly notorious and appeared in many philanthropic articles during the preceding decades as an example of where the great metropolis of London was going wrong. An attempt in the 1870s and early '80s to begin clearance of this district with its numerous slum courts proved slow,[7] and despite the appearance of Lolesworth Buildings and Charlotte de Rothschild Dwellings on the west side of George Street, built for the respectable working classes in 1886, there were still many notorious doss houses remaining. By 1888, the area of which 18 George Street was central had become a pariah.

In the eighteen months that she had been living there, Emma Smith appears to have developed a routine, and, as the deputy of the lodging house, Mary Russell was party to much of Smith's habits and behaviour. According to Mrs Russell, she often left the house at around 6.00 or 7.00 p.m. and would return in the early hours, often drunk. It was the drink which would have appeared to elicit a transformation, for on several occasions Smith would return bruised and battered from brawling and on one occasion even claimed to have been thrown out of a window. When drunk, Mrs Russell claimed, Emma Smith behaved like a 'madwoman'.[8] And so it was on the evening of Monday 2 April, Smith took her leave of the lodging house in her usual manner and, like her fellow lodger Margaret Hayes, ended up in Poplar with its numerous drinking establishments no doubt filled with dockers, sailors and sundry other bank holiday revellers and, therefore, the chance of earning some money.

What happened after Margaret Hayes saw Emma Smith with the man in Burdett Road comes to us from Smith herself, and while the story seems consistent enough, there are a number of vagaries which still remain unresolved. She was making her way back to Spitalfields in the early hours of the Tuesday morning and had reached the western end of Whitechapel Road at about 1.30 a.m. As she passed the church of St Mary, she noticed a group of men standing in the road and, perhaps dubious as to their character, crossed the main road to avoid them and walked up Osborn Street. The men followed her, and as she reached Taylor Bros. cocoa factory at the junction of Osborn Street, Wentworth Street and Brick Lane, they set upon her.[9] What followed was a horrendous attack. They beat her violently – her face was bloodied and one of her ears was partially torn – and stole what little money she had. And, as if that wasn't bad enough, a blunt instrument was rammed into her vagina with great force before the men made their escape.

Between 4.00 and 5.00 a.m., Emma Smith reached her

lodging house in George Street in an obvious state of distress and in great pain. Among the lodgers present were Annie Lee and Mary Russell, who, on being told by Smith what had happened, decided to take her to the London Hospital, about half a mile away. Apart from mentioning that one of the assailants was a young man of about nineteen years, Smith did not describe the attackers to her companions and seemed reluctant to go to the hospital. Nonetheless she agreed, and as the three passed the spot where the assault had taken place, by the cocoa factory opposite 10 Brick Lane, Smith pointed it out.

On arrival at the hospital Russell and Lee left Smith in the capable hands of the house surgeon, Dr George Haslip. While in his care, Emma Smith went into a little more detail about her attack, furnishing him with much of the detail we still rely on today, and eventually he discovered that the blunt object that had been thrust into her had ruptured the perineum. As time passed, Smith began to sink and fell into a coma; at about 9.00 on the morning of Wednesday 4 April, she passed away from the effects of peritonitis. What had started as a brutal and unprovoked attack had become murder.

Dr Wynne Baxter, the coroner for East Middlesex, presided over a brief inquest at the hospital on Saturday 7 April. From what little information we have – essentially from newspaper reports – those in attendance were Mary Russell, Dr Haslip (sometimes referred to as 'Hellier'), Margaret Hayes and Chief Inspector John West, who was representing the Metropolitan Police's H- (Whitechapel) division. In fact, the first the police had heard of this incident was the day before the inquest, when the coroner's office informed them in the standard manner. What is peculiar about the attack is that apparently no constables who would have been in the immediate neighbourhood that morning had heard anything about the assault; nor had they seen any behaviour relating to it, and, unfortunately, none of the inquest witnesses had felt compelled to inform them of the incident when it happened. By all accounts, the streets appeared to be rather quiet at the time. The jury were advised to make a quick decision, as the fact that murder had obviously been committed and the cause of death had been ascertained without doubt, and so, after a brief deliberation, the verdict of 'wilful murder against some person or persons unknown' was given. Coroner Baxter advised that all facts surrounding the case be sent on to the Public Prosecutor, and Inspector Edmund Reid of H-division was given charge of the resulting enquiry. And that is where, owing to the scarcity of official reports, the case of Emma Smith's murder ends.

The mystery of how nobody – particularly police officers on the beat – saw or heard anything of the assault remains, for the unresolved question of what happened to Smith immediately after the attack lingers too. If she was assaulted a little after 1.30 a.m. then a period of anything up to three hours must have passed before she arrived at 18 George Street, which was little more than 200 yards away. Of course, there is a possibility that she was incorrect about the timing of the attack, although the fact that she said she had passed St Mary's Church at 1.30 a.m. could suggest she had got the time from the church clock. Had she been lying in the street unconscious or at the least in great pain and distress for that amount of time, surely somebody would have seen her. The streets might have been described as 'quiet', but in the aftermath of a bank holiday Monday, with the scene of crime being so close to a well-used thoroughfare like Brick Lane, surely they could not have been entirely deserted. Linked to this is Emma Smith's reluctance or inability to describe her attackers in any great detail. There may be reasonable explanations for this – she might not have had a good look at them under the traumatic circumstances, or she might not have been able to recall small details on account of shock and pain from the injuries. But there is also the possibility that, whereas an assault most definitely took place, it might well have been under different circumstances. Was Emma Smith attacked by a gang as she claims, or was it a single assailant? Was robbery the motive (as it appears) or was it the work of a dangerously violent client? There is even the possibility that she had a pimp who turned nasty, inflicting what might have been unintentionally fatal injuries as a warning. We cannot rule out the fact that Emma Smith might have been telling the truth (and why wouldn't she?), but the strange circumstances of her death leave matters open to speculation. Obfuscation, intentional or otherwise, on Smith's part and the dearth of official reports by investigators leave us in the dark.

Emma Elizabeth Smith was buried in a pauper's grave at the City of London Cemetery (Little Ilford) on 12 April 1888. For all we know, this unfortunate woman's funeral might have been attended by very few people; perhaps her lodging house friends were there; maybe the two children made an appearance; maybe nobody came at all. In the aftermath of what transpired to be a shocking attack even by the rough and tough standards of the East End, the culprits were never apprehended, the act itself no doubt becoming a terrible 'one-off' to the residents of Whitechapel and the few newspapers that gave the incident column inches. With the general acceptance that Emma Smith's death was the result of a gang attack, one newspaper felt compelled to make comment:

> The state of our London streets at night is an old subject and a sore one. It cannot be said that at any time within memory of living man their condition has been particularly creditable to

the greatest capital in the world. Still, there certainly was a time, and that not very long ago, when things were very much less disgraceful than they are now. The seamy side of London life which is revealed to anybody whose homeward way lies through Regent-street or Piccadilly at midnight is positively shameful. Cases (one in particular our readers will remember which is not yet decided) are continually arising of riot and assault by women as well as men; and the police are powerless to prevent solicitation and annoyance.[10]

Nobody could foresee that within a few months more brutal crimes would shock the sensibilities not just of those immediately affected, but also of the nation and ultimately the world. The death of Emma Smith would soon be seen as the beginning of the world's most infamous series of killings: the Whitechapel murders.

In June or July of 1888, Martha Tabram, a sometime flower hawker and prostitute, began staying at Satchell's lodging house at 19 George Street, immediately next door to Emma Smith's former residence. John Satchell had been the owner of the three-storey tenement for nearly twenty years and owned numerous other doss houses in the immediate vicinity. Martha Tabram would have been one of anything up to fifty or more lodgers who would be spending that summer in the cramped house, paying fourpence a night for a single bed and using a communal kitchen on the ground floor shared with no. 18.[11] The series of life events which culminated in her arrival in the East End has been well documented.

Martha White was born at 17 Marshall Street, Southwark, on 10 May 1849, the youngest of five children, two boys and three girls, born to Charles White and his wife Elisabeth. Charles and Elisabeth's marriage was not to last, and for reasons unknown they separated in 1865, whereupon Charles took lodgings in the Pitt Street home of Rebecca Glover. He was not in good health at this time; unable to work because of a weak back, he complained of diarrhoea, bad circulation and cold as well as admitting that the family situation troubled him. In October of that year, Elisabeth visited him for the first time since the separation and by November was seeing him regularly. Such visits perhaps cheered him, and he was in a good frame of mind on 15 November, when his estranged wife and daughter Mary Ann had supper at his lodgings. A little later, he made ready for bed and, while undressing, collapsed and died.[12]

On Christmas Day 1869, at Trinity Church in Newington, Martha married Henry Tabram, a furniture packer, and soon after set up home in Marshall Street, close by the White family home. The marriage produced two sons, Frederick John in 1871 and Charles Henry, born in December the following year, but the marriage was to soon feel the strain of Martha's heavy drinking, and the couple separated in 1875.[13] For the first three years of their estrangement, Henry gave Martha an allowance of twelve shillings per week, but felt compelled to reduce it to two shillings and sixpence after she began pestering him for money on the streets. Martha took out a warrant against him; perhaps exasperated by her behaviour, he cut off all financial support in 1878, when he discovered she was living with a man.[14]

The man in question was probably William Turner, a carpenter of slovenly appearance who would go on to live with Martha on and off for the remainder of her life. The unstable nature of their relationship was usually down to her drinking, and it was not unusual for her to go out at night, returning at all hours (or not at all) on a fairly regular basis, blaming fits and subsequent arrests for her lateness. Turner claimed to have seen these fits, which invariably happened when she was drunk.[15] In fact he would later underline her lack of sobriety when he confessed: 'Since she has been living with me, her character for sobriety was not good. If I give her money she generally spent it in drink.'[16]

In 1881, Martha Tabram was recorded as being an inmate at the Whitechapel workhouse infirmary in Thomas Street, where she was registered as a flower hawker,[17] and it was this trade, selling trinkets and menthol cones among other things, which she shared with Turner when he was out of regular work. Eventually, they took up lodgings at 4 Star Place, Commercial Road, the home of Mary Bousfield, who described Martha as somebody who would 'rather have a glass of ale than a cup of tea' but observed that she was not a perpetual drunkard.[18] The situation came to an end in the early summer of 1888, when the couple separated, Turner taking up residence in the Victoria Working Men's Home in Commercial Street. Martha left Star Place without informing Mrs Bousfield, owing two weeks' rent money, but her conscience must have played on her mind as, a while later, she returned secretly one night to drop off her door key.[19] It was around this time that Martha must have taken lodgings at Satchell's lodging house in Spitalfields. The last time Turner saw her was on Saturday 4 August in Leadenhall Street, when he gave her some money to buy trinkets to trade.[20]

The following Monday, 6 August, was a bank holiday. Perhaps in keeping with the cliché of English bank holidays, the weather was not spectacular, rather cool for the time of year (20 degrees centigrade) with occasional light rain. Regardless, it evidently failed to prevent the populace from getting out and about – thousands apparently flocked to venues such as the

Crystal Palace and Alexandra Palace as well as the museums of South Kensington and Madame Tussaud's. The Zoological Gardens at Regent's Park were well patronized, as were the Tower of London and, further afield, Windsor Castle. And as those places closed, the people of London would descend on the theatres and music halls and, of course, the pubs.[21]

It is to that latter option that Martha Tabram was drawn; it is not clear how she spent the best part of her day, but as the evening drew near she went out drinking, and most of what we know about that night comes from the testimony of her companion, Mary Ann Connelly. Unmarried and aged about fifty, Connelly was a prostitute going by the nickname of 'Pearly Poll', a big woman, deep-voiced and with a face reddened by drink[22]. She was at that time a resident of Crossingham's lodging house at 35 Dorset Street, Spitalfields, and had known Martha Tabram for about four or five months, though by the name of 'Emma'.[23] According to Connelly, she and Martha had met two soldiers – a private and a corporal – at about 10.00 p.m. and proceeded to trawl the pubs of Whitechapel with them. The only other sighting of Martha was made by her sister-in-law, Ann Morris, who believed she saw her alone and sober, going into the White Swan pub at 20 Whitechapel High Street at about 11.00 p.m.[24] The absence of Mary Ann Connelly and the two soldiers in this sighting is troublesome, and, assuming that Mrs Morris was not mistaken in her identification (and as she was her sister-in-law this is unlikely), the timing may have been incorrect, or it might have just been a brief sighting when Martha's three companions had been out of sight or already in the pub. The last time Martha was seen alive was at 11.45 p.m., when, on Whitechapel High Street, the group split into pairs. Connelly took the corporal into a tiny thoroughfare called Angel Alley, while Martha went into George Yard with the private.[25] Connelly soon concluded her business and, re-entering Whitechapel High Street, left the corporal at the corner of George Yard and walked off in the direction of Whitechapel, while he departed towards Aldgate.

George Yard[26]was a mean, narrow, cobbled passageway entered from the High Street via a covered arch next to the White Hart pub. Its poor reputation throughout much of the nineteenth century was sealed owing to the slum tenements and common lodging houses that lined it, and its secluded location made it an ideal escape route for criminals and a conveniently isolated venue for prostitution. Following some piecemeal slum clearance in the late 1870s,[27] two 'model dwellings' were built on the western side, essentially homes for the very poor, yet respectable, working classes. One of those, George Yard Buildings, sat at the north-west corner with Wentworth Street, a four-storey tenement of forty-seven rooms which were accessed by a communal staircase running through the centre of the building. These stairs were usually lit, but all lights were extinguished as a rule at 11.00 p.m.

It was at 1.40 on that morning of Tuesday 7 August when residents Joseph and Elizabeth Mahoney trudged up those dark stairwells to their room at no. 47, right at the top of George Yard Buildings. Like so many others, they had made a long day of the bank holiday and were now weary. They were probably hungry too, as, a mere five minutes later, Elizabeth left to go to a chandler's shop in nearby Thrawl Street to buy some supper. On all the occasions that she ascended and descended the stairs in the building she saw nothing out of the ordinary.[28]

But as the Mahoneys casually wound down their day of leisure with more domestic concerns, they appeared to be blissfully unaware of a major disturbance that was taking place nearby. At about 11.30 p.m. a commotion broke out in George Street, just across the way from where George Yard met Wentworth Street. This fracas was heard by John Reeves, a waterside labourer, and his wife Louisa, who lived at 37 George Yard Buildings and whose rooms were accessible from a top-floor balcony at the rear of the dwelling. Further disturbances kept them awake until the situation eventually calmed down after 2.00 a.m. Considering the fact that John Reeves would have to leave for work in a little over two hours' time, the couple must have been relieved.[29] At 2.00 a.m. Police Constable Thomas Barrett was patrolling Wentworth Street when he came across a soldier loitering at the corner with George Yard. Barrett described him as being a private in the Grenadier Guards, aged between twenty-two and twenty-six years, 5 feet 9 inches tall, with a fair complexion, dark hair, a small brown moustache turned up at the ends and sporting a good-conduct badge (but no medals). The soldier told Barrett that he was 'waiting for a chum who had gone with a girl'.[30]

At 3.30 a.m. Alfred Crow, a twenty-one-year-old cab driver who lived with his parents at 35 George Yard Buildings, on returning home, ascended the stone staircase. As he passed the first-floor landing, he noticed somebody lying on the ground in the poor light but, as he was accustomed to seeing the occasional person sleeping rough there, he took little notice. Once home, he went to bed and slept undisturbed until 9.30 a.m.[31] It was only when John Reeves left after his disturbed night to look for work at 4.45 a.m. that Crow's sighting took on considerable significance; Reeves found the body of Martha Tabram on that first-floor landing, lying in a pool of blood. Obviously alarmed at what he had found and without touching the body, he ran into the street looking for assistance, which soon came in the form of PC Barrett; the two men returned to the scene.[32] PC Barrett later noted that the woman's clothes 'were turned up as far as the centre of the body, leaving the lower part of the body exposed; the legs were open, and altogether her position was such as to suggest in my mind that recent intimacy had taken place'.[33] Barrett then went to fetch Dr Timothy Killeen of 68 Brick Lane, who arrived at George Yard buildings at 5.30 a.m. He pronounced life extinct, after which arrangements were made to have the body taken to the small, inadequate 'shed' off Old Montague Street which was officially the Whitechapel workhouse mortuary and was at that time the only such facility in the parish. A violent attack had obviously taken place without any residents being alerted to it; Francis Hewitt, the superintendent of George Yard Buildings, slept a mere twelve feet from where the body was found and had heard not a sound.

As the body of the woman had yet to be identified, a portrait photograph was taken. Dr Killeen conducted the required post-mortem examination, his findings revealing a uniquely horrific attack. There were a total of thirty-nine stab wounds on the body. He estimated that Martha Tabram had been dead for about three hours by the time he had arrived at the scene, putting the time of murder at approximately 2.30 a.m. He estimated that her age was about thirty-six and stated that the body was very well nourished. The left lung was penetrated in five places, and the right lung was penetrated in two places. The heart was penetrated in one place, an injury that would have been sufficient to cause death on its own. The liver was penetrated in five places, the spleen in two places, and the stomach in six places. Dr Killeen did not think all the wounds were inflicted with the same instrument, surmising that thirty-eight were from a small implement like a clasp knife or penknife, whereas the remaining one, which had penetrated the breastbone, was inflicted by a much larger and sturdier weapon, such as a dagger or even a sword bayonet. He disagreed with PC Barrett's observation that recent sexual activity had taken place and felt that all the wounds had been inflicted when Martha was still alive.[34] Interestingly, he also stated, when asked, that one of the injuries could have been made by a left-handed person.[35]

The inquest opened on Thursday 9 August at the Working Lads' Institute beside Whitechapel Underground station, presided over by Deputy Coroner George Collier. Giving evidence were witnesses Alfred Crow, John Reeves, PC Barrett and Dr Killeen, watched over by Local Inspector Edmund Reid, now heading a murder investigation on behalf of the Metropolitan Police. A woman carrying a baby attended the institute early and asserted that she knew the murdered woman and, after seeing the body in the mortuary, identified her as 'Martha Turner'.[36] Mr Collier felt that, as the circumstances of the identification appeared vague at best, despite the fact that it was as good as correct, the woman was not called to testify at the inquest, and thus the identity of the murdered woman remained, for a while at least, elusive.

That same day, Mary Ann Connelly presented herself at Commercial Street police station and furnished them with the details of her night out with Martha Tabram. By this time, PC Barrett had attended two identity parades at the Tower, consisting of a number of Grenadier guardsmen. At the first parade on 7 August he failed to pick any as the soldier he had seen on the night of the murder. The process was repeated again the following day with guardsmen who had been on leave at the time, and Barrett picked out two men. The first was allowed to go when Barrett admitted he had made a mistake, and the second, John Leary, was found to have an impeccable alibi for his movements of the night of the 7th. Now it was Mary Ann Connelly's turn – agreeing to attend a parade at the Tower on 10 August, she failed to turn up, but was found staying at her cousin's home in Fuller's Court, Drury Lane, two days later. On 13 August Connelly finally made it to the Tower but could not identify anybody. She also mentioned that the two soldiers she had been with that night had white bands on their caps, meaning that they were Coldstream Guards stationed at Wellington Barracks, and so, on 15 August, Connelly was taken there for another attempt. It failed, as she picked out two men who, under questioning, were able to give a more than satisfactory account of their movements on 7 August.[37] All further attempts to locate any potential witnesses who may have seen Martha Tabram and her companions on the night of her death ground to a frustrating halt.

The body of Martha Tabram was probably already buried by the time her estranged husband came forward to identify her for definite.[38] The second day of the inquest took place after a lengthy break on 23 August, with Henry Tabram, William Turner, Mary Bousfield, Ann Morris and Mary Ann Connelly testifying. Mr Collier, in his summing-up, said that 'the crime was one of the most brutal that had occurred for some years. For a poor defenceless woman to be outraged and stabbed in the manner which this woman had been was almost beyond belief.'[39] The jury delivered their verdict of 'wilful murder by some person or persons unknown', a result that would become frustratingly familiar in the coming months.

The day after the inquest closed, the *Pall Mall Gazette*, one of the more forthright newspapers of the day,[40] made an early, though perhaps for the time being tenuous, connection:

It is a singular coincidence that the murder was committed during Bank Holiday night, and is almost identical with another murder which was perpetrated near the same spot on the night of the previous Bank Holiday. The victims were both what are called 'unfortunates', and their murderers have up till now evaded capture.[41]

The day after Martha Tabram's inquest closed, James Monro, assistant commissioner of the Metropolitan Police and the man in charge of the CID, handed in his resignation. One of the reasons was due to protracted power struggles with the then serving chief commissioner, Charles Warren. Warren's appointment in 1886 had originally been met with considerable approval; The Times described him as 'precisely the man whom sensible Londoners would have chosen to preside over the policing of the Metropolis'.[42] Public confidence in the new commissioner's abilities soon took several damaging blows in that and the following year, when he was criticized for his heavy handling of a number of public disturbances, culminating in the famous 'Bloody Sunday' of 13 November 1887, when large demonstrations by the unemployed prompted the deployment of troops by Warren, resulting in scenes of violence at Trafalgar Square, with many injuries and one death. Monro was becoming increasingly frustrated with what he felt was unnecessary interference by Warren into the affairs of the CID and was also much displeased when Warren vetoed Monro's choice for chief constable, Melville Macnaghten.

Monro's successor was Dr Robert Anderson, who would take on the role of assistant commissioner on 1 September 1888. Anderson, a millenarist and barrister, had been brought over to London from his native Ireland in 1876 as part of an intelligence branch dealing with Fenianism. When that branch closed he was kept on as a special adviser to the Home Office on matters of political crime relating to the Irish situation and in 1887 he became secretary to the prison commissioners. Unfortunately, by the time of his newest appointment, Anderson had been complaining of ill-health due to overwork and, with the authority of Charles Warren, was granted sick leave.[43] It was unfortunate timing, for the day before he took on his new role, events in the East End of London took an alarming turn.

2.

'I forgive you for what you are,
as you have been to me'

As the light began to fade on the evening of Thursday 30 August 1888, the long, blank walls of Browne and Eagle's wool warehouses, situated on the north side of Buck's Row, began to cast their foreboding shadow over the terrace of workers' cottages opposite. The day had been unsettled: clear and bright to start, but in the early afternoon a thunderstorm had developed, and its passing left a legacy of intermittent showers for the remainder of the day. The little two-up-two-down cottages, populated for the most part by respectable working-class folk, spent much of their days hiding in the semi-daylight afforded by the buildings opposite. At the western end sat New Cottage, which, as its name suggests, was built more recently than its neighbours and abutted on to a small stable yard, protected from the street by a pair of wooden gates. The tracks of the East London Railway passed close by, about twenty feet below ground level, shielded from view by a wall which terminated at the Buck's Row Board School, and the sound of trains arriving and departing from nearby Whitechapel station was an almost constant presence during the day. Just opposite the stable yard stood Essex Wharf, a narrow, handsome building which fronted a small enclave of businesses and the Spitalfields coal depot. Further west, beyond the school, the thoroughfare opened up into a wider space before tapering off into White's Row, which terminated at the junction with Baker's Row.

A few small streets joined this thoroughfare to Whitechapel Road and immediately behind Buck's Row, and running parallel to it, was Winthrop Street, consisting of similar cottages and assorted business premises, one of which was a horse-slaughterer's.

Emma Green, a widow, and her three children lived in New Cottage next to the stable yard; her two sons went to bed at 9.00 and 9.45 p.m. respectively, but Mrs Green stayed up with her daughter until about 11.00 p.m. and, despite being a light sleeper, was not disturbed by anything untoward that night.[1] At about the same time, in Essex Wharf opposite, Mary Ann Purkiss went to bed and was followed by her husband, Walter, manager of the property, about fifteen minutes later. Both had a rather fitful night's sleep and were awake at various times, but both claimed there were no noises coming from Buck's Row outside.[2]

While the residents of Buck's Row lay in their beds, night watchman Patrick Mulshaw was halfway through a lengthy and perhaps tedious night looking after some sewage works off Winthrop Street, at the rear of the Working Lads' Institute. He dozed a few times during the night but saw nobody around except two police constables on their beat, one of whom was PC John Neil.[3] About seventy yards away along Winthrop Street were the open gates of Harrison Barber and Co. slaughterhouse, where Charles Bretton,[4] James Mumford and Henry Tomkins were working through the night. At about 12.20 a.m., Bretton and Tomkins took a stroll down to nearby Wood's Buildings, a narrow passage leading from Whitechapel Road which crossed the railway lines by means of a small bridge which came out on to Winthrop Street by the board school. They were there for about forty minutes before going back to work and at no time did they see anybody or hear anything out of the ordinary.[5]

One resident of Buck's Row, Harriet Lilley, who lived at no. 7 (a few doors along from New Cottage) with her husband William, was having difficulty getting a decent night's sleep. During one of her waking moments in the front bedroom, she heard a luggage train pass on the nearby railway and, as it did so, she was aware of some noises coming from the street. She described them as 'a painful moan – two or three faint gasps – and then it passed away . . . There was, too, a sound as of whispers underneath the window. I distinctly heard voices, but cannot say what was said.'[6] The train passing at that time was calculated as being the 3.07 a.m. goods train from New Cross, putting the time of this curious incident at around 3.30 a.m. Other than that, according to Emma Green and Walter Purkiss, Buck's Row appeared to be unusually quiet that night.[7]

At 3.40 a.m., Charles Cross[8] entered the eastern end of Buck's Row from Brady Street. He had left his home in Doveton Street, Bethnal Green, some ten minutes earlier and was on his way to work at Pickford's in Broad Street, where he was employed as a carman. He was walking along the northern side of Buck's Row and, as he progressed eastwards, he noticed a shape on the other side of the road, at the end of the row of cottages in front of the stable yard gates. Initially he thought it appeared to be a discarded tarpaulin and began to cross the street to have a closer look. At that point, Robert Paul, another carman, was following behind Cross and noticed him in the road; by now, Cross had realized that the form lying on the pavement was a woman. He started to move back towards the footway and, as Paul moved to pass him, Cross tapped him on the shoulder, bringing his attention to the body lying nearby.[9]

The two men went over to the body. The woman was lying on her back with her head pointing east; her arms were by her side, her legs were slightly apart and her clothes were dishevelled.

Her eyes were open, staring at the sky, and a small bonnet sat on the pavement a few feet away. Cross felt the woman's hand, which was cold, causing him to exclaim, 'I believe she is dead,' but, on touching the face, he could detect a little warmth. Paul put his hand on her chest and, believing he had detected some slight movement, said, 'I think she is breathing, but very little if she is.'[10] Cross wanted to lift the woman up, but Paul refused to touch her any further other than to rearrange her clothing, which had been pulled up towards the waist. Once this was done, both men admitted that they needed to get to work and were by now running behind time and so they left the scene, continuing their way westwards, Paul suggesting that he speak to the first policeman they meet on their way. Conveniently, a few minutes after leaving the scene, they saw PC Jonas Mizen in the process of 'knocking up' – waking people up by knocking on their doors or windows, a bit like an alarm call – at the junction of Baker's Row and Old Montague Street and informed him of their find. Cross suggested that the woman was either dead or drunk, and Paul commented that he thought she was dead. With that, the two men continued on their way up Hanbury Street and there parted company, whereupon Paul went to his place of work in Corbett's Court.

While Cross and Paul reported their find, PC John Neil[11] was passing along Buck's Row eastwards from Thomas Street. On his last pass, thirty minutes earlier, there had been nothing to report, but now, as he neared the board school, he could see the body of the woman on the footpath ahead and went over to investigate. Shining his lantern on the body he noticed blood oozing from a deep wound in the throat; he touched the arms and felt warmth from the joints upwards. At that moment, PC Neil heard the footsteps of PC John Thain, passing the end of Buck's Row at the junction with Brady Street, and signalled to him with his lamp. When Thain arrived, Neil immediately sent him off to fetch Dr Rees Llewellyn from his surgery at 152 Whitechapel Road. While waiting for Dr Llewellyn, Neil called upon Essex Wharf, where Walter Purkiss assured him he had heard no disturbance during the night. Very soon, PC Mizen, the policeman alerted to the incident by Cross and Paul, arrived at the scene, finding Neil alone with the body. Neil told Mizen to fetch the ambulance, and he promptly made his way to Bethnal Green police station to collect it.

After being called at 4.00 a.m., Dr Llewellyn arrived at Buck's Row soon after and, making a cursory examination of the woman's body, pronounced life extinct, saying that he would do a further examination at the mortuary. Sergeant Henry Kirby, another officer whose beat took in Buck's Row, arrived and called at New Cottage, where Emma Green assured him that she had heard nothing unusual during the night. Also, the policemen present had been joined by James Mumford and Henry Tomkins (and subsequently Charles Bretton) from the Winthrop Street slaughterhouse, who claimed they had been informed of the murder by PC Thain, who had gone there to pick up his cape. Eventually Mizen arrived with the ambulance – little more than a handcart – and he helped PCs Neil and Thain put the body on it as a small gaggle of onlookers stood by. Much blood had been soaked up by the woman's clothing, and Thain later mentioned that he got quite a bit on him as he handled the body. The ambulance then made its way towards the small mortuary off Old Montague Street, and by the time Inspector John Spratling arrived in Buck's Row just after 4.30 a.m., Emma Green's son James had thrown a bucket of water on the pavement to clear away the blood; despite this attempt at a clean-up, Spratling could still see traces of it between the stones. He then made his way to the mortuary, where he found the body lying on the cart outside the mortuary gates, awaiting the arrival of the attendant. Spratling made a cursory description of the body in the meantime.[12]

Robert Mann, an inmate of the Whitechapel workhouse with responsibility for the little mortuary, arrived at 5.00 a.m. He opened the gates and wheeled the body in; once readmitted, Inspector Spratling made a further examination of the body, noting carefully the woman's characteristics, clothing and possessions.

She was aged about forty-five, height 5 feet 2 inches, with a dark complexion, brown hair turning grey and brown eyes. There were bruises on her lower right jaw and left cheek, her tongue was slightly lacerated, and three teeth were missing. She was wearing a brown Ulster, brown linsey frock, two petticoats (one woollen, one flannel), brown stays, a white chemise, black ribbed woollen stockings and a pair of men's side spring boots. The bonnet was black, of straw, and trimmed with velvet. The only personal possessions, found in the pockets, were a comb and a piece of broken mirror. But it was while inspecting the garments that Spratling made the significant discovery that not only had the woman's throat been cut, but that she had also been disembowelled.[13] It is perhaps a testament to the poor street lighting in Buck's Row and the fact that Charles Cross and Robert Paul had rearranged the clothing that nobody had seen the terrible mutilations before that moment. Under the circumstances, Dr Llewellyn was recalled.

Robert Mann returned to the mortuary after having some breakfast, this time accompanied by James Hatfield, a fellow inmate, and together they stripped the body ready for the post-mortem, despite the fact that they had been told not to. On his arrival, Dr Llewellyn conducted his examination, which revealed the extent of the neck and abdominal injuries:

On the left side of the neck, about an inch below the jaw, there was an incision about four inches long and running from a point immediately below the ear. An inch below on the same side, and commencing about an inch in front of it, was a circular incision terminating at a point about three inches below the right jaw. This incision completely severs all the tissues down to the vertebrae. The large vessels of the neck on both sides were severed. The incision is about eight inches long. These cuts must have been caused with a long-bladed knife, moderately sharp, and used with great violence. No blood at all was found on the breast either of the body or clothes. There were no injuries about the body till just about the lower part of the abdomen. Two or three inches from the left side was a wound running in a jagged manner. It was a very deep wound, and the tissues were cut through: There were several incisions running across the abdomen. On the right side there were also three or four similar cuts running downwards. All these had been caused by a knife, which had been used violently and been used downwards. The wounds were from left to right, and might have been done by a left-handed person. All the injuries had been done by the same instrument.[14]

Dr Llewellyn also concluded that the murderer would have had some rough anatomical knowledge and that the woman had been dead about thirty minutes by the time he first saw her.[15]

The police began careful searches of the Buck's Row neighbourhood, with Inspector Spratling and Sergeant George Godley, among others, checking the embankments of the railway lines and the goods yards nearby, but no clues or murder weapon were found. Enquiries were also being made as to the identity of the dead woman; the key to this turned out to be the words 'Lambeth Workhouse' which were found stencilled on her petticoats, and, following a police visit, several individuals came forward. The workhouse matron viewed the body but could not identify it, and a few others' attempts came out negative until it was ascertained that the woman had been a resident of Wilmott's lodging house at 18 Thrawl Street, Spitalfields. Further enquiries were made there, resulting in the body being identified as that of 'Polly' by Ellen Holland,[16] a resident of the lodging house, who had seen the deceased on the morning of her death. At 7.30 p.m., Mary Ann Monk, a former inmate of the Lambeth workhouse, recognized the body as Mary Ann 'Polly' Nichols, and the following day, 1 September, William Nichols, the estranged husband of the murdered woman, established her identity once and for all. He appeared obviously affected by what he saw and uttered the words 'I forgive you for what you are, as you have been to me.'[17]

Mary Ann Nichols was born Mary Ann Walker on 26 August 1845 in Dawes Court, Shoe Lane, in the City of London. She married William Nichols, a printer, in 1864 at St Bride's church in Fleet Street, and together they had five children between 1866 and 1879, three boys and two girls. They had lodged in Bouverie Street, Fleet Street and with Mary Ann's father in Trafalgar Street, Walworth before moving to no. 6 Block D, Peabody Buildings, Stamford Street, sometime around 1875. The marriage, however, was plagued by disharmony, and William Nichols stated that her drinking was often a cause of their problems.[18] After a number of separations, the final break-up came in 1880, when, according to Mary Ann's father, Edward Walker, William became romantically involved with the woman who nursed Mary Ann through the birth of her last child. Although he never denied the affair, William Nichols said that Mary Ann left the family home of her own accord.

The next seven years of her life have been well documented, giving us a surprisingly good account of her 'progress' from south London to the slums of Spitalfields:

6 September 1880–31 May 1881: Lambeth workhouse.

31 May 1881–24 April 1882: not known.

24 April 1882–18 January 1883: Lambeth workhouse.

18 January 1883–20 January 1883: Lambeth infirmary.

20 January 1883–24 March 1883: Lambeth workhouse.

24 March 1883–21 May 1883: lived with her father but left after a quarrel, probably about her drinking.

21 May 1883–2 June 1883: Lambeth workhouse.

2 June 1883–25 October 1887: Lived with Thomas Stuart Drew at 15 York Street.

25 October 1887: Spent one day in St Giles's workhouse, Endell Street.

26 October 1887–2 December 1887: Strand workhouse, Edmonton.

19 December 1887–29 December 1887: Lambeth workhouse.

29 December 1887–4 January 1888: no record.

4 January 1888–16 April 1888: Mitcham workhouse (Holborn) and Holborn infirmary (Archway hospital).

In mid-April 1888, Mary Ann secured work as a domestic for Samuel and Sarah Cowdrey in Wandsworth and for a moment at least, her fortunes appeared to be improving. On 17 April, she wrote to her father:

I just write to say you will be glad to know that I am settled in my new place, and going all right up to now. My people went out yesterday, and have not returned, so I am left in charge. It is a grand place inside, with trees and gardens back and front. All has been newly done up. They are teetotallers, and very religious, so I ought to get on. They are very nice people, and I have not much to do. I hope you are all right and the boy has work. So goodbye now for the present.

Yours truly, 'Polly'
Answer soon please, and let me know how you are.[19]

Edward Walker replied to the letter but never received a reply. Alas, any optimism for a new start in life was short-lived when, on 12 July, Mary Ann absconded from the Cowdreys' home, taking with her clothing to the value of £3 10s.[20] After a day at Gray's Inn temporary workhouse on 1 August, she arrived at Wilmott's lodging house at 18 Thrawl Street, Spitalfields, and for a while shared a room with three other women, who all paid the going rate of 4d per night for a separate, single bed.[21] On 24 August she moved over to 56 Flower and Dean Street, 'The White House',[22] a rather disreputable lodging house which allegedly permitted men and women to sleep together.

The movements of Mary Ann Nichols on the last night of her life come to us from various sources. Inspector Joseph Helson's official report stated that she had been seen walking along Whitechapel Road at 11.00 p.m. and leaving the Frying Pan public house on Brick Lane at 12.30 a.m. before arriving at 18 Thrawl Street, where she was seen by the deputy at 1.20 a.m.[23] Unable to come up with the required money for a night's lodging, Mary Ann, apparently showing the effects of alcohol, merely laughed and said, 'I'll soon get my "doss" money; see what a jolly bonnet I've got now.'[24] She drew attention to the little black straw and velvet bonnet which had not been seen before and which, before too long, would be lying by her corpse in Buck's Row.

At that time, Ellen Holland was returning to Thrawl Street

after spending some time near the London docks, where a huge fire had been raging for much of the night. Such conflagrations often doubled up as spectator events, and Ellen Holland was probably one of many who went to view at close hand what could actually be seen illuminating the sky for miles. As she approached the corner of Osborn Street and Whitechapel Road, she noticed Mary Ann coming toward her, and they stopped to speak. Mary Ann said she was without money and had not been allowed to stay at the lodging house, but also that she had indeed already had the money three times that day and had spent it. The two women parted company, and Mary Ann said she would find the money and return;[25] it was 2.30 a.m., and the last occasion upon which she was reported as being seen alive. And so ended the account, fabricated from inquest testimony, police intelligence and newspaper interviews, of the demise of Mary Ann Nichols.

The four-day inquest, presided over by Coroner Wynne Baxter on 1, 3, 17 and 22 September, was reported widely in the local and national press. The surge of interest in what was becoming an alarmingly regular occurrence in Whitechapel generated many column inches, and, remarkably, newspapers from overseas had begun to take notice.[26] The press, in their turn, would be responsible for generating a groundswell of sensation surrounding the crimes and, for later students of the case, flesh out the stories of those involved with detail not included in official inquest transcripts and summarized police reports. But they would also create conflicting accounts in their thirst for 'the big story' and, even though they added colour to many aspects of the Whitechapel murders case, it would not always necessarily be the right colour.

But even with the increase in information regarding the events surrounding the murder of Mary Ann Nichols, the inquest jury were once again forced to deliver the verdict of 'wilful murder against person or persons unknown'. There was also serious talk of a connection with the murders of Emma Smith and Martha Tabram:

> Few occurrences of the kind have ever created greater sensa-
> tion, and the sensation is not likely to be allayed, at least in the
> neighbourhood of the murder, until the mystery which at
> present surrounds it has been dispelled, and the criminal dis-
> covered. The identity of the wretched victim may be considered
> fully established, and the very fact that she is shown to have
> belonged to the same unhappy class as the two women previ-
> ously butchered under similar circumstances of brutality and
> mystery adds, if possible, to the horror of the occurrence. It
> tends to show that the three murders are not isolated crimes,
> but are the work of the same hand or the same gang of assas-
> sins; and until some light shall have been thrown upon the
> tragedy the people of Whitechapel may reasonably feel appre-
> hensive that any night fresh horrors may be perpetrated in
> their midst.[27]

On the first day of the Nichols inquest, Dr Robert Anderson officially took up his role as assistant commissioner (CID), albeit in readiness to take his sick leave. And with the investigation into the Buck's Row murder underway, headed by Inspector Helson, another important figure made his first appearance – Inspector Frederick Abberline.

Abberline was brought in to work on the Whitechapel case thanks to his exceptional knowledge of the East End, gained from his fourteen years' previous experience as inspector of H-division (Whitechapel) from 1873. In 1887 he was transferred to A-division (Whitehall) and was effectively removed from field-work on placement at the commissioner's office. When somebody with local clout was required, Abberline was returned to his old stomping ground. Over the years, he has been promoted in popular culture as the head of the Whitechapel murders investigation, which has been somewhat of an exaggeration, but his role was to become important in the autumn of 1888, as he became responsible for coordinating the on-the-ground investigations into those murders which took place on Metropolitan Police territory. The man truly in charge of the investigation overall would be Chief Inspector Donald Swanson, who from mid-September onwards – and in the subsequent absence of Anderson – would be given this great responsibility by Charles Warren:

> [Swanson] must be acquainted with every detail. I look upon him for the time being as the eyes & ears of the Commr. in this particular case. He must have a room to himself, & every paper, every document, every report every telegram must pass through his hands. He must be consulted on every source. I would not send any directions anywhere on the subject of the murder without consulting him.[28]

But between Abberline and Swanson's new appointments, events would take a more dramatic turn than anybody could have imagined.

3.

'A noiseless midnight terror'

After three unsolved murders of an extraordinarily brutal nature, the Metropolitan Police were nowhere near finding any perpetrator, or indeed even establishing once and for all whether these unique crimes were by a single hand. Newspaper reports of Wynne Baxter's lengthy inquest into the death of Mary Ann Nichols made for exciting reading for sure, as did the interviews with some of the witnesses, and the public were now well and truly becoming exposed to the growing sensation that would bolster press coverage of the Whitechapel murders from here on in. The concern caused by the crimes had also generated a public desire for a reward for the capture of those responsible. On 31 August, staff of L. & P. Walter and Son, of Church Street, Spitalfields, wrote to the police on just such a matter.[1] However, as the offer of rewards had for some time been discontinued by the Metropolitan Police because of the problems that offers of money often generated, the suggestion was swiftly turned down.[2]

With the police struggling to gain definitive leads, the newspapers, with one ear to the ground, began to pick up on local hearsay. There was one such rumour in particular which unexpectedly snowballed to become the first major affair to grow around the murders – the individual known as 'Leather Apron'.

The first apparent mention of this alarming figure came the day after the Nichols murder when the *Sheffield and Rotherham*

Independent, talking to a 'woman in a position similar to the deceased', stated:

> that there is a man who goes by the name of the 'Leather Apron' who has more than once attacked unfortunate and defenceless women. His dodge is, it is asserted, to get them in to a house on the pretence of offering them money. He then takes whatever little they have and 'half kills' them in addition.[3]

It was obvious that this report was suggesting that 'Leather Apron' could have something to do with the murders. Within a few days the story had spread, and by 4 September the *Star* – an infamously radical and some would say sensationalist evening newspaper – had latched on, describing him as the 'noiseless midnight terror'. He was, as far as the *Star* was concerned, 'the only name linked with the Whitechapel murders':

> 'Leather Apron' by himself is quite an unpleasant character. If, as many of the people suspect, he is the real author of the three murders which, in everybody's judgement, were done by the same person, he is a more ghoulish and devilish brute than can be found in all the pages of shocking fiction. He has ranged Whitechapel for a long time. He exercises over the unfortunates who ply their trade after twelve o'clock at night, a sway that is based on universal terror. He has kicked, injured, bruised, and terrified a hundred of them who are ready to testify to the outrages. He has made a certain threat, his favourite threat, to any number of them, and each of the three dead bodies represents that threat carried out. He carries a razor-like knife, and two weeks ago drew it on a woman called 'Widow Annie' as she was crossing the square near London Hospital, threatening at the same time, with his ugly grin and his malignant

eyes, to 'rip her up.' He is a character so much like the invention of a story writer that the accounts of him given by all the street-walkers of the Whitechapel district seem like romances. The remarkable thing is, however, that they all agree in every particular.[4]

Much of this account (and what followed) smacks of over-sensation, and whether there really were a hundred women ready to testify against 'Leather Apron' is debatable. But the seeds of uproar were now being sown, and, as other newspapers followed the *Star*'s lead, the man who effectively became the first major suspect in the case began to take on increasingly repellent characteristics, no doubt fuelling considerable anxiety in the East End neighbourhoods and beyond. He was 'a mysterious being',[5] a 'half crazy creature, with fiendish black eyes'[6] and 'unquestionably mad'.[7] The efforts of a *Star* reporter to flesh out this character were published in a number of newspapers:

He is five feet four or five inches in height, and wears a dark close-fitting cap. He is thickset, and has an unusually thick neck. His hair is black, and closely clipped, his age being about thirty-eight or forty. He has a small black moustache. The distinguishing feature of costume is a leather apron, which he always wears, and from which he gets his nickname. His expression is sinister, and seems to be full of terror for the women who describe it. His eyes are small and glittering. His lips are usually parted in a grin which is not only not reassuring, but excessively repellent. He is a slipper-maker by trade, but does not work. His business is blackmailing women late at night. A number of men in Whitechapel follow this interesting profession. He has never cut anybody, so far as is known, but always carries a leather knife, presumably as sharp as leather knives are wont to be. This knife a number of the women have seen. His name nobody knows, but all are united in the belief that he is a Jew or of Jewish parentage, his face being of a marked Hebrew type. But the most singular characteristic of the man is the universal statement that in moving about he never makes any noise. What he wears on his feet the women do not know, but they agree that he moves noiselessly. His uncanny peculiarity to them is that they never see him or know of his presence until he is close by them . . .[8]

In the meantime, Inspector Helson continued enquiries regarding the Buck's Row murder, now with the involvement of Inspector Abberline and other officers. No arrests had been made in connection with Nichols's death, but there was a suggestion that numerous individuals were being watched and that perhaps somebody not directly involved in the crime, but cognizant of the events, might come forward to confess. Such speculation was again the work of the press, and the police, it appears, were keeping any developments close to their chests.[9] What the newspapers were unaware of was that the police had in fact identified a man, possibly 'Leather Apron' himself, whom they wished to question. In a report dated 7 September, Inspector Helson revealed that their enquiries had come across a man named 'Jack Pizer, alias Leather Apron', who had for some time been in the habit of ill-treating prostitutes in the East End and other parts of London.[10] All attempts to locate him had so far failed, but as the matter was of some urgency and a good lead obviously needed, the search continued in earnest, even though there was nothing concrete to suggest that 'Jack Pizer' had killed anybody.

Nevertheless, 'Leather Apron' continued to grace the pages

of the press and it did not go unnoticed by some journalists that there was the distinct possibility that he was 'a mythical outgrowth of the reporter's fancy'.[11] Despite the assurances of the womenfolk he allegedly assaulted, the newspapers who gained much copy from his enigmatic menace and the police's wish to find 'Jack Pizer', it is quite possible that in reality 'Leather Apron' did not actually exist, but was an amalgam of various unpleasant characters who were in the habit of abusing prostitutes. In other words, once the name had been thrown into the public domain, anybody who behaved in the manner of 'Leather Apron' became him.

As Wynne Baxter's inquest into the death of Mary Ann Nichols sputtered on intermittently, the unfortunate woman herself was finally buried, on 6 September, at the City of London Cemetery (Little Ilford) in Manor Park. The cortège consisted of the hearse and two mourning coaches, which carried Edward Walker, William Nichols and Edward Nichols, Mary Ann's eldest son. The funeral arrangements were made by Mr Henry Smith, undertaker of Hanbury Street, and it was that very thoroughfare that would become the centre of outrage and panic only two days later.

At 5.45 a.m. on the morning of 8 September, John Davis, a carman, rose from his bed and made himself a cup of tea before leaving for work at Leadenhall market. He had been living at 29 Hanbury Street, Spitalfields, for two weeks with his wife and three sons, and together they occupied the top-floor front room of the three-storey house, which had seventeen tenants in total. He had gone to bed at 8.00 p.m. the previous night, with the rest of the family following suit at various times until 10.45 p.m. Davis had been awake from 3.00 to 5.00 a.m. and, after dozing for the last forty-five minutes, got up at the sound of the bell of Christ Church on nearby Commercial Street.[12] At around 6.00 a.m., he descended the staircase on his way to the back yard and noticed that the front door was thrown wide open. This was a common enough sight, as, with so many residents coming and going at all hours, locking the front door was perhaps not particularly practical. The door leading to the back yard was closed, and Davis pushed it open before descending the few stone steps which led from the door to the paved yard beyond. As he did so, he saw a sight that was to cause him considerable distress; the body of a woman was lying on the ground, parallel with the fence, her head almost touching the steps. There was a horrid gash in her throat; her skirts had been pushed up above the groin and her abdomen cut open. Bloody pieces of flesh lay over the left shoulder and her intestines, still attached by a string of viscera to the inside of her body, had been pulled out and were lying in a heap over the right shoulder.

John Davis, obviously in a state of shock, ran back through the passage and out into Hanbury Street. A few doors down were James Green and James Kent, two employees of Bailey's packing case makers at 23a Hanbury Street, who were loitering outside their work premises. When he alerted them to what he had found, they followed him back to view the body, but neither dared venture into the yard itself. The three men left together as Henry Holland was passing the house and, after being made aware of what had happened, he went to the back yard with them to see for himself. At that point, Davis went off in the direction of Commercial Street police station, and Holland went looking for a policeman at Spitalfields market, while Green and Kent returned to Bailey's; the latter was so shaken, he procured himself a brandy to steady his nerves before looking for a piece of canvas to throw over the body.[13]

Holland had found a police officer at the market but was disgruntled when the officer said that, as he was on fixed point duty, he was unable to leave his post, an issue which Holland later made a complaint about. Davis had better luck and bumped into Inspector Joseph Chandler at the corner of Commercial Street and Hanbury Street. Immediately the two men returned to no. 29, Chandler remaining with the body while sending for further assistance in the form of Dr George Bagster Phillips, police reinforcements and an ambulance. By the time James Kent returned with the canvas sheet, a crowd had gathered at the front of the house, with any intruders being cleared from the passage by Chandler, who refused any further admittance to the building until Dr Phillips arrived at 6.30 a.m:[14]

> I found the body of the deceased lying in the yard on her back, on the left hand of the steps that lead from the passage. The head was about 6in in front of the level of the bottom step, and the feet were towards a shed at the end of the yard. The left arm was across the left breast, and the legs were drawn up, the feet resting on the ground, and the knees turned outwards. The face was swollen and turned on the right side, and the tongue protruded between the front teeth, but not beyond the lips; it was much swollen. The small intestines and other portions were lying on the right side of the body on the ground above the right shoulder, but attached. There was a large quantity of blood, with a part of the stomach above the left shoulder. I searched the yard and found a small piece of coarse muslin, a small-tooth comb, and a pocket-comb, in a paper case, near the railing. They had apparently been arranged there. I also discovered various other articles, which I handed to the police. The body was cold, except that there was a certain remaining

heat, under the intestines, in the body. Stiffness of the limbs was not marked, but it was commencing. The throat was dissevered deeply. I noticed that the incision of the skin was jagged, and reached right round the neck. On the back wall of the house, between the steps and the palings, on the left side, about 18in from the ground, there were about six patches of blood, varying in size from a sixpenny piece to a small point, and on the wooden fence there were smears of blood, corresponding to where the head of the deceased laid, and immediately above the part where the blood had mainly flowed from the neck, which was well clotted.[15]

By 7.00 a.m. the body had been taken by Sergeant Badham to the Whitechapel workhouse mortuary, the same 'shed' that had previously received the bodies of Martha Tabram and Mary Ann Nichols. Once the yard was clear, Inspector Chandler made an inspection of the scene. A portion of envelope was found, which contained two pills and bore the crest of the Sussex Regiment and the letter 'M'. These objects had been noted by Dr Phillips earlier, who later said that they looked as if they had been 'arranged'.[16]

Before long, the woman had been identified as Annie Chapman, alias 'Annie Sievey', a woman of the same class as the previous victims, who had been residing at Crossingham's lodging house at 35 Dorset Street, Spitalfields. Her life story was typical of the downward path that the 'unfortunates' of the East End travelled and arguably was the most tragic of the Whitechapel murders victims.

She was born Annie Eliza Smith in Paddington on 25 September 1840,[17] the eldest child of George Smith, a soldier, and Ruth Chapman, the couple being unmarried at the time of her birth. The family were living in Knightsbridge, west London, for a time and later in Clewer, Berkshire, before returning to London, when, in 1860, and at his own request, George was pensioned off from the army and became a valet. The family appeared to move back to Clewer, but this time without Annie, who probably stayed in London, and her life at this time is unknown. George Smith died at Clewer in 1866.

On 1 May 1869, Annie married coachman John Chapman, and they lived at various addresses in west London thereafter. Their first child, Emily, was born in 1870, followed by Annie Georgina in 1873, after which John got a job as a coachman and domestic servant to a wealthy family in Berkshire, which necessitated a return to Clewer. Their final child, Alfred, was born in 1880; he was crippled, and it seems that from here the Chapman's fortunes began to falter. By now Annie was drinking heavily and was apparently often in custody for drunkenness,[18] and eventually this situation reached the point where it was no longer advisable for her to be living on the estate of a respectable Berkshire family. Annie and John separated sometime around 1881, and she returned to London, with John giving her a weekly allowance of 10 shillings, a not inconsiderable sum at the time. In 1882, the eldest daughter, Emily, died of meningitis, and Annie's life took a further downturn in 1886, when, on Christmas Day, John died of cirrhosis of the liver, ascites and dropsy, taking his generous maintenance payments with him. That year, Annie took up with a man named Jack, who made sieves for a living and was known as 'Jack Sievy', no doubt the source of Annie's nickname. They lived at 30 Dorset Street, Spitalfields, a common lodging house, and Annie attempted to support herself by making antimacassars and selling articles in the street,[19] being described as 'very industrious when sober . . . a very clever little woman'.[20] Such descriptions came from Amelia Palmer, a resident of 30 Dorset

Street, who claimed to have known Annie for quite some time; much of what we know about Annie Chapman's life in Spital-fields comes from her inquest testimony and interviews.

After breaking up with the sieve-maker, Annie got together with Ted Stanley, known generally as 'The Pensioner', even though he was not particularly old, nor had he drawn a pension from the army. He would occasionally stay with Annie at her latest lodging house of choice, Crossingham's at 35 Dorset Street, where they were regarded as man and wife.[21] He had been away from the East End from 6 August until 1 September and had last seen Annie alive in Brushfield Street the day after his return. He noticed that she had a blackened eye.[22]

Annie had indeed received a black eye and other bruising during a quarrel with Eliza Cooper, a fellow lodger at Cross-ingham's. However the reasons for the fight and the exact location where it took place differ according to various accounts. One explanation was that it had been caused by jealousy over the attentions of Stanley,[23] the other that it was over a bar of soap.[24] Also, according to Eliza Cooper, the argument began at Crossingham's and continued afterwards at the Britannia, the pub on the corner of Dorset Street and Commercial Street, where the fight took place.[25] John Evans, the night watchman of Crossingham's, stated that the fight took place at the lodg-ing house itself as early as Thursday 30 August.[26] Whatever the date or venue for the incident, a number of people were made aware of Annie's bruises, including Timothy Donovan, the lodging house deputy, and Amelia Palmer. She had met Annie in Dorset Street on 3 September, where they had had a brief chat about the bruising, Annie complaining that she was not feeling too well. They met again the following day, and again Annie commented on her health and that she had not eaten all day. With that, Palmer gave her twopence to get something, advising her not to spend it on alcohol. It is believed that Annie spent some time at the infirmary,[27] for by Friday 7 September, she had acquired a bottle of medicine and some pills. Amelia Palmer again saw her in Dorset Street at 5.30 that afternoon, and things were not good. Annie's health was obviously deteriorating, and she felt too ill to do anything, but said, 'I must pull myself together and go out and get some money or I shall have no lodgings.'[28]

And so to Annie Chapman's final hours. At 11.30 p.m. on the night of Friday 7 September she asked for permission to be readmitted to the lodging house and forty minutes later shared a pint of beer with fellow lodger Frederick Stevens. At about 12.15 a.m. Stevens was with Annie – who appeared sober – in the kitchen, and, while there, she took out a box of pills, which immediately broke open. She fashioned a makeshift wrap from a piece of envelope found on the kitchen mantelpiece. With that she left, Stevens thinking she may have gone to bed. However, he saw her leave Crossingham's at 1.00 a.m. She had returned a little over thirty minutes later and was sitting in the kitchen eating a baked potato when John Evans was sent to collect her doss money, but she did not have it. Deputy Timothy Donovan chastised her for seemingly always having money for beer rather than rent, and with that, in a situation very similar to Mary Ann Nichols's a week earlier, she promised to get the money quickly and asked Evans to keep her regular bed free for when she returned. Evans watched as she left by a door into Little Paternoster Row, turned right and walked up to Brushfield Street. It was 1.45 a.m.[29]

A number of newspapers[30] mentioned that a woman of a similar description to Annie Chapman was seen in the Ten Bells pub at the corner of Commercial Street and Church Street at around 5.00–5.30 a.m., one account saying she was drinking with a man, others claiming that a man wearing a skull cap beckoned her outside. However, without further proof that the woman was indeed Annie Chapman, these reports are hardly conclusive.

At about 5.30 a.m., Elizabeth Long was walking along Hanbury Street on her way to Spitalfields market and, as she passed no. 29, she saw a woman whom she later identified as Annie standing against the shutters of the house with a man. She felt certain of the time as she had just heard the clock of Truman's brewery strike the half-hour. Mrs Long saw the woman's face but she did not see the man's, except to notice that he was dark. She described him as wearing a brown deerstalker hat, and she thought he had on a dark coat, but was not quite certain. She could not say what the age of the man was, but he looked to be over forty and appeared to be a little taller than the woman. He seemed to be a foreigner and had a 'shabby genteel' appearance. She could hear them talking loudly and she overheard him say to the woman, 'Will you?', to which she replied, 'Yes.' They remained there as Mrs Long passed, and she continued on her way without looking back.[31] Thirty minutes later, John Davis found Annie Chapman's brutally mutilated body in the back yard.

At the time of her death, Annie Chapman was described as five feet tall, stout, with a pallid complexion, blue eyes and dark-brown wavy hair. Her teeth were good, although there were two missing in the lower jaw. She had been wearing a long black figured coat that came down to her knees, a black skirt, two bodices, two petticoats, lace-up boots, red and white striped woollen stockings and a red and white neckerchief. There were also some slight abrasions on her fingers where three brass rings that she had been seen wearing prior to her death had been removed. The cause of Annie's apparent ill-health was ascertained in Dr Phillips's post-mortem examination, in that she was 'far advanced in disease of the lungs and membranes of the brain'.[32] She was already dying.

The post-mortem findings were effectively cut short during the inquest on the wishes of Dr Phillips. However, the medical journal the *Lancet* published an account of his findings:

> the uterus and its appendages, with the upper portion of the vagina and the posterior two-thirds of the bladder, had been entirely removed. No trace of these parts could be found, and the incisions were cleanly cut, avoiding the rectum, and dividing the vagina low enough to avoid injury to the cervix uteri. Obviously the work was that of an expert – of one, at least, who had such knowledge of anatomical or pathological examinations as to be enabled to secure the pelvic organs with one sweep of a knife.[33]

This judgement was important, for although Dr Rees Llewellyn commented that the killer of Mary Ann Nichols may have had some rough anatomical knowledge, Dr Phillips was convinced that Annie Chapman's murderer was blessed with significant expertise, adding that:

> I myself could not have performed all the injuries I saw on that woman, and effect them, even without a struggle, under a quarter of an hour. If I had done it in a deliberate way, such as would fall to the duties of a surgeon, it would probably have taken me the best part of an hour.[34]

Wynne Baxter's inquest, which took place at the Working Lads' Institute and lasted five days spread over a fortnight, generated more evidence in addition to that gleaned from those party to Annie Chapman's final days. One witness was her younger brother, Fountain Smith, who claimed to have last seen her on the Commercial Road a fortnight before her death, giving her two shillings. Importantly, the residents of Hanbury Street itself gave tantalizing glimpses of what occurred on that fateful morning.

John Richardson was the son of Amelia Richardson, a widow who rented out the first two floors of no. 29 and ran a small packing-case business from the cellar and the back yard. Mrs Richardson was very trusting of those who lived in the house, and it was not unusual for the front door to be unlocked; perhaps as a result of this, some tools had been stolen from the cellar some time before.[35] Subsequently, John Richardson, who lived in nearby John Street, would often visit the house on his way to work and check that the cellar doors were locked. This he did at 4.45 on the morning of 8 September and, after doing so and satisfying himself that all was well, sat on the steps leading from the back door in order to cut a piece of leather from his boot that had been annoying him. It was just getting light, and he could see the yard all around him, noticing nothing unusual. He declared, 'I could not have failed to notice the deceased had she been lying there.'[36]

Albert Cadosch, a Parisian-born carpenter, lived next door at no. 27. At about 5.20 a.m. he said that he went outside to his back yard (probably to use the outdoor privy) and on his return he heard somebody say, 'No.' A few minutes later, he had to go back and as he passed the fence that divided the yards of nos. 27 and 29 he heard what he believed was something falling against it from the other side. When he left the house immediately after, he noted that the time was 5.32 a.m. on the clock of Christ Church as he passed it.[37] Had Cadosch heard the murder taking place? Despite this, the residents of no. 29 heard nothing out of the ordinary until the commotion surrounding the discovery of the body erupted around 6.00 a.m.

And what a commotion it was. Large crowds assembled outside Commercial Street police station, Buck's Row and Hanbury Street.[38] At the latter, the street was heaving with onlookers, local residents were leaning out of windows to catch the spectacle, and some entrepreneurial characters even profited from the situation, selling refreshments and, in some cases, charging money to view the murder site from the windows of neighbouring houses. Fear, excitement and anger were tangible; never, said one newspaper,

> have the streets of East London presented such an appearance of mingled excitement, awe, and indignation, until within the last few days. Poor murdered Polly Nicholls, lying butchered outside the Essex Wharf in Buck's-row, was bad enough in all conscience, and sent every spectator of the spot where the body was found away with a desire for vengeance against the perpetrator of so foul a deed; but the latest butchery of Annie Chapman at Hanbury-street has driven the inhabitants of Whitechapel nearly crazy.[39]

Occasionally the crowds would burst into sporadic unruliness, giving the police cause to break up 'lynch mobs' who responded furiously to the many rumours sweeping the neighbourhood. Some men, pointed out as somehow suspicious, would find themselves fleeing for their safety, and unfounded stories of potential arrests saw excitable hordes descend upon police stations. 'Leather Apron' was still the name on everybody's lips, perhaps exacerbated by the news that a leather apron had been found in the yard of no. 29 near the body – an item which was proven to belong to Mrs Richardson. Further supposed sightings of him were made, each time causing considerable excitement, regardless of whether it was truly the man himself or just a sensational claim by an overexcited and perhaps ignorant bystander. The police continued their search for 'Jack Pizer', and on the 10 September got their man when Sergeant William Thick went with a fellow officer to 22 Mulberry Street in Whitechapel, the home of John Pizer, and arrested him. Alas, the breakthrough would not be a long-lasting one, for, under questioning, Pizer – who indeed fitted several of 'Leather Apron's' attributes – could prove where he was at the times of the two preceding murders. He was staying at Crossman's lodging house in Holloway, north London, at the time of Nichols's murder and had spoken to a policeman on Seven Sisters Road about that night's dock fire, which was visible even from that distance. On 6 September, he had returned to Mulberry Street, where his family, aware that he may be at risk from those who thought of him as 'Leather Apron', kept him at home. His alibis were impeccable, and even though accounts vary as to whether Pizer was indeed 'Leather Apron' or was even believed as such by the public at large, he took the singular opportunity of appearing at the Chapman inquest on 12 September to clear his name.[40]

The police, however, had other leads to follow. At 7.00 on the morning of Annie Chapman's death, a Mrs Fiddymont, landlady of the Prince Albert pub on Brushfield Street, was standing in the 'first compartment' of the bar, talking with her friend Mary Chappell. A man entered the pub whose appearance frightened her. He was wearing a brown stiff hat, a dark coat and no waistcoat; his hat was pulled down over his eyes, and with his face partly concealed he asked for half a pint of 'four ale'. Mrs Fiddymont was struck by the fact that there were blood spots on the back of his right hand, on his collar and below his ear and that he behaved furtively. The man drank the beer in one gulp and immediately left. Mary Chappell followed the man into Brushfield Street and, noting that he was heading in the direction of Bishopsgate, pointed him out to a bystander, Joseph Taylor, who followed before losing sight of him.[41]

The sighting was soon linked to another early suspect, Jacob Isenschmid, who had come to the attention of the police on 11 September. Isenschmid, a butcher, had spent time in Colney Hatch asylum and since release had led a very unsettled life before being found by the police and placed at Fairfield Road asylum in Bow. Inspector Abberline felt that Isenschmid's description fitted that of the man seen by Mrs Fiddymont *et al.*, and an identity parade was arranged.[42] However, Isenschmid's mental health was unsatisfactory, and it is now not known if Mrs Fiddymont was ever called to identify him.

4.

'How can they catch me now?'

Following the death of Annie Chapman, the East End deto-
nated. Thanks to the widespread news coverage of the murder
and the resultant panic, the realities of East London, its populace, characteristics and far-reaching problems, exploded into
the faces of the public in a way that could not be ignored.
More than was the case for any of the women who fell victim
to the Whitechapel murderer, Annie's life was a most dramatic
demonstration of the journey taken by those unlucky enough
to be driven to the doss houses of Spitalfields, via the workhouse
and the park bench, through a combination of circumstance,
personal weakness and just plain bad luck. What the public now
had to face was the fact that these women were by no means
unique in the mighty city that was London. The *Daily Telegraph*
made this perfectly clear in an editorial:

'Dark Annie's' spirit still walks Whitechapel, unavenged by
Justice. Most miserable, most desolate, most degraded, most
forgotten and forsaken of all her sex in this vast Metropolis,
Destiny also reserved for her to perish most awfully and
mysteriously of all the recent martyrs of neglect by the hand
of some horrible assassin, who, not content with slaying, dese-
crated and mutilated the body of his victim. The inhuman
murderer still comes and goes about our streets free and
unpunished, hiding in his guilty heart the secret known only to

him, to Heaven, and to the dead. And yet even this forlorn and despised citizeness of London cannot be said to have suffered in vain. On the contrary, she has effected more by her death than many long speeches in Parliament and countless columns of letters to the newspapers could have brought about. She has forced innumerable people who never gave a serious thought before to the subject to realise how it is and where it is that our vast floating population – the waifs and strays of our thoroughfares – live and sleep at nights, and what sort of accommodation our rich and enlightened capital provides for them, after so many Acts of Parliament passed to improve the dwellings of the poor, and so many millions spent by our Board of Works, our vestries, and what not . . . but 'Dark Annie's' dreadful end has compelled a hundred thousand Londoners to reflect what it must be like to have no home at all except the 'common kitchen' of a low lodging-house; to sit there, sick and weak and bruised and wretched, for lack of fourpence with which to pay for the right of a 'doss'; to be turned out after midnight to earn the requisite pence, anywhere and anyhow; and in course of earning it to come across your murderer and to caress your assassin.[1]

The problems of the East End, the 'second square mile' that sat in complete opposition to its eminently wealthy neighbour, the City, were many. Throughout the industrial revolution of the early nineteenth century, it became a magnet for migrant workers from the shires and provinces looking to earn a living in the factories and workshops placed there by a city wary of 'noxious trades'. Breweries, slaughterhouses, tanneries and smithies flourished in an area where prevailing winds would blow pollutant fumes and smoke away from the financial quarter. Some, disposed to working at home or in less industrial surroundings, would settle into smaller industries like cigar and cabinet making, matchbox assembly or tailoring. The creation and subsequent growth of London's docks had seen to it that areas close to the river grew phenomenally quickly as London became a hub of world trade. But could the East End comfortably cope with the rapidly growing population? It appeared not; fields gave way to the urban sprawl and orchards and tenter grounds disappeared under new housing, crammed dangerously into the limited spaces available and often accessible only through small alleyways and dark passages. The average population density in London in 1888 was 50 people per acre, but in Whitechapel it was 176; shockingly, in the Bell Lane district of Spitalfields it was 600 people per acre.[2] Such a vast population made the availability of work for all practically impossible, and with the ravages of a long-standing recession, 'unemployment', a word coined in the 1880s, became a condition which touched many. By 1888, it is believed that out of a population of 456,877 in Tower Hamlets, over a third lived below the margins of subsistence, with a total of 13 per cent being 'chronically distressed' – in other words, facing daily starvation.[3]

Some of the most notorious neighbourhoods existed in the back streets of Whitechapel and Spitalfields; namely those districts where property owners had seized on the needs of a transient and fundamentally poor population, providing them with beds in common lodging houses. Spitalfields became particularly notorious; once the prosperous home of immigrant Huguenot silk weavers in the seventeenth and eighteenth centuries, the area had suffered with the passing of time. As the silk-weaving industry faltered in the early nineteenth century, the French settlers moved on, allowing their once handsome properties to become sublet or converted into doss houses, and their gardens, once planted with fruit and mulberry trees, were replaced by cramped tenements. The most notorious district consisted of the streets around Commercial Street, a road which had been built in the 1850s with the intention of clearing slums as well as extending trade routes from the London docks. It cut through leprous, overcrowded warrens, but the displaced population did not disperse far and wide, and the already crammed thoroughfares on either side filled up with the exiled poor. Flower and Dean Street, Thrawl Street and Dorset Street were names that even today are historically synonymous with the worst of London poverty. And it was in the common lodging houses here where could be found the Ted Stanleys, the Eliza Coopers, the Pearly Polls and of course the Mary Ann Nichols, Martha Tabrams and Annie Chapmans of this world. As one correspondent described it:

> Thieves, loose women, and bad characters abound, and, although the police are not subject, perhaps, to quite the same dangers as they were a few years ago, there is still reason to believe that a constable will avoid, as far as he can, this part of his beat, unless accompanied by a brother officer. The district, in short, is one of common lodging-houses, and it is believed by some that if the mysteries of their ownership were exposed to the public eye much would be made clear.[4]

Philanthropy, however, was not scarce. Commercial Street was home to Toynbee Hall, set up in 1884 by Canon Samuel Barnett of St Jude's Whitechapel to bring help, education and culture to the impoverished east Londoner. The Salvation Army, formed by William Booth in 1865, saw its genesis on these very streets. And Thomas Barnardo, a former medical student at the London Hospital on Whitechapel Road, was moved to provide care and shelter for the destitute children of the East End in the 1880s after seeing so much impoverishment. But these well-meaning social reformers were taking on a resilient adversary, and the problems endured, with many of the solutions failing or being too slow to effect positive change. East London had become a Gordian knot – a problem insoluble in its own terms. With the murder of Annie Chapman, the dark underbelly of the East End slums was brought into focus like never before. Suddenly, newspaper readers around the globe were made aware of the conditions, and it did not reflect favourably on what was then the world's largest and wealthiest city.

One other ingredient impacted on the life of the East End significantly during those turbulent 1880s – immigration. Proximity to the river Thames meant that this quarter of the capital would invariably receive waves of immigrants who would go on to stamp their mark on the area. After the Huguenots came Irish travellers, fleeing problems caused by the potato famine of 1845–52, and from 1881 onwards Jews from Eastern Europe, and it was this latter wave of settlers whose presence was felt by many to exacerbate the already ingrained problems.

On 1 March 1881, Tsar Alexander II of Russia was assassinated, provoking a wave of persecution against Jews in Eastern Europe, even though only one of the five assassination conspirators was Jewish. Anti-Jewish 'pogroms' ensured huge migration as thousands attempted to flee dire poverty and unremitting maltreatment, and for many the only way to escape the relentless hardship and enforced transience was to go overseas. London, and specifically the East End, with its small, previously established Jewish communities, was an ideal choice for many. Whitechapel became the first point of entry to the United Kingdom for those who disembarked at St Katherine's Dock near the Tower of London. The influx was more like an avalanche – by 1888, it is estimated that in the district of Whitechapel, over 40 per cent of the population were Jewish settlers, forming micro-communities or 'ghettos' of their own. With the unemployed scraping to survive, these newcomers, who needed work as much as anybody else, were blamed for inflaming the situation. Large numbers of unskilled and semi-skilled Jewish workers were prepared to work long hours for poor wages, effectively putting the indigenous workers out of the job market. As these newcomers began to descend upon specific areas of Whitechapel and Spitalfields, further resentment was forthcoming from those who believed that they were responsible 'for pushing up rents by accepting overcrowded conditions, therefore forcing native East Enders to move out'.[5] As the alarm surrounding the Whitechapel murders took hold during September 1888, eyes inevitably turned to the Jews, again the ideal scapegoat:

On Saturday in several quarters of East London the crowds who had assembled in the streets began to assume a very threatening attitude towards the Hebrew population of the district. It was repeatedly asserted that no Englishman could have perpetrated such a horrible crime as that of Hanbury-street, and that it must have been done by a Jew – and forthwith the crowds proceeded to threaten and abuse such of the unfortunate Hebrews as they found in the streets. Happily, the presence of the large number of police in the streets prevented a riot actually taking place.[6]

Just as our correspondent was writing a gang of young vagabonds marched down Hanbury-street shouting 'Down with the Jews!' 'It was a Jew who did it!' 'No Englishman did it!'

After these the police were prompt, and whenever there was a stand they quickly, and without ceremony, dispersed them. There have been many fights, but the police are equal to it, as men are held in reserve under cover, and when there is a row they rush out and soon establish order. As the night advances the disorderly mobs who openly express antipathy to the Jews increase, and a request has been forwarded to headquarters for extra men.[7]

The heady mix was, of course, being continually stirred by the sensationalist newspapers. The *Star*, perhaps the most lurid of them all,[8] boasted that its circulation on the Monday after Annie Chapman's murder was 261,000 – 55,000 more than any other evening paper in London. The *Star* could also be said to have been responsible for one more unwitting victim of the Whitechapel horrors, when Mary Burridge, a resident of Blackfriars Road, collapsed in a fit after reading one of their reports. After regaining consciousness for a brief while after, she promptly died.[9]

Such unrest led to the formation of the Mile End Vigilance Committee, a group of local businessmen who felt that the scares surrounding the murders were affecting trade. At a meeting of the committee on 10 September, George Lusk, a painter and decorator of Tollet Street, Mile End, was nominated chairman. The question of rewards was now a major concern, and the Mile End Vigilance Committee, along with the already extant St Jude's District Committee, were committed to pressurizing the authorities to offer them. A long list of subscribers was drawn up with the aim of securing £100 from private contributors to bolster the same amount already being offered privately by Samuel Montagu MP. Direct pleas to the home secretary, Henry Matthews, were unsuccessful, with the reply stating that 'such offers of reward tended to produce more harm than good, and the Secretary of State is satisfied that there is nothing in the circumstances of the present case to justify a departure from this rule'.[10]

But all was not well as far as the investigation was concerned; with the newspapers reporting fresh incidences of knife crime and threats against women around London and the East End, it was becoming difficult to separate the wheat from the chaff. Detectives were now increasingly irritated by using precious time sifting through innumerable reports and claims which had no foundation.[11] One example was the case of Edward McKenna, who was arrested on suspicion of being a man seen in Flower and Dean Street with a knife on the day of Chapman's murder. Several members of the public were found who had seen suspicious individuals that morning, including the potman of the Ten Bells and Joseph Taylor, the man who had followed the suspicious individual from the Prince Albert pub,[12] but all to no avail. As Annie Chapman lay cold in the Whitechapel workhouse mortuary, Dr Robert Anderson was on his way to Switzerland for his first day of sick leave and, despite not mentioning his inconvenient absence, the radical press were apoplectic at the investigating authorities' lack of progress:

And when public opinion is at last aroused, and the whole East-end is under a Red Terror, our authorities refuse to take the most obvious and elementary precautions for ensuring detection. All we can say is that if a mad panic sweeps through the quarters desolated by a maniac's knife, the Home Office and Scotland-yard will be alone to blame. It is impossible to exaggerate the utter want of confidence in the whole police system which this frightful tragedy has evoked; and if sheer fright grows into crazed fury we shall hold Mr MATTHEWS and Sir CHARLES WARREN responsible.[13]

On 10 September, the *Evening Standard* made a passing mention that a message had been found on a wall in the back yard of 29 Hanbury Street, reading 'Five; 15 more, and then I give myself up.' This story, mentioned in other forms and with different wording, would remain unsubstantiated; however it did hint at a more tangible and genuine phenomenon to come – alleged communications from the murderer, namely in the form of letters. The first known example[14] was written on 24 September and sent to Charles Warren:

Dear sir

I do wish to give myself up I am in misery with nightmare I am the man who committed all these murders in the last six months my name is so [drawing of coffin] and so I am horse slauterer and work at Name [blacked out] address [blacked out]

I have found the woman I wanted that is chapman and I done what I called slautered her but if any one comes I will surrender but I am not going to walk to the station by myself so I am yours truly [drawing of coffin]

Keep the Boro road clear or I might take a trip up there
Photo
[drawing of knife]
of knife
this is the knife that I done these murders with it is a small handle with a large long blade sharpe both sides

It was seemingly given little consideration and was certainly not made public, but, unbeknownst to the author, it was to be the first of its kind in a case that would be deluged with such missives on a scale never seen before. Soon after, a second letter was received by the Central News Agency on New Bridge Street, London on 27 September. Written in red ink, it read:

25 Sept 1888
Dear Boss,

I keep on hearing the police have caught me but they wont fix me just yet. I have laughed when they look so clever and talk about being on the right track. That joke about Leather Apron gave me real fits. I am down on whores and I shant quit ripping them till I do get buckled. Grand work the last job was. I gave the lady no time to squeal. How can they catch me now. I love my work and want to start again. You will soon hear of me with my funny little games. I saved some of the proper red stuff in a ginger beer bottle over the last job to write with but it went thick like glue and I cant use it. Red ink is fit enough I hope ha. ha. The next job I do I shall clip the ladys ears off and send to the police officers just for jolly wouldn't you. Keep this letter back till I do a bit more work, then give it out straight. My knife's so nice and sharp I want to get to work right away if I get a chance. Good Luck.

Yours truly
Jack the Ripper

Dont mind me giving the trade name

PS Wasnt good enough to post this before I got all the red ink off my hands curse it No luck yet. They say I'm a doctor now. ha ha [15]

The letter was sent to the Metropolitan Police on 29 September with a covering note in the handwriting of Central News journalist Thomas Bulling, which claimed that the agency had treated the thing as 'a joke'.[16] What the police initially felt about it is unclear, but in accordance with the author's wishes, they did indeed keep the letter back until the murderer struck again. And they did not have long to wait.

'No, not tonight, some other night'

As Elizabeth Stride served customers in the Poplar coffee shop she ran with her husband, she must have felt that, for once in her life, things were going fine. The establishment offered some security for a woman living far away from her native country and newly married to an Englishman. But it had not always been that way.

She was born Elisabeth Gustafsdotter on 27 November 1843 at a small farm called Stora Tumlehed, in Torslanda parish, north of Gothenburg, Sweden. Her parents, Gustaf Ericsson and Beatta Carlsdotter, had four children, two girls and two boys, of which Elizabeth was the second eldest. Very little of her childhood is known, save for records of her religious instruction between 1848 and 1854, which commented that her biblical knowledge was good. In 1859, she applied to work in Gothenburg and was accepted, her behaviour being deemed 'good' and her biblical knowledge 'extensive'.[1]

At the age of seventeen, she secured a job as a maid for Lars Frederick Olofsson and his family, staying there until 1864, after which her life began to crumble. In August of that year her mother died, and by the following month Elizabeth had become pregnant. There were complications – she had been diagnosed with a venereal disease (condyloma, or genital warts) and on 21 April 1865 gave birth to a stillborn daughter. Soon after, she was treated for chancre, a highly contagious ulcer which forms in the early stages of syphilis, but by November, she was given a clean bill of health, appearing in police records as a professional prostitute. Her eventual discharge from the records was helped by her obtaining further employment as a maid, but by 1866 Elizabeth had inherited a respectable sum of money from her mother's estate, enabling her to go to Britain, and in February 1866 she arrived in London.

She was registered at the Swedish church in Princess Square, St George-in-the-East, in July 1866 and, according to some who knew her later in life, she went into the service of a 'foreign gentleman' or a family living near Hyde Park.[2] A life in the West End of London during this period is borne out by her address in 1869, given as 67 Gower Street at the time of her marriage to a carpenter, John Stride, on 7 March at the church of St Giles-in-the-Fields. By the following year they had opened the coffee shop in Upper North Street in Poplar, moving the business a few years later to 178 Poplar High Street, where they remained until 1875. From then on, records show that Elizabeth's life began to take the same problematical course that she might have thought had been left behind in Sweden.

At the Thames Magistrates Court on 21 March 1877 she is recorded as being sent by the police to the Poplar workhouse for reasons unknown. The Swedish church in London records that Elizabeth sought financial assistance in January 1879 owing 'to her husband's illness'.[3] By 1881, Elizabeth and John were living in Usher Road, Old Ford, Bow,[4] and it is believed that they were at this address when the couple separated. From 28 December until 4 January 1882 Elizabeth was admitted to the Whitechapel workhouse infirmary on Baker's Row, suffering from bronchitis, where her address was given as Brick Lane. After her discharge, she entered the workhouse on

South Grove for three days – it was after this that she found lodgings at 32 Flower and Dean Street, Spitalfields, the doss house which became her favoured residence for much of the remainder of her life. In the meantime, the illness that had seemingly afflicted John Stride resulted in his death from heart disease in 1884 – he was sixty-three years old. We cannot be sure how John's death affected Elizabeth, but many accounts from those who knew her said that she claimed to have been involved in the *Princess Alice* disaster in 1878, when the paddle-steamer *Princess Alice* was struck by the collier boat *Bywell Castle* at Galleon's Reach, a terrible incident which resulted in over 600 deaths and which remained the Thames's worst boating disaster for many decades. Elizabeth claimed that she lost her husband and children in the tragedy, which was blatantly untrue and which has led many to believe that Elizabeth had wilfully created a fantasy to account for her predicament.

A few weeks after John's funeral, Elizabeth appeared before Thames Magistrates Court on a charge of being drunk and disorderly and soliciting, for which she received seven days' hard labour.[5] In 1885, she began a stormy relationship with Michael Kidney, a waterside labourer seven years her junior, and together they took up lodgings in Devonshire Road, off Commercial Road. The couple separated frequently, and occasionally Elizabeth would absent herself for days at a time – in the three years they were together, Kidney reckoned they had been apart for a total of five months, and that it was abuse of alcohol that caused the separations.[6] There were also suggestions of violence on Kidney's part, for on 6 April 1887 Elizabeth accused him of assault, only for the case to be thrown out when she failed to turn up at the Magistrates Court. In all fairness, there is little to suggest that Kidney was physically abusive. However their chaotic lives do appear to have been fuelled by alcohol: Kidney himself was sentenced to three days' hard labour for being drunk and disorderly and using obscene language in July 1888. Elizabeth was also no stranger to the Magistrates Courts during 1887–8, appearing no fewer than seven times for numerous drink and disorder misdemeanours. Financially, things must also have been hard, for she also petitioned twice for monetary assistance from the Swedish church.[7]

The last time Kidney saw Elizabeth was on Tuesday 25 September 1888 in Commercial Street. She was sober, and the couple parted on good terms, Kidney assuming they would reunite a little later. However, it was not to be.[8]

Elizabeth returned to 32 Flower and Dean Street, and during the next few days Dr Thomas Barnardo visited the lodging house. The women there complained bitterly of their plight and the threat from the murderer, one exclaiming, 'We're all up to no good, and no one cares what becomes of us. Perhaps some of us will be killed next! If anyone had helped the likes of us long ago we would never have come to this.'[9] Dr Barnardo later confirmed that one of the women assembled was Elizabeth Stride. She was present at the lodging house on Saturday 29 September and that afternoon earned herself sixpence for cleaning two rooms, paid by Elizabeth Tanner, the deputy, who knew Elizabeth as 'Long Liz'. Subsequently, both spent some time in the Queen's Head public house at the corner of Commercial Street and Fashion Street before returning to no. 32, where they parted company.[10]

Fellow lodger Charles Preston saw Elizabeth between 6.00 and 7.00 that evening in the kitchen of the lodging house, where he claimed she was 'dressed ready to go out', and she asked him for the loan of a clothes brush. She was wearing a black jacket trimmed with fur and a coloured silk handkerchief round her neck. He was not told where she was going that evening or what time she would be returning. Catherine Lane was also present, and Elizabeth asked her to look after a piece of velvet while she was away; both Preston and Lane concurred that Elizabeth was sober when she left.[11]

Shortly before 11.00 p.m., John Gardner and J. Best[12] entered the Bricklayer's Arms at the corner of Fordham Street and Settles Street. As they did so a man and a woman left the pub, having already been served, and, owing to the heavy rain, the couple stood in the shelter of the doorway. The man was of English appearance and respectably dressed in a black morning suit with a morning coat. He appeared to have no eyelashes but was sporting a thick black moustache. He wore a rather tall black billycock hat and had on a collar. The woman, on the other hand, was poorly dressed, with a flower in her jacket, and the fact that the couple hugged and kissed came as some surprise to Best, judging by their outward differences. The two men offered them a drink and suggested that the man treat his woman companion and when they refused said, 'That's Leather Apron getting round you,' at which point, perhaps tired of the two labourers' jibing, the couple departed 'like a shot'.[13] They later identified the woman as Elizabeth Stride.

Berner Street was a long but narrow thoroughfare leading from Commercial Road southwards to Ellen Street in the parish of St George-in-the-East. In 1888 Berner Street contained a variety of buildings, most notably a row of houses on the east side, broken by Sander Street and Dutfield's Yard, which formed a passage between nos. 40 and 42. No. 40 was the International Working Men's Educational Club, patronized mostly by Jewish workers, a place for socialist political

meetings and with a printing works at the rear, the offices of
Der Arbeter Fraint (Worker's Friend), a radical Yiddish newspaper.
Opposite was a board school, and at no. 46, on the corner with
Fairclough Street, was the Nelson beer house. At 11.45 p.m.
William Marshall, a resident of no. 64 Berner Street, was
standing at the door of his house and observed a couple standing a few doors away on the opposite side of the road. They
were kissing, so Marshall could not see the man's face clearly,
but he was able to note other particulars – he was middle-aged
and stout, about 5 feet 6 inches tall, respectably dressed in a
small black cut-away coat and dark trousers. He was wearing a
small peaked cap, 'something like a sailor would wear'. All in
all, he had the appearance of a clerk. The woman was wearing
a black jacket and skirt and a black crape bonnet, but Marshall
did not notice if there was a flower pinned to her jacket. Just
before the couple walked on, the man was heard to say, 'You
will say anything but your prayers.'[14]

Matthew Packer, a greengrocer who served from the front
window of his home at 44 Berner Street, told police that he
had seen nothing unusual that night and had locked up his
shop early as trade was slack owing to the heavy rain that had
developed by that time. Unfortunately, Packer was approached
again twice about that night and on both occasions changed
his story, to the effect that he had seen Elizabeth Stride with a
man who bought grapes from his shop. His description
appeared to fit others that had already been published, leading
Donald Swanson, in his official report of 19 October, to
declare:

> Packer, who is an elderly man, has unfortunately made differ-
> ent statements so that apart from the fact of the hour at
> which he saw the woman (and she was seen afterwards by

the P. C. and Schwartz as stated) any statement he made would be rendered almost valueless as evidence.[15]

Dr George Bagster Phillips, who was called upon to perform the post-mortem, noted that there was no trace of grapes – pips, skin or otherwise – in Elizabeth's stomach, a fact which served to give Matthew Packer even less credibility as a witness. The presence of a grape stalk in Dutfield's Yard had been widely reported after the event, with some press reports even stating that Elizabeth was found holding some grapes in her hand when she was discovered.[16] However, the story was soon refuted as, according to those actually there, there was no such thing.

The officer mentioned in Swanson's report was PC William Smith, who, at 12.30 a.m. on 30 September, saw a man and a woman (whom he later felt certain was Elizabeth Stride) standing on the pavement a few yards up Berner Street, on the opposite side to Dutfield's Yard. He described the man as being about twenty-eight years of age, 5 feet 7 inches tall, wearing a dark overcoat and trousers. He also wore a hard felt deer-stalker hat and was described as 'respectable' looking. The man was also holding a newspaper parcel, about eighteen inches in length and six or eight inches wide. He also noticed that the woman had a flower in her jacket. PC Smith heard no conversation, and as the couple appeared sober and were not acting in a suspicious manner, he continued his beat along Berner Street towards Commercial Road.[17] Fifteen minutes later, James Brown, a dock labourer on his way to a chandler's shop, saw a woman with a man in Fairclough Street. The woman had her back to the wall of the board school, facing the man, who had his arm up against it. Brown heard the woman say, 'No, not tonight, some other night,' which is what attracted his attention. There was no trace of an accent in the woman's voice. Brown said the man was about 5 feet 7 inches tall and stoutly built, wearing a long overcoat which went down almost to his heels. He was wearing a hat, but Brown was unable to describe it. It was quite dark, so he could not tell if the woman was wearing a flower on her jacket, but both appeared sober.[18]

Curiously, the reliability of Brown's sighting – in terms of timing at least – could be called into question by a remarkable incident that also took place at 12.45 a.m. Israel Schwartz, on his way home to Ellen Street, was passing along the western side of Berner Street, having come from Commercial Road. By the entrance to Dutfield's Yard he had a most curious and alarming experience. Donald Swanson's official report takes up Schwartz's story:

> he saw a man stop and speak to a woman, who was standing in the gateway. He tried to pull the woman into the street, but he turned her round and threw her down on the footway and the woman screamed three times, but not very loudly. On crossing to the opposite side of the street, he saw a second man lighting his pipe. The man who threw the woman down called out, apparently to the man on the opposite side of the road, 'Lipski', and then Schwartz walked away, but finding that he was followed by the second man, he ran as far as the railway arch, but the man did not follow so far. Schwartz cannot say whether the two men were together or known to each other.
>
> He thus describes the first man, who threw the woman down:– age, about 30; ht, 5 ft 5 in; comp., fair; hair, dark; small brown moustache, full face, broad shouldered; dress, dark jacket and trousers, black cap with peak, and nothing in his hands.

Second man: age, 35; ht., 5 ft 11 in; comp., fresh; hair, light brown; dress, dark overcoat, old black hard felt hat, wide brim; had a clay pipe in his hand.[19]

'Lipski' was a direct reference to the notorious case of Israel Lipski, convicted of the murder of Miriam Angel at 16 Batty Street in 1887 and who was hanged at Newgate for the crime. Since then the word had been used 'by persons as mere ejaculation by way of endeavouring to insult the Jew to whom it has been addressed'.[20] Schwartz, a young Hungarian immigrant, was of decidedly Jewish appearance. The *Star* was the only newspaper to cover the incident in any depth, interviewing Schwartz with the aid of an interpreter. Their report[21] added other details, some of which contradicted the original statement, despite the basic story being essentially the same. Schwartz described the attacker as intoxicated in the *Star* interview. In the police statement, he tried to pull the woman *from* the passage, whereas in the *Star*, he tried to push her *into* the passage. In the *Star* interview, it was the second man (not the attacker) who yelled 'a warning' (as opposed to 'Lipski!' in the police statement). In the interview, the second man had a red moustache, but no mention of this is made in Swanson's report. And, significantly, the *Star* stated that the second man was holding a *knife*, not a pipe.

Another intriguing press account came in the form of Fanny Mortimer, a resident of 36 Berner Street, a mere two doors down from Dutfield's Yard. She stated that she was standing at her door for much of the time between 12.30 and 1.00 that morning. She heard no noise and the only person she saw was a man holding a black bag who walked along Berner Street, looking up at the club as he passed, before turning the corner by the school.[22] Moments after going back into her house, she claimed she heard a commotion from the working men's club. Mrs Mortimer's account flies in the face of testimony from PC Smith and Israel Schwartz – it raises questions regarding the accuracy of her timekeeping and the duration of her stay at the door. She did see a man with a black bag, a man who was a member of the International Working Men's Educational Club named Leon Goldstein and who had been encouraged to come forward after the sighting was made public.[23] The commotion she heard from the club was not 'another row', as she described it, but the activity surrounding the discovery of a dead woman in Dutfield's Yard.

It was the steward of the club, Louis Diemschitz, who found the body of Elizabeth Stride in the yard at 1.00 a.m. As would be normal after a long day's work (Diemschitz was a market trader who that day had been working in Sydenham), he was driving his pony and cart into Dutfield's Yard with the purpose of dropping off some unsold goods before stabling the pony in George Yard, Cable Street. On this occasion the pony stopped at the entrance and pulled to one side. Diemschitz could see something in the way and prodded it with his crop before getting off the cart and striking a match to get a better view in the dark. Before the wind blew the match out, he could see a woman lying on the ground. Initially worried that it was his wife, he went into the club and, finding her safe and well, went back into the yard with Morris Eagle and Isaac Kozebrodsky, at which time he wasn't sure if the woman was dead. By the light of a candle, the men could see blood on the cobbles near the body. Without touching anything, the men went out into Berner Street and separated, looking for the police. Diemschitz and Kozebrodsky, running towards Fairclough Street and beyond, encountered only Edward Spooner, but Eagle, going north into Commercial Road found PCs

Henry Lamb and Henry Collins, who accompanied him back to Dutfield's Yard.

PC Collins was sent to fetch Dr Frederick Blackwell from his surgery at 100 Commercial Road, but, as he was still in bed, Blackwell's assistant Edward Johnson went to Berner Street first. PC Lamb sent Morris Eagle to fetch an inspector from Leman Street police station and examined the body, noting there was no pulse and that the face was quite warm. As he did so, people began to enter Dutfield's Yard, but he told them to keep back, eventually closing the gates to the yard assisted by Edward Spooner, who had followed Diemschitz and Koze-brodsky back to the scene. A constable was put on the gate, allowing nobody to leave or enter, and PC Lamb made an examination of Dutfield's Yard and the club building. In the club, he checked the hands of attendants for bloodstains.[24] Edward Johnson made initial observations on the body before Dr Blackwell arrived at 1.16 a.m. He observed that

> The deceased was lying on her left side obliquely across the passage, her face looking towards the right wall. Her legs were drawn up, her feet close against the wall of the right side of the passage. Her head was resting beyond the carriage-wheel rut, the neck lying over the rut. Her feet were three yards from the gateway. Her dress was unfastened at the neck. The neck and chest were quite warm, as were also the legs, and the face was slightly warm. The hands were cold. The right hand was open and on the chest, and was smeared with blood. The left hand, lying on the ground, was partially closed, and contained a small packet of cachous wrapped in tissue paper. There were no rings, nor marks of rings, on her hands. The appearance of the face was quite placid. The mouth was slightly open. The deceased had round her neck a check silk scarf, the bow of

which was turned to the left and pulled very tight. In the neck there was a long incision which exactly corresponded with the lower border of the scarf. The border was slightly frayed, as if by a sharp knife. The incision in the neck commenced on the left side, 2 inches below the angle of the jaw, and almost in a direct line with it, nearly severing the vessels on that side, cutting the windpipe completely in two, and terminating on the opposite side 1 inch below the angle of the right jaw, but without severing the vessels on that side. I could not ascertain whether the bloody hand had been moved. The blood was running down the gutter into the drain in the opposite direction from the feet. There was about 1lb of clotted blood close by the body, and a stream all the way from there to the back door of the club. [25]

More police officers arrived at the scene, as did Dr George Bagster Phillips. It was not until 4.30 a.m. that the body of Elizabeth Stride was removed to the nearest mortuary, a small brick building within the grounds of St George-in-the-East church at the junction of Cannon Street Road and Cable Street. Within the hour, PC Collins had washed the blood away from the yard. But by this time news was rapidly circulating that another murder had taken place, this time within the bounds of the City of London.

6.

'Good night, old cock'

At 1.30 a.m., City Police Constable Edward Watkins entered Mitre Square from Mitre Street, something he had done several times since commencing his beat at 10.00 the previous night and, with his lantern turned on and attached to his belt, he examined the various corners and passages. Mitre Square was surrounded mostly by tall warehouses, and there were also two dwelling houses in the north-east side, one of which was unoccupied. Other than the entrance from Mitre Street, the small covered St James's Passage gave access to St James's Place (also known as 'the Orange Market') and on the opposite corner, narrow Church Passage ran to Duke Street. The south-east corner, at the rear of Tayler's picture-framing shop in Mitre Street, was the darkest part of the square, gaining little illumination from the two gas lamps which served the immediate area. Satisfied that all was well, PC Watkins continued on his way. He returned at 1.44 a.m., immediately turned right into the dark corner and, on shining his lamp into the darkness, found the body of a woman in a terrible state of mutilation:

> I saw the body of the woman lying there on her back with her feet facing the square, her clothes up above her waist. I saw her throat was cut and her bowels protruding. The stomach was ripped up, she was lying in a pool of blood.[1]

Watkins immediately ran across the square to the warehouse of Kearley and Tonge and alerted the night watchman there, retired Metropolitan Police officer George Morris. On being told that there had been 'another woman cut to pieces', Morris fetched his lamp and accompanied Watkins to the body. Being in possession of his old police whistle (City police did not carry them), he blew it and ran into Mitre Street towards Aldgate, whereupon he was approached by two officers, PCs James Harvey and Frederick Holland. Returning with Morris to the scene, Holland immediately went to fetch Dr George Sequeira from his surgery in Jewry Street, and Harvey remained by the body with Watkins. Joining them were Detectives Edward Marriott, Robert Outram and Daniel Halse, who had heard the alarm being raised as they stood talking at the bottom of Houndsditch a few hundred yards away. At Bishopsgate police station, Inspector Collard got word of the murder and sent for Dr Frederick Gordon Brown before rushing to Mitre Square, finding the various police officers by the body with Dr Sequeira, who had arrived at about 1.55 a.m. From then on, officials began to assemble quickly as the small gaggle of men were joined by Dr Brown and Superintendents James McWilliam and Alfred Foster, who set about instructing their men to make a search of the immediate vicinity and surrounding streets.

Sometime after 2.20 a.m., the body was conveyed to the mortuary on Golden Lane and stripped, Inspector Collard making a list of her clothing and possessions. Dr Brown conducted the post-mortem that afternoon, assisted and observed by Dr Sequeira, Dr George Bagster Phillips and Dr William Sedgewick Saunders. The woman's injuries were extensive:

The face was very much mutilated. There was a cut about a quarter of an inch through the lower left eyelid, dividing the structures completely through. The upper eyelid on that side, there was a scratch through the skin on the left upper eyelid, near to the angle of the nose. The right eyelid was cut through to about half an inch. There was a deep cut over the bridge of the nose, extending from the left border of the nasal bone down near the angle of the jaw on the right side of the cheek. This cut went into the bone and divided all the structures of the cheek except the mucous membrane of the mouth. The tip of the nose was quite detached by an oblique cut from the bottom of the nasal bone to where the wings of the nose join on to the face. A cut from this divided the upper lip and extended through the substance of the gum over the right upper lateral incisor tooth. About half an inch from the top of the nose was another oblique cut. There was a cut on the right angle of the mouth as if the cut of a point of a knife. The cut extended an inch and a half, parallel with the lower lip. There was on each side of cheek a cut which peeled up the skin, forming a triangular flap about an inch and a half. On the left cheek there were two abrasions of the epithelium under the left ear.

The throat was cut across to the extent of about six or seven inches. A superficial cut commenced about an inch and a half below the lobe below, and about two and a half inches behind the left ear, and extended across the throat to about three inches below the lobe of the right ear. The big muscle across the throat was divided through on the left side. The large vessels on the left side of the neck were severed. The larynx was severed below the vocal cord. All the deep structures were severed to the bone, the knife marking intervertebral cartilages. The sheath of the vessels on the right side was just opened. The carotid artery had a fine hole opening, the internal jugular vein was opened about an inch and a half – not divided.

The blood vessels contained clot. All these injuries were performed by a sharp instrument like a knife, and pointed.

The cause of death was haemorrhage from the left common carotid artery. The death was immediate and the mutilations were inflicted after death.

The front walls were laid open from the breast bones to the pubes. The cut commenced opposite the enciform cartilage. The incision went upwards, not penetrating the skin that was over the sternum. It then divided the enciform cartilage. The knife must have cut obliquely at the expense of that cartilage. Behind this, the liver was stabbed as if by the point of a sharp instrument. Below this was another incision into the liver of about two and a half inches, and below this the left lobe of the liver was slit through by a vertical cut. Two cuts were shewn by a jagging of the skin on the left side. The abdominal walls were divided in the middle line to within a quarter of an inch of the navel. The cut then took a horizontal course for two inches and a half towards the right side. It then divided round the navel on the left side, and made a parallel incision to the former horizontal incision, leaving the navel on a tongue of skin. Attached to the navel was two and a half inches of the lower part of the rectus muscle on the left side of the abdomen. The incision then took an oblique direction to the right and was shelving. The incision went down the right side of the vagina and rectum for half an inch behind the rectum.

There was a stab of about an inch on the left groin. This was done by a pointed instrument. Below this was a cut of three inches going through all tissues making a wound of the peritoneum about the same extent. An inch below the crease of the thigh was a cut extending from the anterior spine of the ilium obliquely down the inner side of the left thigh and separating the left labium, forming a flap of skin up to the groin.

The left rectus muscle was not detached. There was a flap of skin formed by the right thigh, attaching the right labium, and extending up to the spine of the ilium. The muscles on the right side inserted into the frontal ligaments were cut through. The skin was retracted through the whole of the cut through the abdomen, but the vessels were not clotted. Nor had there been any appreciable bleeding from the vessels. I draw the conclusion that the act was made after death, and there would not have been much blood on the murderer. The cut was made by someone on the right side of the body, kneeling below the middle of the body.

I removed the content of the stomach and placed it in a jar for further examination. There seemed very little in it in the way of food or fluid, but from the cut end partly digested farinaceous food escaped. The intestines had been detached to a large extent from the mesentery. About two feet of the colon was cut away. The sigmoid flexure was invaginated into the rectum very tightly. Right kidney was pale, bloodless with slight congestion of the base of the pyramids. There was a cut from the upper part of the slit on the under surface of the liver to the left side, and another cut at right angles to this, which were about an inch and a half deep and two and a half inches long. Liver itself was healthy. The gall bladder contained bile. The pancreas was cut, but not through, on the left side of the spinal column. Three and a half inches of the lower border of the spleen by half an inch was attached only to the peritoneum. The peritoneal lining was cut through on the left side and the left kidney carefully taken out and removed. The left renal artery was cut through. I would say that someone who knew the position of the kidney must have done it. The lining membrane over the uterus was cut through. The womb was cut through horizontally, leaving a stump of three quarters of an inch. The rest of the womb had been taken away with some of the ligaments. The vagina and cervix of the womb was uninjured.

Attention was also drawn to a dirty linen apron worn by the deceased over her skirts, a portion of which was missing. It transpired that the fragment had already been found, at 2.55 a.m. by PC Alfred Long, a Metropolitan Police officer on his beat walking through Goulston Street, Whitechapel. The portion was found in the open doorway to 108–119 Wentworth Dwellings and appeared to be partly wet with blood. He at once searched the staircases and other parts of the building without any result, but he had noticed, on the wall above the apron, some writing in white chalk upon the black brickwork. According to PC Long's transcription of the message in his notebook, it read: 'The *Juews* are the men that will not be blamed for nothing.'[2] He was sure that neither the apron piece nor the writing were there when he passed along Goulston Street at 2.20 a.m. Detective Halse had also passed through the street at about that time while conducting his neighbourhood searches and had not noticed anything out of the ordinary then. Once news of the discovery had reached Leman Street police station, numerous officers from both the Metropolitan and City forces converged on Goulston Street. Directions were given by Inspector McWilliam of the City Police to have the writing photographed;[3] however, Superintendent Thomas Arnold from the Metropolitan force was desirous that the writing be erased lest it cause a riot against the local Jewish community in the wake of the recent accusations against them and excitement that had surrounded 'Leather Apron'.[4] Arnold's concern was vindicated following the arrival of Sir Charles Warren, who at 5.30 a.m., despite the urgings of some officers to have the offending part of the message covered prior to photographs being taken, ordered the erasure of the writing. A police constable who had been standing by with a wet sponge for some time awaiting further instructions did the deed. Warren later gave an explanation to the home secretary:

> A discussion took place whether the writing could be left covered up or otherwise or whether any portion of it could be left for an hour until it could be photographed; but after taking into consideration the excited state of the population in London generally at the time, the strong feeling which had been excited against the Jews, and the fact that in a short time there would be a large concourse of the people in the streets, and having before me the Report that if it was left there the house was likely to be wrecked (in which from my own observation I entirely concurred) I considered it desirable to obliterate the writing at once.[5]

Of course, there is little to suggest that the message was *actually* written by the murderer, and the possibility of it being anti-Semitic graffiti (of which there was much at the time) cannot be ignored. However, Warren's decision may have averted a disaster of great magnitude, even though he was roundly criticized for his judgement – Sir Robert Anderson later described the erasure as an act of 'crass stupidity'.[6]

The inquests into the two murders, for a time, ran concurrently, the Stride inquest being the longest, as was a characteristic of Wynne Baxter's proceedings. A number of witnesses were called who were able to give more details about the night of Stride's death; William West furnished the inquest with a detailed description of the crime scene and the club and testified that he had left the premises at 12.15 a.m. and had seen nothing unusual, noting that the gates of Dutfield's Yard were wide open.[7] Club member Joseph Lave also stated that he had left at 12.40 a.m. to catch some air and again saw nothing unusual – the yard was so dark he had to feel his way along the wall to reach the street.[8] Identification of Stride's body came quickly, but not without a little trouble; Mary Malcolm, a resident of Red Lion Square, Holborn, claimed that on the night of the murder she had felt a hand on her chest as she lay in bed and was kissed three times by a presence she was convinced was her sister Elizabeth Watts. Concerned for the well-being of her sibling, Mary visited the mortuary twice and identified the body as that of her sister, pointing out some distinguishing marks into the bargain.[9] The whole claim was reduced to a sham when Mrs Malcolm's sister, now remarried as Elizabeth Stokes, made an appearance to vouch for her safety.

Identifying the woman found in Mitre Square was a different matter. The body lay in the Golden Lane mortuary for several days until John Kelly, a labourer living at a lodging house at 55 Flower and Dean Street, identified the woman as his common-law wife, Catherine Conway. Soon after, Eliza Gold, a widow living in Thrawl Street, identified her as her sister, Catherine Eddowes.

Catherine Eddowes was born in Wolverhampton on 14 April 1842, the sixth of twelve children born to George Eddowes and his wife Catherine. The family moved to Bermondsey in London before Catherine was two years old, and she was subsequently educated at St John's Charity School, Potter's Field, Tooley Street. Her mother died in 1855, and her father two years later, from which point most of her siblings entered Bermondsey workhouse and industrial school. According to later press reports, she returned to the care of her aunt in Bilston Street, Wolverhampton, and found employment as a tin-plate stamper.[10] Around 1862 she began a relationship with an army pensioner named Thomas Conway (formerly enlisted in the 18th Royal Irish Regiment under the name Quinn and drawing a regimental pension under that name), who at that time was earning a living writing and selling chapbooks, cheap books sold on the streets by pedlars, the content usually being political or religious tracts, histories, nursery rhymes or accounts of current events. Together, they eked out a living this way around Birmingham and the Midlands, and in 1863, their first child, Catherine Ann Conway ('Annie'), was born in Norfolk.[11]

By 1868, the family had moved back to London, and that year son Thomas was born in Westminster. Their last child, Alfred, was born in Southwark in 1873. The family obviously moved home a lot, and in the last record of them together they were listed as living in Chelsea.[12] However, Thomas and Catherine's relationship ended around 1881. There was never any evidence that the couple had ever married, but the bond must have been strong for some time, as Catherine had had the initials 'TC' tattooed on her arm and took his name as if she was his wife. The cause of the split was uncertain; Annie Conway believed it was because of her mother's behaviour when in drink,[13] whereas Catherine's elder sister, Elizabeth Fisher, stated that Conway would occasionally be violent.[14]

After the separation, Catherine met John Kelly and for the remainder of her life lived with him at the doss house at 55 Flower and Dean Street known as 'Cooney's'. Kelly admitted that Catherine drank, though not to excess, but was not aware that she ever went out on the streets for 'immoral purposes'.[15] All in all, despite obvious difficulties at times, the relationship seemed relatively harmonious: 'I have lived with that girl a long while, and we never quarrelled,' said Kelly.[16]

In September 1888 the couple went hopping in Kent, a regular endeavour for them and others of their class, who would look forward to the opportunity of making a little money picking hops whilst reaping the health benefits of time in the countryside, away from the grime of the city. Unfortunately, owing to the poor crop that season, the trip had been an unsuccessful one, and they trudged wearily back to London, accompanied part of the way by Emily Birrell and her partner, who gave Catherine a pawn ticket for a shirt. It was the same pawn ticket that was found on the body in Mitre Square and which, when mentioned in the press, alerted Kelly to her death. They reached London on 27 September, spending the night at the casual ward in Shoe Lane. The following day, in order to get money for provisions, Catherine pawned a pair of Kelly's boots at Jones's pawnbroker in Church Street,[17] Spitalfields, and they spent the night apart. The last time the couple were together was on Saturday 29 September at 2.00 p.m. on Houndsditch, when Catherine told Kelly that she was going to Bermondsey to see her daughter with the intention of getting some money. They parted on good terms, and apparently Catherine was sober when she went off.

At 8.30 that evening PC Louis Robinson of the City Police was on duty in Aldgate when his attention was diverted by a small crowd outside no. 29 Aldgate High Street. Investigating, he found Catherine Eddowes, by now drunk and incapable, lying on the pavement. The fact that she was effectively penniless when she last saw Kelly begs the question of where and indeed how she acquired enough money in six hours to get herself extremely intoxicated. He tried to prop her up against the shutters of the shop, but she keeled over and, when asked her name, replied, 'Nothing.' PC Robinson, assisted by PC George Simmons, lifted her up and carried her, perhaps with some difficulty, to Bishopsgate police station. Station Sergeant James Byfield booked Catherine in, and she was taken to a cell to sleep off the drink. PC George Hutt made regular checks on the new prisoner and at 12.55 a.m. he could see that she was now sober enough to be released. She gave her name as 'Mary Ann Kelly' of 6 Fashion Street, Spitalfields, and as Hutt led her from the cells to the exit, she asked the time, to which he commented that it was too late to get any more drink. She muttered that she would get 'a damn fine hiding' when she got home, at which Hutt chastised her for her drunkenness. At 1.00 a.m. she left with a cheery 'Good night, old cock,' and was seen to turn left out of the station exit towards Houndsditch.

At 1.35 a.m., Joseph Lawende, Harry Harris and Joseph Hyam Levy left the Imperial Club on Duke Street and, as they walked towards Aldgate, they noticed a man and a woman on the opposite side of the road, at the corner of Church Passage, one of the entrances to Mitre Square. Harris found the couple disconcerting, saying, 'I don't like going home by myself when I see those characters about,' but Levy had no such qualms. Lawende, walking just ahead of the other two, was later able to furnish the police with more information – the woman had had her hand on the man's chest and was wearing the same clothing he saw later at the mortuary. The man was described as 'of shabby appearance, about thirty years of age and 5ft. 9in. in height, of fair complexion, having a small fair moustache, and wearing a red neckerchief and a cap with a peak'.[18] Unfortunately, Lawende also believed that he would not recognize the man again.[19]

It was five minutes later that PC James Harvey, one of the

1. Mortuary photograph of Martha Tabram, considered by many as an early, or even the first, victim of the Whitechapel murderer.

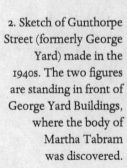

2. Sketch of Gunthorpe Street (formerly George Yard) made in the 1940s. The two figures are standing in front of George Yard Buildings, where the body of Martha Tabram was discovered.

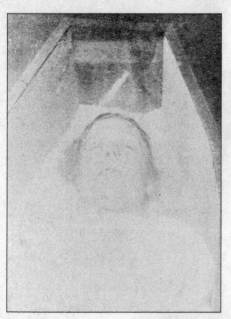

3. Mortuary photograph of Mary Ann Nichols. Pictures such as these were taken to record the face in case the body was not identified before burial.

4. Buck's Row, Whitechapel, in the late 1920s. By this time it had been renamed Durward Street.

5. Mortuary photograph of Annie Chapman.

6. 29 Hanbury Street in the 1960s, a few years before demolition.
Annie Chapman would have accompanied her killer through the left-hand
door to the back yard (the other door was a later addition).

7. Mortuary photograph of Elizabeth Stride.
The throat wound, just visible in this picture,
was the only one inflicted on the victim.

8. Berner Street in April 1909. The narrow entrance to Dutfield's Yard
is marked by the cartwheel jutting out from the wall. The International
Working Men's Educational Club is the taller property behind.

9. Catherine Eddowes in the mortuary 'shell', prior to the post-mortem.

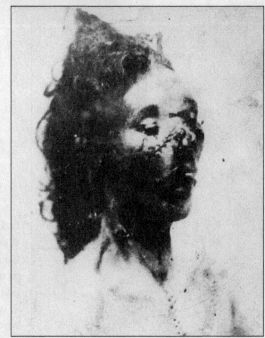

10. Catherine Eddowes after the post-mortem stitching, showing the injuries to the face.

11. Contemporary sketch of Catherine Eddowes's body as found in Mitre Square. It was drawn by city surveyor Frederick Foster and would have been used at the inquest.

12. Entrance to 108–119 Wentworth Dwellings, Goulston Street, where the missing portion of Catherine Eddowes's apron was found, as well as the controversial writing on the wall.

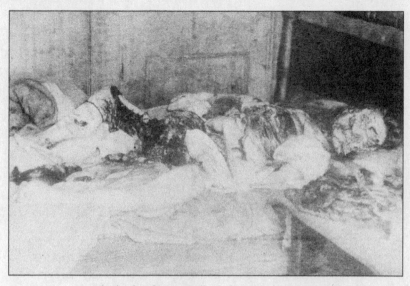

13. The body of Mary Kelly as found in her room in
Miller's Court, Dorset Street.

14. Exterior of Mary Kelly's room
at 13 Miller's Court. The passageway
leading from Dorset Street is visible
to the right.

15. Mortuary photograph of
Alice McKenzie, whom Dr Thomas
Bond believed was murdered by
Jack the Ripper.

16. Mortuary photograph of Frances Coles, the last Whitechapel murder victim. James Sadler, her 'companion' on the night of her death, was initially suspected but soon released without charge.

17. Crowds gathered at the entrance to Swallow Gardens after the death of Frances Coles; a contemporary press illustration showing how fear of the Ripper still prevailed years after the autumn of 1888.

first officers at the scene following the discovery of the murder, passed down Church Passage, stopping at the entrance to Mitre Square. He heard nobody and heard no cry. Feeling that all was well, he turned and went back up Church Passage into Duke Street, whereupon he continued his beat in the direction of Aldgate. Minutes later, watchman Morris's whistle alerted him and other nearby officers to PC Watkins's discovery of Catherine Eddowes's mutilated body.

If Lawende and friends had seen the murderer only nine minutes prior to the murder being discovered, then the extensive mutilations were executed fast and at great risk. Evidence of that risk was forthcoming during the Eddowes inquest, with a number of witnesses testifying to their proximity to the murder scene at the crucial time. George Clapp, the caretaker of 5 Mitre Street, his wife and Mrs Tew, a nurse, had a night of undisturbed sleep, even though their bedroom windows looked out on to Mitre Square. Similarly, off-duty City PC Richard Pearce and his family, living in the only occupied house in Mitre Square, heard nothing out of the ordinary until being called at 2.20 a.m. Pearce could see the murder spot from his bedroom window, behind which he, his wife and three children slept without disturbance that night. James Blenkinsopp, a night watchman looking after some road works in St James's Place (the 'Orange Market'), did state that a respectably dressed man came up to him at 1.30 a.m. and asked if he had seen a couple passing through, to which he replied that he had not.[20] This was a curious event because if Blenkinsopp's timing was correct, then it happened minutes before the sighting in Duke Street made by Lawende and company. If Blenkinsopp was *incorrect* with the timing, then it is possible that it was one of the detective constables who were making enquiries *after* the discovery of Eddowes's body. Either way, Blenkinsopp, like everybody else in the vicinity, heard nothing of the murder.

Dr George Bagster Phillips believed that the two murders were not committed by the same person[21] but made no comment as to the medical skill of Catherine Eddowes's killer as he had done in the case of Annie Chapman. Dr George Sequeira believed that the murderer would have had sufficient light in Mitre Square to perform the mutilations and that he needn't have any anatomical skill,[22] but Dr Frederick Gordon Brown hinted at some considerable ability and knowledge – even that possessed by someone used to cutting up animals for a living.[23]

News of the two murders was quick to spread, and great crowds assembled outside the gates of Dutfield's Yard, and the entrances to Mitre Square as east London woke to tales of more horrors on their doorstep.

All day long there were yesterday mobs of people assembled in the vicinity of the two dead-houses in which the victims are at present laid, and Berner-street was at one time during the day greatly thronged. During the working dinner hour people poured down into the neighbourhood in a continuous stream, and a densely packed crowd stood before the closed gates beside the International Club, discussing the events, as though the sight of the gates and the club assisted them to realise what the morning papers had been narrating to them. Thousands of the people about this part of London cannot read English papers; but they can more or less perfectly understand spoken English, and up and down the street and all the corners persons were to be seen reading aloud the newspaper accounts to listening throngs clustering round, every detail of the shocking occurrences being earnestly debated.[24]

'O have you seen the devle?'

The events of 30 September triggered a new groundswell of opinion from the public and press alike. Newspapers around the globe were now becoming more than familiar with the unravelling events, reporting on the crimes as if they were happening on their own doorstep. Back in London, the radical press was becoming extremely vocal in its condemnation of the police, especially Sir Charles Warren and Henry Matthews, who as home secretary was deemed complicit in the perceived malfunction of the Metropolitan Police. One element of this which continued to surface was the matter of rewards, as picked up by the *Star*:

> Mr MATTHEWS has neatly tapped in the last nail in his political coffin by again refusing to issue the reward which the City authorities, the majority of the Unionist Press in London, and all sensible officials now favour. Whitechapel now knows the measure of the interest which its lords and governors take in its welfare. No one asks for a reward as an absolutely certain method of discovering the murderer. We ask for it as one of a series of methods – such as drawing the cordon, setting on bloodhounds, reorganising the detective agencies of the metropolis, and modifying the clumsy military drill of the police in favour of a system more especially directed to the pursuit of

criminals – which have occurred to everybody but Sir CHARLES WARREN and Mr MATTHEWS.[1]

The Home Office stood its ground, despite the increasing number of private individuals and organizations offering rewards of their own. As suggested by the comments above, the lord mayor of London had offered a reward of £500 on behalf of the City authorities, which, combined with contributions from other private businesses and institutions, made a total of £1,200.[2]

Another newspaper, the *Pall Mall Gazette*, now spoke of a 'headless C.I.D.' and made a direct reference to Dr Robert Anderson's absence:

> At a time when all the world is ringing with outcries against the officials who allow murder to stalk unchecked through the most densely crowded quarter of the metropolis, the chief official who is responsible for the detection of the murderer is as invisible to Londoners as the murderer himself. You may seek for Dr Anderson in Scotland-yard, you may look for him in Whitehall-place, but you will not find him, for he is not there. Dr Anderson, with all the arduous duties of his office still to learn, is preparing himself for his apprenticeship by taking a pleasant holiday in Switzerland![3]

The *Star* printed extracts from what it deemed were 'hundreds' of letters it had received from the general public. Suggestions were many, such as having a number of prostitutes working alongside the police and even having officers dressed as women to act as lures. One of the most common suggestions was the introduction of bloodhounds, a matter that was being discussed heavily by the Metropolitan Police at that time. They had concerns, however – the possibility of such a dog attacking the wrong person was an issue, as were the difficulties faced by dogs which had not been trained for use in the urban environment. Even the financial expenditure for keeping bloodhounds was discussed. Despite these reservations, behind the scenes the idea was certainly gaining momentum.[4]

So the perceived inactivity of the police by the radical press was not necessarily the reality. Following the double murder, extensive enquiries were made; reports made by Chief Inspector Donald Swanson, now well and truly in the thick of his new post, showed that a colossal manhunt was underway. Eighty thousand leaflets were distributed to home occupiers requesting information; 2,000 lodgers from common lodging houses were interviewed and examined; the Thames Police were enquiring into the movements of sailors; the activities of three supposedly insane medical students were investigated; seventy-six butchers and slaughtermen along with their employees were questioned, as were visiting Greek gypsies and cowboys; upwards of 300 people were detained.[5]

Another development had come on 1 October, when a postcard was received by the Central News Agency from 'Jack the Ripper'. The writing was the same as that found on the original 'Dear Boss' letter of 27 September and its content was equally chilling:

I was not codding dear old Boss when I gave you the tip, you'll hear about Saucy Jacky's work tomorrow double event this time number one squealed a bit couldn't finish straight off. had not the time to get ears for police. thanks for keeping last letter back till I got to work again.
   Jack the Ripper

It bore the postmark 'LONDON OC 1 88' and, despite the apparent prediction of a 'double event', it could easily have been written and posted the day before, when news of the murders was already common knowledge. The police had been keeping the previous letter back, as requested by the author, until there was another murder. Now the time seemed to be right to issue the text of the 'Dear Boss' letter. It appeared in the evening newspapers later that day[6] along with the text of the postcard, and both were soon to be reproduced on posters which were displayed on police station notice-boards around the country. The result could not have been predicted. In the following weeks, a multitude of letters descended upon the newspaper offices, police stations and homes of private individuals, each one claiming to have been written by the murderer and many of them bearing the name 'Jack the Ripper'. Like 'Leather Apron' before it, the name became a byword for fear, the difference being that this one prevailed.

Elizabeth Stride was buried in a modest ceremony at the East London cemetery in Plaistow on 6 October, and Catherine Eddowes's funeral took place at the City of London cemetery (Little Ilford) two days later, her body being interred only a few yards from that of Mary Ann Nichols. As Catherine's funeral cortège made its way from Golden Lane mortuary, crowds of people gathered or leaned out of windows as the procession passed, marking a tremendous outpouring of sympathy for the plight of the Whitechapel murderer's latest victim.[7] Ironically, it was only after so much bloodshed that Robert Anderson returned to London, as a matter of great urgency, to take up his duties as Assistant Commissioner (CID). It was hardly an auspicious start.

Meanwhile, the Vigilance Committees continued their

work and the Central Vigilance Committee, formed in the West End of London in the mid-1880s, but now focusing its attention on events unravelling in Whitechapel, joined the cause.[8] George Lusk, chairman of the Mile End Vigilance Committee, had by now become a prominent resident of the East End, and his name and address had been made public several times in the press. As a result of this, he had been subjected to a number of letters from the alleged murderer. One, however, took on considerable significance. On 16 October, he received a parcel in the evening post; contained within were a letter and half a kidney. The letter, in a less-than-educated hand, peppered with spelling mistakes, read:

> From hell
>> Mr Lusk,
>> Sir
>> I send you half the Kidne I took from one woman and prasarved it for you tother piece I fried and ate it was very nise. I may send you the bloody knif that took it out if you only wate a whil longer
>> signed Catch me when you can Mishter Lusk

Lusk was immediately of the opinion that it was all a gruesome stunt, but he did not dispose of the kidney immediately. After mentioning it to members of the committee two days later, he was encouraged to have it examined by a medical expert, bearing in mind that a similar organ had been taken from Catherine Eddowes. The kidney was taken to the surgery of Dr Frederick Wiles at 56 Mile End Road, but in his absence it was examined by his assistant, Mr Francis Reed. Reed, feeling that it warranted further inspection, took the piece to Dr Thomas Horrocks Openshaw, curator of the

Pathology Museum at the London Hospital. From there it was taken, along with the accompanying letter, to Leman Street police station. The kidney was passed on to the City of London Police for further examination by Dr Frederick Gordon Brown, and the letter went to Scotland Yard.[9]

Mr Reed believed the kidney to be human, that it was divided longitudinally and that it had been preserved in spirits of wine. He was also reported as stating that it was probably genuine.[10] The initial reports on Dr Openshaw's findings were highly misleading. According to a press interview with Vigilance Committee member Joseph Aarons, Dr Openshaw had claimed that it was part of a left kidney, that it had belonged to a female in the habit of drinking and that it had probably been removed around the same time as the previous murder.[11]

However, interviewed in the press the following day, Dr Openshaw refuted nearly all the claims attributed to him:

Dr Openshaw told a Star reporter to-day that after having examined the piece of kidney under the microscope he was of opinion that it was half of a left human kidney. He couldn't say, however, whether it was that of a woman, nor how long ago it had been removed from the body, as it had been preserved in spirits.[12]

Various claims and counter-claims would result from this obviously important piece of potential evidence, particularly regarding the condition of the kidney portion in relation to the other organ remaining in Catherine Eddowes's body. One consideration, suggested by the original press accounts, is that it was described as a 'ginny' kidney, an idea that was bolstered by the later opinion of Major Henry Smith, in 1888 the acting commissioner of the City Police; specifically that the organ showed signs of Bright's Disease, an affliction allegedly present in the kidney which remained in Catherine Eddowes's body.[13] Conflicting press statements and missing doctor's reports have only served to cloud the mystery of the kidney over the years, but during October 1888 the claims of the letter's author certainly added more shock to an already outrageous story as limbs of the press, disposed toward the kidney piece being genuine, described the murderer as a 'cannibal'.[14]

As October progressed, the two police forces of London continued to be inundated with the efforts of tireless letter-writers. The City Police received an inordinately large amount of correspondence from the public, including offers of help, suggestions on investigative techniques and the exposure of suspicious individuals. Some, like those which professed to garner information from the spirit world or which accused police officers of the crimes, were generally given short shrift. Some claimed to be from the murderer, including this unusual one written on 2 October from a 'M. Puddig' of 'Thrall Street, London E':

> You offer certainly a handsome reward but I have sworn that nobody shall earn it, this the one thousand eight hundred and eighty eighth year of our Lord. shall find me still at liberty untill its close, for not till I hear the first chimes of the church bells on watch night will I be tired of gloating over my work for hard work it has indeed been. thanks to my thorough proficiency in anatomical matters I gave them little or no pain, for humanity – they had to die, and at my hand. Still only a few more weeks and my task is done, when I shall ornament the scaffold that in short hours then and not till then shall you become acquainted with the motive of my crimes as you are pleased to style them was stern duty. They will forgive me when we meet in paradise, in celestial bliss. Amen[15]

Another, addressed to Dr Thomas Openshaw, arrived at the London Hospital on 29 October. In a similarly uneducated hand to the Lusk letter (though by no means identical) it read:

> Old boss you was rite it was the left kidny i was goin to hoper-ate agin close to you ospitle just as i was going to dror mi nife along of er bloomin throte them cusses of coppers spoilt the game but i guess i wil be on the jobn soon and will send you another bit of innerds
> Jack the Ripper
> O have you seen the devle with his mikerscope and scalpul a-lookin at a kidney with a slide cocked up.

It is hard to assess how much credence the authorities gave to missives like these, or how much time they spent following up letters which named specific individuals as the killer. But sensational letters like the one sent to George Lusk would certainly have kept the investigation ticking over and the press well fed with more outrageous news, despite no 'Ripper'-type murders being committed in October. These unique crimes had appeared to follow a pattern, being committed during the first week or the last days of the month, and at weekends or bank holidays, so it would have been logical to assume that any further crimes would possibly take place at the start or end of October, but it was not to be. That month, a thick fog descended over London, a matter that might have had some bearing on when the killer felt disposed to act next – poor visibility might well have benefited the murderer in the act of escaping the scene of the crime, but it could also prove risky should a passer-by or policeman suddenly loom out of the smog at the wrong moment.

And in the first week of November, with the police no

closer to finding out the identity of their elusive assassin, Sir Charles Warren resigned as chief commissioner of the Metropolitan Police. He had tendered his resignation on three previous occasions (the last being in the early summer of 1888), but this time it was final. In early November, *Murray's Magazine*, a small London newspaper, published an article written by Warren in which he attempted to describe how the Metropolitan Police worked. However, rather than limiting itself to this seemingly safe subject, the article managed to criticize government ministers past and present; even the public were harangued for their fickle opinions on the police, which appeared to fluctuate on the basis of how much the people of London felt they needed the protection of the force at any given time.

Unbeknownst to Warren, this article was in direct contravention of an 1879 ruling stating that no police officer was to publish any material without the prior consent of the Home Office. He claimed not to know about such a ruling and stated that, if he had, he would never have taken his position as chief commissioner in the first place, believing that he had a right to defend himself and his men from unfair condemnation.[16] Home Secretary Henry Matthews fired off an immediate communiqué to Warren, but the chief commissioner was adamant that his duties were governed by statutes which meant the home secretary was not in any position to give orders to the police. Warren, now at the end of his tether with such interference, tendered his resignation on 8 November 1888, the day before the Lord Mayor's Show.

Word spread about Warren's resignation the following day, mixed with the excited reports of yet another murder, which, for its sheer brutality, was unsurpassed.

'I hope I may never see such a sight again'

At about 10.45 on the morning of 9 November 1888 Thomas Bowyer walked from Dorset Street into the narrow, grimy passageway leading to Miller's Court with the intention of calling upon the young resident of room 13, Mary Kelly. He had been sent by John McCarthy, who owned the shop at 27 Dorset Street where Bowyer worked as well as the various furnished rooms in Miller's Court and who was aware that Mary owed him a considerable amount of money in unpaid rent. Bowyer, arriving at room 13, knocked on the door. As there was no reply, he knocked again, with the same result, so, not put off, he walked round to the windows, where one pane of glass was missing in the window nearest the door. Assuming Mary was in the room, he put his hand in the open window frame, pulled aside an old curtain and peered into the dark room. At first he saw what he thought were two lumps of flesh on the bedside table; looking again, he could see a body lying on the bed and a large amount of blood on the floor. Obviously shocked, he immediately ran to McCarthy's shop by the entrance to Miller's Court and informed his master of what he had seen.[1] Once McCarthy had seen the body for himself, the two men ran to Commercial Street police station, where Inspector Walter Beck was on duty. Beck, accompanied by PC Walter Dew, followed the two men back to Dorset Street. Immediately Beck closed Miller's Court off so that nobody could leave or enter and sent for Dr George Bagster Phillips.

Soon news of the murder had been telegraphed to police stations across London. A number of constables were called down from Commercial Street police station and were used to guard Miller's Court and to cordon off each end of Dorset Street. Dr Phillips arrived at 11.15 a.m. and, looking into the room, saw immediately that Mary Kelly was in no need of medical attention. Inspector Abberline arrived soon after with the word that entry to the room would have to wait for the arrival of the much-debated bloodhounds. However, the situation deteriorated into farce when the dogs were not forthcoming, and it was not until 1.30 p.m. that Inspector Thomas Arnold arrived with instructions to enter the room. John McCarthy, curiously having no key of his own, forced the door open with a pickaxe. The sheer horror of the spectacle that confronted the men as they entered was summed up by McCarthy in a later interview:

> The sight we saw, I cannot drive away from my mind. It looked more like the work of a devil than of a man. I had heard a great deal about the Whitechapel murders, but I declare to God I had never expected to see such a sight as this. The whole scene is more than I can describe. I hope I may never see such a sight again.[2]

Mary Kelly was lying in the middle of the bed, her body inclined to the left and her head resting on the left cheek. The face was unrecognizable, as the nose, cheeks, eyebrows and ears had been partly removed. Mary's neck had been severed down to the bone and the vertebrae notched by the murder weapon. The left forearm was stretched across her abdomen, her right arm resting on the mattress; both arms had been mutilated. The breasts had been cut off, with one being placed under her head, the other put by the right foot. The heart was 'absent'. The whole of the surface of the abdomen and thighs had been removed and the contents of the abdomen emptied and distributed around the body: the uterus and kidneys under the head, her liver between the feet, intestines on her right side, the spleen by her left. On the bedside table parts of the abdomen and thighs had been placed. The front of the right thigh was entirely stripped of skin, and the left thigh was denuded of flesh to the knee.[3]

A great number of officers descended upon the scene, and at 1.50 p.m. even Robert Anderson made an appearance. A tarpaulin-covered horse-drawn cart pulled into Dorset Street at 3.50 p.m., at the sight of which great excitement ensued:

> The news that the body was about to be removed caused a great rush of people from the courts running out of Dorset-street, and there was a determined effort to break the police cordon at the Commercial-street end. The crowd, which pressed round the van, was of the humblest class, but the demeanour of the poor people was all that could be described. Ragged caps were doffed and slatternly-looking women shed tears as the shell, covered with a ragged-looking cloth, was placed in the van.[4]

As the body was transported to the small mortuary in the grounds of St Leonard's Church, Shoreditch, room 13 was closed, the windows boarded up, and the door padlocked. Later in the day, the police cordon was lifted as the crowds began to disperse, their curiosity exhausted.[5]

According to various individuals who knew her, Mary Jane

Kelly was about twenty-five years old at the time of her death, five foot seven inches tall and stout. She had blue eyes and a fair complexion; however, press reports after the murder variously gave her hair colour as blonde, ginger, light or dark.[6] PC Walter Dew later said that he knew Kelly by sight and that she invariably wore a clean white apron, but never a hat.[7] Sir Melville Macnaghten, later assistant chief constable of the Metropolitan Police, had heard that she was 'said to be of considerable personal attractions'.[8] But Mary Kelly's appearance and character are as much of a mystery as her past. Much of what is known about her life came from Joseph Barnett, her former lover, and a few others. Any of it, or none of it, may be true.

She said she had been born in Limerick, Ireland, but whether she meant County Limerick or the town of Limerick is not clear. She said her father was named John Kelly and she had six or seven brothers and one sister. The family had moved to Wales when she was very young, and her father worked as foreman in an ironworks in either Caernarvonshire or Carmarthenshire, probably the latter. She had married when only sixteen years old, but her husband, a collier named Davis or Davies, was killed in a mine explosion some two or three years later. Mary then went to live with a cousin in Cardiff, where she turned to prostitution. From Cardiff she moved to London, where she said that she had worked for a French woman in a high-class bordello in the West End; she claimed that she had been dressed well, had been driven about in a carriage and had gone across to France several times in the company of 'a gentleman'. However, she had not been enamoured by this life and had returned to London in 1884 – the time in France may have inspired her to use the alternative spelling of her name, 'Marie Jeanette'. Her first residence on her return to London was with a Mrs 'Buki'[9] in St George Street, near the London Docks.[10] She then moved to Breezer's Hill, off Pennington Street, staying with a 'Mrs Carthy',[11] who later said that some time in 1886 Mary had left to live with a Joseph Fleming, and although Mrs Carthy believed that Fleming would have married Mary, the relationship soon ended.[12]

By 1887 Mary Kelly was living at a lodging house at 16–17 Thrawl Street. On 8 April that year – Good Friday – she met Joseph Barnett, a porter at Billingsgate Market and sometime fruit hawker, in Commercial Street. They went for a drink, arranged to meet the following day and at that meeting decided to live together. The couple took up lodgings in George Street, Spitalfields, then moved on to Little Paternoster Row, off Dorset Street. After some time in Brick Lane they acquired room 13, Miller's Court, in January or February of 1888, paying John McCarthy a weekly rent of four shillings and sixpence.

In July or August 1888 Joseph Barnett lost his job, and the resulting financial hardship began to put a strain on the relationship. Mary may have returned to prostitution, and Barnett certainly complained that she let prostitutes use their room. As a result they had many arguments, the window of their room being broken during one of them. In the early evening of 30 October, Barnett walked out. There appears to have been no hard feelings, as he called in on her often and gave her money when he had some to spare. On Thursday 8 November he visited her at about 7.30 p.m. Mary was with Lizzie Allbrook, who left soon after he arrived, and Barnett stayed on for about half an hour. Conflicting statements by Maria Harvey and Elizabeth Foster make Mary's movements after that difficult to ascertain,[13] but the next reliable sighting of Mary was made by a neighbour, Mary Ann Cox, a widow who lived at 5 Miller's Court. At about 11:45 p.m. she turned into Dorset Street from Commercial Street and ahead of her she could see Mary walking with a man. They turned into the passage leading into Miller's Court, and, as Mrs Cox turned down the passage herself, she saw them going into room 13. Mrs Cox bid Mary goodnight, Mary replying in a slurred manner that she was 'going to have a song'. She was obviously quite drunk, and her companion was described as about thirty-six years of age, stout, with a blotchy face, small side whiskers and a thick 'carroty' moustache. He was dressed in shabby dark clothes, a long dark overcoat and a round, hard billycock hat. In his hand he held a quart can of beer.[14]

Mary could soon be heard singing 'A Violet I Plucked From Mother's Grave' and half an hour later she was still singing the same song. Catherine Pickett, a flower-seller who lived in Miller's Court, was not best pleased and was all ready to complain, but her husband stopped her.[15] Elizabeth Prater, a prostitute living in a room above Mary, returned home after a night drinking at about 1.00 a.m. She loitered at the entrance to Miller's Court for about half an hour and had a chat with John McCarthy in his shop before going up to her room. Not bothering to undress, she lay on her bed and immediately fell asleep. By now there was no sound from Kelly's room.

At 2:00 a.m. George Hutchinson, a friend, was walking along Commercial Street from Romford when he met Mary near the junction with Thrawl Street. She asked if he could lend her some money, but Hutchinson had spent what he had in Romford. Kelly, who seemed 'spreeish', said goodbye and walked on towards Thrawl Street. Hutchinson's statement to the police takes up the story:

A man coming in the opposite direction to Kelly tapped her on the shoulder and said something to her. They both burst out laughing. I heard her say alright to him. And the man said you will be alright for what I have told you. He then placed his right hand around her shoulders. He also had a kind of a small parcel in his left hand with a kind of strap round it. I stood against the lamp of the Queen's Head Public House and watched him. They both then came past me and the man hid down his head with his hat over his eyes. I stooped down and looked him in the face. He looked at me stern. They both went into Dorset Street I followed them. They both stood at the corner of the Court for about 3 minutes. He said something to her. She said alright my dear come along you will be comfortable He then placed his arm on her shoulder and gave her a kiss. She said she had lost her handkercheif he then pulled his handkercheif a red one out and gave it to her. They both then went up the court together. I then went to the Court to see if I could see them, but could not. I stood there for about three quarters of an hour to see if they came out they did not so I went away.[16]

Hutchinson's rather detailed description of the man said that he was:

about 34 or 35. height 5ft6 complexion pale, dark eyes and eye lashes slight moustache, curled up each end, and hair dark, very surley looking dress long dark coat, collar and cuffs trimmed astracan. And a dark jacket under. Light waistcoat dark trousers dark felt hat turned down in the middle. Button boots and gaiters with white buttons. Wore a very thick gold chain white linen collar. Black tie with horse shoe pin. Respectable appearance walked very sharp. Jewish appearance. Can be identified.

Shortly before 4.00 a.m. Sarah Lewis, who was staying with friends at 2 Miller's Court, heard 'a scream like that of a young woman, which seemed to be not far away. The voice screamed out "murder".' In her room above Mary's, Elizabeth Prater was awakened by her little black kitten Diddles walking across her neck. She too heard the cry in a faint voice but, being used to such cries in the neighbourhood, she went back to sleep.[17] She woke at 5.00 a.m. and went to the Ten Bells for a glass of rum. The only people she saw in the street were two or three men harnessing some horses. Mary Ann Cox heard a man's footsteps leaving Miller's Court at about 5.45 a.m., and at 7.30 a.m. Catherine Pickett knocked on Mary's door with the intention of borrowing a shawl, but there was no reply. A little over four hours later, Thomas Bowyer made his shocking discovery.

Mary Kelly's post-mortem was conducted the following day by Dr George Bagster Phillips and his assistant, Dr William Dukes, assisted and observed by Dr Frederick Gordon Brown and Dr Thomas Bond. Dr Bond believed that rigor mortis had begun between six and twelve hours after death, from which he roughly calculated that death could have taken place between 2.00 a.m. and 8.00 a.m. The remains of a meal – fish and potatoes – were found in the stomach and intestines, so reasonably assuming that Kelly had eaten no later than between 10.00 and 11.00 the previous night, time of death was narrowed down to 1.00 a.m. or 2.00 a.m., which makes the claims of two witnesses, Maurice Lewis and Caroline Maxwell, stand out as strange, almost unbelievable.

Lewis, who had known Mary for five years, claimed to have seen Mary Kelly leave her room at 8.00 a.m. and return a few moments later. Then, at 10.00 a.m., he was playing 'pitch and toss' in Miller's Court, after which he and his companions went to the Britannia. There, Lewis was certain he saw Mary drinking with some other people.[18] Caroline Maxwell, of 14 Dorset Street, had an even stranger tale to tell. She saw Mary at the corner of Miller's Court between 8.00 and 8.30 a.m. She spoke to Mary, asking her why she was up so early, to which Mary replied that she had the 'horrors of drink' upon her, as she had been drinking for some days previously. Mrs Maxwell suggested she go and have a drink in 'Mrs Ringers' (the Britannia), but Mary replied that she had already done so and had brought it up, pointing to some vomit in the road. Maxwell left, saying that she pitied her feelings. On returning from an errand in Bishopsgate, Maxwell saw Mary again at about 8.45–9.00 a.m. outside the Britannia, talking to a man. He was about thirty years of age, stout of build, about 5 feet 5 inches tall and dressed like a market porter. The statements made by Lewis and Maxwell flew in the face of medical evidence, and Mrs Maxwell was warned about her evidence by the inquest coroner, Roderick MacDonald, as it was 'different to other people's'.[19] MacDonald's inquest lasted a single day, in complete contrast to Wynne Baxter's often interminably long proceedings, that being all that was needed to ascertain the circumstances of Mary Kelly's death. The verdict was the all too familiar 'wilful murder against person or persons unknown'.

The murder of Mary Kelly prompted a number of unique events. Owing perhaps to the secure nature of the crime scene, photographs of the body were taken *in situ*, the only time this was done in the whole case. Queen Victoria, via a telegram sent to Prime Minister Lord Salisbury on 10 November, spoke of her grave concern:

This new most ghastly murder shows the absolute necessity for some very decided action. All these courts must be lit, &

our detectives improved. They are not what they should be. You promised, when the 1st murders took place to consult with your colleagues about it.[20]

Henry Matthews also received a letter three days later, demonstrating that her Majesty was as exasperated as everybody else with the lack of progress:

The Queen fears that the detective department is not so efficient as it might be. No doubt the recent murders in Whitechapel were committed in circumstances which made detection very difficult; still, the Queen thinks that, in the small area where these horrible crimes have been perpetrated, a great number of detectives might be employed, and that every possible suggestion might be carefully examined and, if practicable, followed.

Have the cattle boats and passenger boats been examined?

Has any investigation been made as to the number of single men occupying rooms by themselves?

The murderer's clothes must be saturated with blood and must be kept somewhere.

Is there sufficient surveillance at night?

These are some of the questions that occur to the Queen on reading the account of this horrible crime.[21]

The Metropolitan Police finally capitulated – in part – to the reward lobbyists by making a most unusual offer of:

Her Majesty's Gracious pardon to any accomplice not being a person who contrived or actually committed the murder who shall give such information and evidence as shall lead to the discovery and conviction of the person or persons who committed the murder.

And Dr Thomas Bond, who, after completing the lengthy post-mortem on Mary Kelly, was made familiar with the particulars surrounding the previous deaths, produced an overview of the sort of person he thought the murderer might have been. Bond believed that the five murders from Nichols to Kelly were 'no doubt' committed by the same person but, contrary to the views of other doctors, he thought the murderer lacked anatomical knowledge, even that of a butcher or horse-slaughterer. He also thought that the murderer's hands and arms would have been bloodied, as would his clothes, and as such would probably wear an overcoat or similar apparel to hide the stains.

Dr Bond described the murderer as physically strong, but quiet and inoffensive in appearance, probably middle-aged and neatly and respectably dressed, although probably not in regular employment. He would therefore have had a small regular income or pension or lived with people of respectable character who likely entertained suspicions they evidently were not communicating to the police. The murderer was probably solitary and eccentric in his behaviour.[22]

What Thomas Bond did, in effect, was create the first example of what has become a modern police tool used to assist investigations into the behaviour of serial murderers like 'Jack the Ripper' – offender profiling.

9.

'Where have I been Dear Boss . . .'

The funeral of Mary Kelly took place on 19 November, paid for in full by Mr H. Wilton, clerk of St Leonard's church, Shoreditch, from where the cortège began its journey to St Patrick's Roman Catholic cemetery in Leytonstone. The coffin bore the inscription 'Marie Jeanette Kelly, died November 9, 1888, aged 25 years', and on it were placed two crowns and a cross, made of heartsease and white flowers. The funeral itself was sparsely attended by associates of Mary from Miller's Court and Joseph Barnett. However, the show of grief and sympathy from the public was considerable:

> At half-past twelve, as the coffin was borne from the mortuary, the bell of the church was tolled, and the people outside, who now numbered several thousands, manifested the utmost sympathy, the crowd, for an East-end one, being extremely orderly. Vehicles of various descriptions took oppositions outside the church railings, and traffic was completely blocked until the hearse moved off. The funeral procession, which left Shoreditch Church at a quarter to one, made but slow progress through the crowds of people and vehicles. All along the route through Whitechapel and Cambridge Heath signs of sympathy were to be seen on every hand.[1]

The awful affair in Miller's Court was seen as yet one more atrocity in an escalating series with seemingly no predictable end, and, needless to say, tensions were still running high in the East End. A good example of the sensational release of such tensions came two days after Mary's funeral, in the heart of the very district of doss houses frequented by the unfortunate victims of the Whitechapel murderer, when a prostitute claimed to have been attacked by a man who she said was 'Jack the Ripper'.

At 7.30 on the morning of 21 November, Annie Farmer had picked up a potential client whom she described as 'shabby genteel' and took him back to her lodging house at 19 George Street, the same doss house that had once been home to Martha Tabram only months before. The man paid for both of them, but the arrangement descended into violence, as two hours later a piercing scream was heard, after which the man was seen running from the house. Passing two men standing in the street, he was heard to exclaim, 'What a ----- cow!' before disappearing from view.[2] Annie seemed obviously distraught, for her throat had been cut, and she said she had been attacked by Jack the Ripper himself. It was not long before word got out of another outrage, and crowds began to assemble excitedly in front of no 19. Before long a panic ensued.

The uproar was probably all for nothing, for the throat injury she had sustained was rather superficial, and subsequently it was discovered that Annie had been hiding coins in her mouth. This led the police to assume that she had attempted to rob the man, who had obviously remonstrated with her and, following her scream, made a run for it. In truth, the wound may well have been self-inflicted, but, despite this, Annie never recanted her story. The man never came forward to give an account of himself, and thus the case was dropped. The police were obviously circumspect about the whole issue, and no official record of any investigation survives. However, they were of the belief that Annie Farmer might well have known her attacker, hence her reluctance to give any information that might have led to his discovery.[3]

Another Ripper scare erupted following the discovery of the body of Catherine (a.k.a. Rose) Mylett in Clarke's Yard, Poplar High Street on 20 December. The Mylett case was a peculiar one – at her inquest, four doctors stated that the evidence pointed to death by strangulation, as there were signs that a cord had been used around her neck. Dr Thomas Bond, directed by Robert Anderson to make a late examination, changed his opinion from homicide to 'natural causes', and the whole affair led to some rather acrimonious exchanges between the officials.[4] Anderson appeared to be wilfully pushing for a non-homicide verdict, as there were no signs of a struggle. Coroner Wynne Baxter also favoured death by natural causes, but in the face of weighty medical opinion a verdict of 'wilful murder against some person or persons unknown' was given. The evidence to suggest that Mylett was killed by Jack the Ripper was flimsy at best, even non-existent, but perhaps it was more the timing of the homicide, combined with the nature of the crime scene and the character of Mylett herself, rather than the way it was done that made the public at least show concern that Jack the Ripper had attempted another outrage.

Alice McKenzie, like Mary Kelly before her, had a mysterious past. It is believed she was born around 1849 and was brought up in Peterborough, moving to the East End sometime before 1874. She was known by many as 'Clay Pipe Alice' on account of her regular habit of smoking a pipe. She had scars on her forehead and was missing part of a thumb, the result of an industrial accident some years previously. In about 1883, she had got together with a man named John McCormack, an Irish porter who had been doing casual work for Jewish traders in Hanbury Street, and together they lodged at various doss houses in the district over the years before settling at 'Mr Tenpenny's' lodging house at 52 Gun Street, near Spitalfields market.[5]

Between 3.00 and 4.00 on the afternoon of 16 July 1889 McCormack had returned to the lodging house after his morning's work. He found Alice there and, having money, he gave her 1s 8d, the 8d for the rent and the rest to do with as she saw fit, before going to bed. It was the last time he would see her, and it would later transpire that she left without paying the deputy for their bed.[6] At 7.10 p.m., a blind boy named George Dixon claimed that Alice had taken him to a pub near the Cambridge music hall on Commercial Street. He heard Alice ask someone if they would stand a drink, and the reply was 'yes'. After remaining a few minutes, he was led back to Gun Street and left there.[7]

Elizabeth Ryder, the deputy of Mr Tenpenny's, saw Alice between 8.00 and 9.00 p.m. at the lodging house; Alice was on her way out, and it was noted that she had some money in her hand. It was believed for a while that she had gone out with a fellow lodger named Margaret 'Mog' Cheeks, and, according to Mrs Ryder, both women had not returned to the house when she checked at 3.30 the following morning, 17 July.[8] The final sighting of Alice McKenzie was made at 11.40 p.m. by a Margaret Franklin in Flower and Dean Street, where she was sitting on the steps of her lodging house with two friends. Alice passed by, seemingly in a hurry, and when asked how she was, merely replied, 'All right, can't stop now,' before turning into Brick Lane.[9]

At 12.50 a.m., PC Walter Andrews found the body of Alice McKenzie in Castle Alley, a narrow thoroughfare which ran off Whitechapel High Street. Blood had flowed from two stabs in the throat, and her abdomen was superficially mutilated. What made this latest victim a contender for the next Ripper murder was the opinion of some of the medical officials. Although Dr George Bagster Phillips, a doctor who by sheer experience of the Whitechapel murders was probably well informed enough to confidently assert that this was not the work of 'Jack the Ripper',[10] Dr Thomas Bond disagreed,[11] and his opinion was shared by the new commissioner of the Metropolitan Police, James Monro, who stated, 'I need not say that every effort will be made by the police to discover the murderer, who, I am inclined to believe, is identical with the notorious Jack the Ripper of last year.'[12] Robert Anderson, inconveniently on holiday at the time of McKenzie's murder, did not share this opinion and later wrote that it was committed by 'another hand', at the same time suggesting that Monro had changed his mind as he had intimated to Anderson that it was 'an ordinary murder and not the work of a sexual maniac'.[13]

The last of the Whitechapel murders took place on 13 February 1891 after a considerable lull. The victim, thirty-one-year-old prostitute Frances Coles, was found at 2.15 that morning by PC Ernest Thompson in Swallow Gardens, a rather pleasant name for what was effectively a grim railway arch that ran between Chamber Street and Royal Mint Street, not far from the Tower of London. As PC Thompson approached the railway arch, he believed he could hear footsteps walking at a normal pace east towards Mansell Street. When he found Frances Coles, she was still alive and opened one eye as he bent to examine her.[14] She apparently died on the ambulance, the result of a large cut in her throat.

The movements of Frances on the day of her death were

well documented on account of her undertaking a lengthy pub-crawl with James Sadler, a ship's fireman with whom Frances had been before and who reacquainted himself with her the day before her death. The night of 12 February was not a happy one by all accounts, and both of them got very drunk visiting numerous public houses. After Sadler was attacked and robbed by a small group of ruffians in Thrawl Street, the couple had an argument and parted, reuniting at their lodging house in White's Row, Spitalfields, several hours later. Frances was found drunk and crying, and Sadler was bloodied from a fight he'd had at the London docks; now very drunk, he had tried to be readmitted to his ship but was refused and found himself in an abusive confrontation with some men who promptly beat him up as a result. He left Frances drunkenly sleeping at a table in the lodging house, the last time he saw her alive, but returned around 3.00 a.m. so drunk he could barely speak. He was turned away again. The night became too much for him, and he went to get his wounds attended to at the London Hospital, spending the remainder of the night there.[15]

Sadler immediately became prime suspect for the murder, and he was arrested on 15 February and charged the following day, but thanks to the testimony of favourable witnesses in the absence of hard evidence, as well as good legal representation by the Seamen's Union, charges against him were dropped on 2 March, before the case even went to court. Whether Sadler did murder Frances Coles will probably never be known, but one thing is for certain: he was not 'Jack the Ripper', as he was at sea on the fateful nights of the previous murders.

And so ended the Whitechapel murders. But their legacy carried on long after the death of Frances Coles, as the police continued to make enquiries and file reports for many years after, and the press somehow managed to keep the story ticking over, despite the lack of new crimes. The taunting letters from potential 'Jack the Rippers' had begun to dwindle to a trickle compared to the frenzied days of 1888, but it seems appropriate to mention the last recorded communication, which was sent on 14 October 1896:

Dear Boss

You will be surprised to find that this comes from yours as of old Jack-the-Ripper. Ha. Ha. If my old friend Mr Warren is dead you can read it. You might remember me if you try and think a little. Ha. Ha. The last job was a bad one and no mistake, nearly buckled, and meant it to be the best of the lot & what curse it, Ha Ha I'm alive yet and you'll find it out. I mean to go on again when I get the chance wont it be nice dear old boss to have the good old times once again. You never caught me and you never will. Ha Ha.

You police are a smart lot, the lot of you could nt catch one man Where have I been Dear Boss you'd like to know, abroad if you would like to know, and just come back. Ready to go on with my work and stop when you catch me. Well good bye Boss wish me luck. Winters coming 'The Jewes are people that are blamed for nothing' Ha Ha have you heard this before.

Yours truly
Jack the Ripper[16]

Police reports and communications discussing this latest missive – and ultimately dismissing it – would become the final official documents in the Whitechapel murders file.

PART TWO

Theories

Murder and Motive

Jack the Ripper has often been described as the 'world's first serial killer'. This is frankly not true, as there are many examples throughout history of serial murder stretching back through the centuries. However, he might more accurately be described as the first 'modern' serial killer; that is to say, not only did extensive news coverage at the time make the murders known to much of the civilized world, but also the sheer weight of theorizing about the Ripper's identity over the ensuing years would make it *de rigueur* to analyse the behaviour and possible motives of not just Jack the Ripper, but also those killers that came before and after.

In his memoirs, Sir Melville Macnaghten, who became assistant chief constable of the Metropolitan Police in 1889, was moved to write that even by 1913 not many people outside of the legal and medical professions had much of a concept of 'motiveless murder', or 'killing for its own sake'.[1] Individuals disposed to this sort of behaviour were deemed by medical authorities as far back as the mid-nineteenth century to be suffering from 'moral insanity', described by one doctor in 1855 as 'a form of mental derangement which consists in a morbid perversion of the feelings, affection and active powers, without any illusion or erroneous state impressed on the understanding; it sometimes coexists with an unimpaired state of the intellectual faculties'.[2] Such lack of moral conscience coupled with an outward normality would later been seen as elements of psychopathy. The press of 1888 were having difficulty coming to terms with the concept of murder for mere personal gratification, but one correspondent attempted to set the record straight early on:

> It may interest your readers to learn in connection with the Whitechapel murders that a number of parallel cases occurred some seven years ago near Bochum in Westphalia. The murderer was in the habit of lassoing women, and treating them in exactly the same manner as his confrère of Spitalfields. After many fruitless efforts on the part of the police to catch the perpetrator of the outrages, they at last arrested a gipsy, who was duly sentenced to death and beheaded. Unfortunately, a few days after his execution the murders recommenced! The assassin had the impudence to write to the magistrate of the district that he meant to kill a certain number of victims and would then give himself up. The papers applied to such a murder the expressive term of lustmord (pleasure murder).[3]

The *British Medical Journal* also published a brief article in which 'an eminent surgeon' speculated that those individuals who were not of the medical profession 'are prompted rather by a desire to account for them (the murders) – that is to say, to find some motive for them – than by any knowledge of the subject'.[4] The London *Evening News*, perhaps unable to understand this concept, treated the report rather disparagingly but chose to mention an important point, namely that laymen had 'treated the occurrences as though they were unprecedented in the annals of crime' but that the eminent surgeon stressed that 'it seems desirable to point out that such is by no means the case'.[5]

Nonetheless, for many there simply *had* to be a reason for the Whitechapel murders in order for people to attempt to come to terms with what was happening in the world's most powerful city. An early correspondent, and probably the most prominent one, was Lyttleton Forbes Winslow, a noted and distinguished medical man who, having grown up at his father's asylums (and running them after his death in 1874), had a formidable experience of the insane. In September 1888 he wrote to *The Times*:

> I think that the murderer is not of the class of which 'Leather Apron' belongs, but is of the upper class of society, and I still think that my opinion given to the authorities is the correct one – viz., that the murders have been committed by a lunatic lately discharged from some asylum, or by one who has escaped. If the former, doubtless one who, though suffering from the effects of homicidal mania, is apparently sane on the surface, and consequently has been liberated, and is following out the inclinations of his morbid imaginations by wholesale homicide.

He also wrote to Scotland Yard in November 1888, stating that the murderer was a 'homicidal lunatic' and put his services at the disposal of the government.[6] It is difficult to say how much notice the police took of Winslow's claims, but early suspects were those with some medical background or history of insanity or both. The former category was no doubt influenced by Dr George Bagster Phillips's assertion that the murderer of Annie Chapman possessed significant anatomical skill, added to which was coroner Wynne Baxter's announcement at the end of the Chapman inquest that an American doctor had apparently been offering £20 for specimens of uteri with the intention of giving them away with a medical publication he was producing.[7]

One early suspect who fitted both criteria was Oswald Puckeridge, born at Burpham, near Arundel in Sussex, in 1838. He became a chemist and married Ellen Buddle in 1868, and they had a son. Oswald suffered bouts of insanity and was often a patient in mental hospitals, generally being discharged after a few days. The record shows a subsequent series of admissions and discharges over the next few years, at one point it being noted that he was a 'danger to others'. It is not known when or by whom Puckeridge came to the attention of the police in 1888, or how seriously they took him as a suspect, but he was obviously someone who needed to be investigated. The only mention of him was contained in a report by Sir Charles Warren:

> A man called Puckeridge was released from an asylum on 4 August. He was educated as a surgeon and has threatened to rip people up with a long knife. He is being looked for but cannot be found as yet.[8]

The same report mentioned Jacob Isenschmid, who had come to the attention of the police at around the same time. He was born in Switzerland in 1843, married Mary Ann Joyce in 1867 and had five children. On 11 September 1888, Dr Cowan and Dr Crabb of Holloway, North London, informed the police that they believed Isenschmid to be the Whitechapel murderer. Police learned that he had been lodging with a Mr Tyler at 60 Milford Road, Holloway, since 5 September and that he was frequently out of the house and was missing on the night of Annie Chapman's murder. He had later left his wife following an argument. By 17 September, he had been confined to Fairfield Road asylum, Bow, where Sergeant William Thick learned that he had told a number of women in

Holloway that he was 'Leather Apron'. He had been maintaining a living by collecting sheep's heads, feet and kidneys from the market, which he dressed and sold in the West End, and perhaps this casual work explained his absences from his lodgings.[9]

Two days later, Inspector Abberline reported that Isenschmid was known to a publican named Gehringer of Wentworth Street, Whitechapel, and that he was known locally as the 'mad butcher'. Significantly, he was believed to be the man with a bloodstained hand seen by Mrs Fiddymont and others at the Prince Albert following the murder of Annie Chapman and that this would be confirmed as soon as the doctors thought he was fit to appear for identification.[10] It is unclear whether any confirmed identification was made by Mrs Fiddymont, and Isenschmid was subsequently returned to Colney Hatch asylum.

Another early suspect of note was the volatile Charles Ludwig, a German hairdresser, who had come to London from Hamburg in 1887 or 1888 and found employment with Mr C. A. Partridge in the Minories, lodging with a German tailor named Johannes in Church Street, Minories, until his disorderly habits made him unwelcome, and he moved to a hotel in Finsbury. His landlord presented the press with a rather alarming picture of him:

He is . . . a most extraordinary man, is always in a bad temper, and grinds his teeth in rage at any little thing which puts him out. I believe he has some knowledge of anatomy, as he was for some time an assistant to some doctors in the German army, and helped to dissect bodies. He always carries some razors and a pair of scissors with him, and when he came here again on Monday night last he produced them. He was annoyed because I would not him sleep here, and threw down the razors in a passion, swearing at the same time.[11]

In the small hours of Tuesday 18 September 1888 he accompanied prostitute Elizabeth Burns to Three Kings Court, Minories, which led to some railway arches. There, he pulled a knife on her, and her cries of 'Murder!' attracted a police officer from his beat. He dismissed Ludwig and walked Miss Burns to the end of his beat, where she said, 'Dear me, he frightened me very much when he pulled a big knife out,' and explained that she was too afraid to make the complaint in Ludwig's presence. Johnson searched unsuccessfully for Ludwig and alerted other constables to the situation.

Ludwig then appeared at a coffee stall in Whitechapel High Street at 3.00 a.m. and pulled a knife on a bystander, for which he was arrested and remained in custody for a week. They also learned that he was believed to have had blood on his hands on the day of Annie Chapman's murder. His remands continued, as he was the most promising arrested suspect hitherto. For a moment, elements of the press regarded him as being 'connected by popular imagination with the murder'.[12] However, he, and Isenschmid, would later be exonerated of the crimes, when it became apparent that both were safely in custody when the later atrocities occurred.

Another interesting line of enquiry at the time, and one which fitted the notion of suspects with experience in medical fields, was the case of a group of three 'insane medical students' who had gone missing. Enquiries were made, and two were located and accounted for, but the third, John Sanders, could not be traced. Sanders studied at the London Hospital in 1879, but his mental condition had deteriorated to the extent that by 1887 he was becoming increasingly violent. His mother was traced to the leafy suburbia of St John's Wood, north-west London, but she told the police that he had 'gone abroad' two years earlier.[13] From what is known from the surviving documents, the hunt for John Sanders came to a dead end.

So the policemen on the ground, the press and the general public, few of whom knew about motiveless murders and struggled to rationalize a succession of crimes apparently committed by the same person on a class of society who had nothing of value, were looking for more prosaic explanations. The attack on Emma Smith was perceived, owing to her account, to be the work of a gang, a theory that still held sway following the death of Martha Tabram and maintained at the time of the murder of Mary Ann Nichols:

> The officers engaged in the case are pushing their inquiries in the neighbourhood as to the doings of certain gangs known to frequent these parts, and an opinion is gaining ground among them that the murderers are the same who committed the two previous murders near the same spot. It is believed that these gangs, who make their appearance during the early hours of the morning, are in the habit of blackmailing these poor unfortunate creatures, and when their demands are refused, violence follows, and in order to avoid their deeds being brought to light they put away their victims.[14]

'High Rip' gangs were mentioned frequently in the press during the autumn of 1888, the most notable being the gang of that name from Liverpool, who were known for their extreme violence. The 'High Rips' were often portrayed as having some level of organization, which they used to plan criminal activities. However, one of the most terrifying features of the gang was their willingness to engage in random acts of violence. There was often no attempt at theft, and it seemed that nobody could pass without some form of abuse or assault being inflicted upon them.[15] They had their equivalents elsewhere, such as the notorious 'Scuttlers' of Manchester; these were essentially youth gangs, deprived of moral values and self-discipline and downtrodden by the monotony of the city's slums. Extreme violence was usually meted out between rival gangs, and by 1890 it was believed that more young people were in Strangeways prison for scuttling than for any other crime.[16] Both examples appear to demonstrate violence for its own sake.

London, like any large metropolis, was also the home of similar gangs; in November 1888 an American newspaper listed the 'Marylebone Gang', the 'Fitzroy Place Gang', the 'Jovial Thirty-two' and the 'Black Gang', to name but a few.[17] In the East End there were immigrant gangs from Eastern Europe such as the rival 'Bessabarabians' and 'Odessians', as well as the 'Hoxton Mob' (or 'Hoxton High Rips') and the 'Monkey Parade'. The disruptive and often dangerous activities of the latter were reported weekly in the local press. However, what they got up to was not a patch on what was happening to the unfortunates on the streets of Whitechapel.

Of course the idea of 'aliens', or foreigners, being to blame was also very much a part of the picture, with the incitement of suspicion against the Jewish community being prevalent early on. The scare surrounding the mysterious – and perhaps non-existent – 'Leather Apron' was a significant element of that suspicion, especially when the newspapers began circulating sinister descriptions of the 'mad Jew'. Enter Edward Knight Larkins, a clerk in the HM Customs statistical department, who had the idea that the murderer was a Portuguese sailor who came to London from Oporto on cattle-boats. Over several years, Larkins approached many authorities, including the senior police officials involved in the Ripper case, and surviving official documentation shows that they took his highly detailed endeavours very seriously, at least early on. Two specific boats, the *City of Cork* and the *City of Oporto*, were earmarked by Larkins as being in the London docks at the time of each of the Whitechapel murders, all of the crews being Portuguese, which was important to Larkins, as he felt a need to comment on what he considered to be the 'vengeful character' of that nation.[18] He initially settled on Manuel Cruz Xavier and José Lourenço as individuals to be followed up, and Scotland Yard did indeed make enquiries of the consulate in Oporto. Even Montague Williams QC, nobody's fool, was convinced that Larkins was on to something. Larkins was extremely persistent, and initially the police were of the opinion that the theory was of 'great practical interest', until the inconvenient absence of the names of the suspects from the relevant crew lists led Larkins to construct more elaborate scenarios based on them changing ships, or travelling as stowaways, or even the involvement of a third ship. Robert Anderson eventually stated that Larkins was 'a troublesome "faddist" & it is idle to continue the subject with him'.[19] Nonetheless, Edward Knight Larkins, through his persistence, could be considered the first 'Ripperologist'. However, his case illustrates a problem that would continue to beset researchers, writers and readers even to this day – namely the extent to which it is legitimate to modify a theory as new information emerges. If Jose Lourenço, for example, had been found hunched over Mary Kelly's body, bloody knife in hand, he would not have been released simply because his name wasn't on a crew list. An explanation for the anomaly would have been sought, and the idea he had entered the country as a stowaway would then have seemed plausible enough.

The London docks were very much a focus for investigation even before Larkins's Portuguese sailor theory hit the desks of Scotland Yard. Chief Inspector Donald Swanson's report detailing police efforts following the double murder noted the work of the Thames Police as they made enquiries into sailors at the docks and rivers, making a particular effort regarding the presence of 'asiatics', which resulted in upwards of eighty people being detained.[20] As early as September 1888 the *Daily Telegraph* hoped that the detective service was energetic enough to 'direct the persistent, unrelaxing, inexorable inquiry which should be made in every court and alley, not only in Whitechapel but in maritime London, among the waterside characters and on board every vessel in the docks'.[21] In the aftermath of the double event it was reported that 'every vessel that has left the harbour since the hour of the commission of the last crime has been thoroughly overhauled'.[22]

In early October 1888, the police reacted with great interest to a telegram sent from New York from somebody who called himself 'Dodge', suggesting that the murderer was a Malay cook named 'Alaska'. This enigmatic character (who was never traced) had claimed to have been robbed of all he had by a 'woman of the town' and that 'unless he found the woman and recovered his property, he would kill and mutilate every Whitechapel woman he met'.[23] Intensive investigative activities in the world's busiest port were therefore taking place almost from day one, a fact apparently unknown to many who subsequently advanced what they thought were original 'seaman' theories. One recent commentator wrote, 'I suspected that Jack the Ripper may have been a merchant seaman. I could find nothing to suggest that the police pursued this line of inquiry at the time.'[24]

Even the police themselves were not exempt from suspicion during these tentative forays into identifying the murderer. Somebody calling himself 'An Accessory', who wrote to the City Police on 19 October 1888, stated that:

> The crime committed in Mitre Square City and those in the district of Whitechapel were perpetrated by an Ex Police Constable of the Metropolitan Police who was dismissed from the force through certain connection with a prostitute. The motive for the crimes is hatred and spite against the authorities at Scotland Yard one of whom is marked as a victim after which the crimes will cease.[25]

PC Edward Watkins was also suspected by an anonymous correspondent from Trowbridge, who suggested that the authorities 'keep an eye on him', later adding: 'Please be careful and keep this quiet not let him know you are watching him.'[26] Another name familiar to the case was Sergeant William Thick, the well-respected and prominent officer who has become probably the best-known police character after Frederick Abberline. Thick was suspected by Henry T. Haselwood in a letter to the Home Office of 14 October 1889:

> I beg to state that through the information I have received I believe that if Sergt. T. Thicke otherwise called 'Johnny Upright' is watched and his whereabouts ascertained upon other dates where certain women have met their end, also to see what deceace he is troubled with, you will find the great secreate this is to be strictly private and my name is not to be mentioned.

A note made on a covering letter made the police opinion very clear: 'I think it is plainly rubbish – perhaps prompted by spite.'[27] Even police suspects had to have a motive or disease which caused them to kill, it seems, but other correspondents merely felt that the culprit dressed as a policeman to evade capture without necessarily offering a reason why they were killing in the first place.

Or was the Whitechapel murderer a religious fanatic, exacting brutal punishment upon the fallen women of Whitechapel? So thought Edgar Sheppard MD, who wrote to *The Times*, believing that the murderer might not necessarily have been an escaped or recognized lunatic, but that he was on 'a mission from above to extirpate vice by assassination. And he has selected his victims from a class which contributes pretty largely to the factorship of immorality and sin.'[28] Whitechapel and neighbouring Spitalfields would have been seen as the epitome of 'immorality and sin' – the police estimate of around 1,200 prostitutes was a staggering statistic for so small a district and enquiries were made to ascertain the number of disreputable houses in the area. In reply to a query from the Home Office on the very subject, Sir Charles Warren stated that:

> during the last few months I have been tabulating the observations of Constables on their beats, and have come to the conclusion that there are 62 houses known to be brothels on the H or Whitechapel Divn and probably a great number of other houses which are more or less intermittently used for such purpose.[29]

And so, any such fanatical religionist would be well placed in such a district to conduct their own unique brand of 'street cleaning'.

In late 1889 the figure of Lyttleton Forbes Winslow re-emerged. He had been persistent in his attempts to get the police to employ his apparently expert services but was constantly rebuffed. He had convinced himself that he knew the identity of the Ripper and, facing persistent indifference from the investigating authorities, he went on to expound his theories to the newspapers. By now he actually had a suspect, who, it emerged, was one G. Wentworth Bell Smith, who had been lodging at the house of Mr and Mrs Callaghan of Sun Street, Finsbury, since August 1888. Mr Callaghan had noted that Smith was in the habit of writing reams of religious tracts and had delusions about women, prostitutes in particular, whom he said should be drowned. Smith also claimed to have performed 'operations' on them. Apparently he would stay out at all hours of the night, wearing silent, rubber-soled shoes, and on his return would collapse on the sofa and foam at the mouth. The Callaghans logically considered him to be insane.[30]

The theory surrounding Wentworth Bell Smith was discussed by the police, and the story of a man answering to his description, acting suspiciously in the Finsbury area between the murders of Tabram and Nichols, was investigated by Inspector Abberline and detailed in a report circulated by Donald Swanson.[31] Forbes Winslow eventually published his memoirs in 1910, the first book to discuss the Ripper correspondence at length which printed facsimiles of letters that he had claimed were sent to him personally.[32] One letter, apparently written on 19 October 1888, predicted that the next murder would take place on 8 or 9 November (subsequently the date of the Kelly murder). Forbes Winslow obviously accepted such letters as genuine; however, enquiries found that the address given by the sender, 22 Hammersmith Road, did not exist. It was also noted that the date on this letter, 'Oct. 19th 88', was actually '89', the last digit being altered to make the date more relevant to the murders.[33] It is fair to say that only Forbes Winslow could have made such a 'convenient' adjustment and, allied to his conviction that once he had made public his theories on the Ripper the murders ceased (he believed Alice McKenzie was a genuine Ripper victim), the whole scenario began to appear as a seemingly desperate attempt to be recognized for solving the case. Unlike Edward Knight Larkins, who was prepared to alter a theory to reflect new discoveries, Forbes Winslow could be seen as an early example of a theorist who was obviously willing to manipulate facts to suit a theory.

Speculation about a religious motive got off on a new tack when word got around, via the press, that a similar series of murders had been committed in Austria a few years before. A Galician Jew by the name of Mosheh Ritter had been sentenced to death for outraging a young Christian girl named Francis Mnich in Krakow and then instructing a Pole named Stochlinski to murder and mutilate her. Each time the verdict was reversed by a higher court on the grounds that the evidence was not sufficient, and Ritter was finally let go. So whoever the actual murderer was might have escaped to carry on his dreadful butchery in the East End.

The interesting feature of the Ritter case was that witnesses had come forward at the trials to testify that among fanatical Jews it was held that, if ever a Jew succumbed to temptation and had illicit intercourse with a Christian woman, it was his duty to atone for the offence by killing her and carrying out atrocious sexual mutilations. However, no such authorization is given in the Talmud. The press made a link between this case and a more sinister motive:

In various German criminal codes of the seventeenth and eighteenth centuries, as also in statutes of a more recent date, punishments are prescribed for the mutilation of female corpses with the object of making from the uterus and other organs the so-called 'diebalichter' or 'schlafslichter', respectively 'thieves' candles' or 'soporific candles.' According to an old superstition, still rife in various parts of Germany, the light from such candles will throw those upon whom it falls into the deepest slumbers, and they may, consequently, become a valuable instrument to those of the thieving profession.[34]

Thieves' candles also played an important part in the trials of robber bands at Odenwald and in Westphalia, in 1812 and 1841 respectively. They were heard of at the trial of the notorious German robber Theodor Unger, who was executed at Magdeburg in 1810. It was on that occasion discovered that a regular manufactory had been established by gangs of thieves for the production of such candles. Their use was believed to have survived among German thieves, as was proved by a case at Biala, in Galicia, in 1875.[35]

It wasn't just elements of the arcane that were suggested as motives for the murders; some went as far as to use spiritualism in their endeavours to track down the killer. Following the death of Alice McKenzie, Stuart Cumberland, a medium and 'thought reader', published a description of the Ripper in his own illustrated Sunday publication, the *Mirror*. It was accompanied by a drawing of the supposed murderer, the appearance of whom came to Cumberland in a dream.[36]

A story first published in the *Chicago Sunday Times Herald* in April 1895 said that spiritualist and medium Robert Lees had tracked the Whitechapel Murderer to the home of an eminent London physician. Lees, dogged by visions and premonitions, claimed to have attempted to use his gifts to help the police during the autumn of 1888 but was rejected as a 'crank' a number of times. However, on one occasion he was apparently accompanied in his endeavours by a police officer:

> After an earnest appeal from the inspector, Lees consented to try and track the Ripper, much in the same way as a bloodhound pursues a criminal. All that night Lees traversed swiftly the streets of London. The inspector and his aids followed a few feet behind. At last, at 4 o'clock in the morning, the human bloodhound halted at the gates of a West End mansion. Pointing to an upper chamber where a faint light gleamed, he said: 'There is the murderer you are looking for.'
>
> 'It is impossible,' returned the inspector. 'That is the residence of one of the most celebrated physicians in the West End; but, if you will describe to me the interior of the doctor's hall, I will arrest him.'[37]

Apparently, the interior of the mansion matched Lees's description. The doctor in question was examined and certified insane. However, such was his profile that, to avoid embarrassment, a fake funeral was arranged and an empty coffin interred in Kensal Green cemetery, whilst the physician himself was placed in an asylum under the false name of Thomas Mason, alias 'No. 124'.

But even the full-blown use of black magic was suggested. In December 1888, self-styled occultist Roslyn D'Onston Stephenson (writing as 'one who knows') sent a suggestion to the *Pall Mall Gazette*, blatantly putting forth the idea that the Whitechapel murders were committed by a Frenchman; his reasoning was that the word 'Juwes' as found on the wall in Goulston Street probably said 'Juives', the feminine French form of 'Jews', and that prostitute murder was 'considered to be almost peculiarly a French crime'. The motive was indulgence in 'unholy rites', in that the sexual organs missing from the victims could be used with other ingredients in black magic rituals and that the locations of the murders – except Mary Kelly's – formed a perfect sacrificial cross.[38]

Sir Arthur Diosy, later a member of 'Our Society',[39] was aggrieved by this suggestion, mainly because he claimed to have had similar ideas as early as October 1888.

> According to him, among the quests of these people in the East is the elixir vitae, one of the ingredients of which must come from a recently killed woman. Diosy got quite excited when he heard of the bright farthings and burnt matches which he said might have formed the 'flaming points' of a magical figure called a 'pentacle' at each angle of which such points were found, and according to ritual certain 'flaming' articles had to be thus disposed. Diosy said later that he had paid a visit to Scotland Yard to place his theories before the authorities, but had been received without enthusiasm, as one can well understand.[40]

As for Stephenson, he later became a Ripper suspect himself.[41] In 1890 he was living in Southsea with his lover, the novelist Mabel Collins, and it was here that he met Collins's friend Baroness Vittoria Cremers. After first finding Stephenson inoffensive, Cremers would later become uncomfortable in his company and on one occasion she saw him drawing an upside-down triangle on his door, apparently to keep out an evil presence. In the late 1920s or '30s, Cremers told journalist Bernard O'Donnell[42] that she once went into Stephenson's room without him knowing and under the bed she found seven neck-ties in a tin case that were stained with what appeared to be dried blood. Cremers became convinced, along with Mabel Collins, that Stephenson was Jack the Ripper. The ties later supposedly came into the possession of notorious occultist Aleister Crowley, who boasted that they had belonged to the Ripper. He went on to name the man as Stephenson.[43]

One other singularly notable theory as to the identity of the killer made its debut in September 1888, when Lord Sydney Godolphin Osborne wrote to *The Times* with a lengthy correspondence which made a case that probably would have had its readers puffing with exasperation:

> All strange, Sir, as it may appear to you and the generality of your readers, it is within the range of my belief that one or both these Whitechapel murders may have been committed by female hands. There are details in both cases which fit in well with language for ever used where two of these unfortunates are in violent strife; there is far more jealousy, as is well known, between such women in regard to those with whom they cohabit than is the case with married people where one may suspect the other of sin against the marriage vow.
>
> There are, I have no doubt, plenty of women of this class known for their violent temper, with physical power to commit such a deed. As to the nature of their sex forbidding belief that they could so act, how many of them are altogether unsexed, have no one element in character with female feeling?[44]

Strange though it may have seemed to people at the time, the idea of a female Ripper (or 'Jill the Ripper' as the theory is often called) would be picked up more than once in the first half of the following century. It has been said that Arthur

Conan Doyle, creator of that most famous fictional detective Sherlock Holmes, felt that the murderer could have been a woman or at the very least a man who dressed as such to evade detection, an idea posited by many correspondents to the press and police throughout 1888. Such potentially wayward conjecture was a demonstration of the great lengths that contemporary theorists were prepared to go to in order to find meaning in what appeared to be a completely meaningless series of murders, bereft of any potential benefit to the perpetrator. To this extent some, like Mrs L. Painter from the Isle of Wight – after suggesting a female killer – could only assume that the murders were committed by some animal which had escaped from a private menagerie and in a letter to the police on 3 October 1888 stated that the creature:

> would be swift, cunning, noiseless and strong, standing over its work until a footstep was heard and then vaulting over fence or wall, disappearing in a moment, hiding its weapon perhaps high up in a tree or other safe place, and returning home to shut itself up in its cage'.[45]

Anecdote and Memory

By the final years of the nineteenth century the Jack the Ripper murders, seemingly now past, were perhaps far enough away for commentators to begin *naming* their suspects, although much of the reasoning behind this was often anecdotal. What began was a new era of theorizing which relied on specific sources of information, rather than trying to fit the murderer into some form of preconceived archetype.

In February 1894, the *Sun* published a series of articles under the title of 'The Story of Jack the Ripper. Solution of the great murder mystery. His personality, career and fate' which claimed to have identified the murderer.[1] Although no name was given, the suspect under discussion was actually Thomas Hayne Cutbush, who had been sent to Broadmoor in 1891 after he had maliciously wounded a woman by stabbing her in the buttocks. Apparently he had also stabbed six girls, committed murderous assaults on a co-worker, a servant girl and a relative and had threatened to murder a doctor and another individual. His general behaviour obviously suggested insanity, hence his committal to the asylum, and the *Sun* believed that it had its man.

The publication of these confident claims led Melville Macnaghten to react in an official capacity on 23 February 1894. Macnaghten was appointed assistant chief constable of the CID in July 1889, too late to be directly involved with the main Ripper investigation. Nonetheless, his new position and connections would have made his knowledge of the case significant, and it was with this in mind that he penned a memorandum refuting the *Sun's* claims, as well as naming Cutbush. But the report had greater significance than just disproving a theory, for in his attempt to exonerate Cutbush, Macnaghten named what appeared to be three other contemporary suspects:

No one ever saw the Whitechapel murderer; many homicidal maniacs were suspected, but no shadow of proof could be thrown on any one. I may mention the cases of 3 men, any one of whom would have been more likely than Cutbush to have committed this series of murders:

(1) A Mr M. J. Druitt, said to be a doctor & of good family – who disappeared at the time of the Miller's Court murder, & whose body (which was said to have been upwards of a month in the water) was found in the Thames on 31st December – or about 7 weeks after that murder. He was sexually insane and from private information I have little doubt but that his own family believed him to have been the murderer.

(2) Kosminski – a Polish Jew – & resident in Whitechapel. This man became insane owing to many years indulgence in solitary vices. He had a great hatred of women, specially of the prostitute class, & had strong homicidal tendencies: he was removed to a lunatic asylum about March 1889. There were many circumstances connected with this man which made him a strong 'suspect'.

(3) Michael Ostrog, a Russian doctor, and a convict, who was subsequently detained in a lunatic asylum as a homicidal maniac. This man's antecedents were of the worst possible type, and his whereabouts at the time of the murders could never be ascertained.[2]

On the face of it, Macnaghten seemed to be merely stating that *any* of the three individuals mentioned were more likely than Cutbush to be the murderer, without appearing to favour any one in particular or saying that any were indeed Jack the Ripper. The notes also stated, quite unequivocally, that 'the Whitechapel murderer had 5 victims – & 5 victims only', they being Nichols, Chapman, Stride, Eddowes and Kelly.

The first name on Macnaghten's list, 'M. J. Druitt', was Montague John Druitt. A rather unhappy character, it seems, he was born into a respectably well-heeled family, was Oxford-educated and became a schoolmaster before being called to the Bar in 1885. However, he was no doubt of unsound mind and left a note in his pocket, found after his death, which apparently read: 'Since Friday I felt that I was going to be like mother, and it would be best for all concerned if I were to die.'[3] Though he was not a medical man himself (and this is where Macnaghten got it wrong), there were many doctors in his immediate family, and his cousin Lionel had a surgery in the Minories in the 1870s, on the edge of the City of London near Aldgate and close to the murderer's theatre of operations. But he *was* found dead in the Thames on the date Macnaghten specified.[4] Interestingly, three years prior to the memoranda being written, a story about the Ripper's supposed suicide appeared in the provincial press, stating that a 'West of England' Member of Parliament had declared that he had solved the Ripper mystery and that the murderer was 'the son of a surgeon' who suffered from 'homicidal mania' and committed suicide on the date of the final murder.[5] The following year, the *Western Mail*[6] stated that Henry Farquharson MP was credited with such a theory, which on the face of it appeared to pre-empt Macnaghten in terms of what he said about Montague Druitt.

In 1898, Arthur Griffiths in his *Mysteries of Police and Crime*, had this to say about the Whitechapel murders and the close similarity with Macnaghten's statements cannot be ignored:

> But the police, after the last murder, had brought their investigations to the point of strongly suspecting several persons, all of them known to be homicidal lunatics, and against three of these they held very plausible and reasonable grounds of suspicion. Concerning two of them the case was weak, although it was based on certain colourable facts. One was a Polish Jew, a known lunatic, who was at large in the district of Whitechapel at the time of the murder, and who, having afterwards developed homicidal tendencies, was confined in an asylum. This man was said to resemble the murderer by the one person who got a glimpse of him – the police-constable in Mitre Court. The second possible criminal was a Russian doctor, also insane, who had been a convict both in England and Siberia. This man was in the habit of carrying about surgical knives and instruments in his pockets; his antecedents were of the very worst, and at the time of the Whitechapel murders he was in hiding, or, at least, his whereabouts were never exactly known. The third person was of the same type, but the suspicion in his case was stronger, and there was every reason to believe that his own friends entertained grave doubts about him. He also was a doctor in the prime of life, was believed to be insane or on the borderland of insanity, and he disappeared immediately after the last murder, that in Miller's Court, on the 9th of November, 1888. On the last day of that year, seven weeks later, his body was found floating in the Thames, and was said to have been in the water a month. The theory in this case was that after his last exploit, which was the most fiendish of all, his brain entirely gave way, and he became furiously insane and committed suicide.[7]

And as early as 1899 George R. Sims – a journalist and play-wright with very good police connections – had been talking of a suspect who had drowned himself in the Thames at the end of 1888.[8] What is evident from the statements of Mac-naghten, the press reports about Farquharson, Griffiths's reminiscences and Sims's hints is that much of the informa-tion they put forward is obviously similar. Indeed, Griffiths's mention of 'the police-constable in Mitre Court' as the only person who got a look at the murderer could be found in a draft version of Macnaghten's notes, transcribed by his daugh-ter Christobel (later Lady Aberconway),[9] which were not for official consumption, although the mistake of referring to 'Mitre Court' appeared to be Griffiths'. As far as official records were concerned, no City policeman saw a man near Mitre Square, and the possibility that Macnaghten is referring to another officer (perhaps Metropolitan PC William Smith, who saw a man with Elizabeth Stride on the same night) sug-gests that, coming late to the Whitechapel murders case, Macnaghten was using second-hand or anecdotal information passed down by those who were more active at the time. In fact, Griffiths probably got his information in the same man-ner, most likely from Macnaghten, and Sims used Griffiths as his source.

Macnaghten's notes (or the 'Macnaghten memoranda' as they are popularly known), in mentioning two other individu-als, Michael Ostrog and Kosminski, serve up more food for thought. Ostrog's inclusion was somewhat of a mystery; from what is now known of him he appears to be little more than an audacious confidence trickster and thief, using a number of aliases throughout his criminal career and exhibiting no homi-cidal characteristics. In July 1888 he was arrested for stealing a microscope and sentenced on 14 November, which goes a long way to suggest that he was in France at the time of the murders. But the veracity of Macnaghten's suggestions was not necessarily nullified by such odd inclusions, thanks to the citation of Druitt and the other suspect, 'Kosminski', who is somewhat more problematical. In the anecdotal world of police reminiscences, his inclusion is significant.

In 1907 Sir Robert Anderson (he was knighted on his retirement in 1901) published comments on the Whitechapel murders in his book *Criminals and Crime*,[10] where he declared that the perpetrator had been 'caged in an asylum'. As early as 1895, he was reported as stating that 'Jack the Ripper was a homicidal maniac, temporarily at large, whose hideous career was cut short by committal to an asylum'[11] and again in 1901, in a short article on penology.[12] Anderson published his memoirs[13] in 1910, in which he shed some light on the supposed author of the 'Dear Boss' letter and expanded on his previous brief comments:

And the conclusion we came to was that he and his people were certain low-class Polish Jews; for it is a remarkable fact that people of that class in the East End will not give up one of their number to Gentile justice.

And the result proved that our diagnosis was right on every point. For I may say at once that 'undiscovered murders' are rare in London, and the 'Jack-the-Ripper' crimes are not within that category. And if the Police here had powers such as the French Police possess, the murderer would have been brought to justice. Scotland Yard can boast that not even the subordinate officers of the department will tell tales out of school, and it would ill become me to violate the unwritten rule of the service. So I will only add here that the 'Jack-the-Ripper' letter which is preserved in the Police Museum at New Scotland Yard is the creation of an enterprising London journalist.

Having regard to the interest attaching to this case, I am almost tempted to disclose the identity of the murderer and of the pressman who wrote the letter above referred to. But no public benefit would result from such a course, and the traditions of my old department would suffer. I will merely add that the only person who had ever had a good view of the murderer unhesitatingly identified the suspect the instant he was confronted with him; but he refused to give evidence against him.

In saying that he was a Polish Jew I am merely stating a definitely ascertained fact. And my words are meant to specify race, not religion. For it would outrage all religious sentiment to talk of the religion of a loathsome creature whose utterly unmentionable vices reduced him to a lower level than that of the brute.

But in a serialized version of the memoirs published in *Blackwood's Magazine* prior to the book, Anderson had also said that the suspect was put into an asylum, after which he was identified by the witness. Anderson obviously stuck to his story, and his comments were given some weight by pencilled annotations made by his good friend Chief Inspector Donald Swanson in a copy of the *Lighter Side of My Official Life*, sometime between 1910 and Swanson's death in 1924. Where Anderson had written about the identification, Swanson's 'marginalia' added that the witness would not testify:

because the suspect was also a Jew and also because his evidence would convict the suspect, and witness would be the means of murderer being hanged which he did not wish to be left on his mind. D.S.S

On the endpaper of the book, Swanson added that:

After the suspect had been identified at the Seaside Home where he had been sent by us with difficulty, in order to subject him to identification, and he knew he was identified.

On suspects return to his brothers house in Whitechapel he was watched by police (City CID) by day & night. In a very short time the suspect with his hands tied behind his back, he was sent to Stepney Workhouse and then to Colney Hatch and died shortly afterwards – Kosminski was the suspect. DSS

The combination of references to 'Kosminski' as being a Polish Jew, his indulgence in 'solitary' or 'unmentionable vices' as set down by Macnaghten and Anderson and the apparent confirmation of the identification and incarceration in an asylum by Swanson sets up the seemingly obvious chain of thought that Macnaghten's 'Kosminski' was the same man discussed by Anderson and Swanson. But was 'Kosminski' Jack the Ripper? None of these obviously well-informed men gave a first name to this most intriguing of suspects, and it was not until just after Swanson's marginalia were made public in 1987 that a suggestion was made – Aaron Kosminski.

Aaron Kosminski,[14] born in Kłodawa, central Poland, in 1865, appears in the records of Colney Hatch asylum, where he was incarcerated in February 1891. The cause of his insanity was 'self abuse', which again appears to confirm what had been said about him in the observations of those former senior officers. Swanson mentions 'Kosminski' being taken from his brother's house for the identification; Aaron was taken from his brother Wolf's house to the Mile End Old Town workhouse in 1890 (where he was deemed as having been insane for two years) prior to being sent to Colney Hatch. Unfortunately, there is also much about Aaron's life that conflicts with the claims of those senior police officials. Macnaghten and Swanson said that he died soon after being admitted to the asylum, but Aaron Kosminski died at Leavesden Asylum in 1919. Except for one alleged incident where he threatened his sister with a knife, he appeared to be non-violent, later becoming an incoherent imbecile and in fact, when researching this matter in 1987, author Martin Fido was so unimpressed by the lack of any violent or homicidal characteristics that he rejected him and chose another Colney Hatch inmate, the more volatile David Cohen, as a potential candidate for the insane Polish Jew suspect.[15] According to Fido, Cohen seemed to be the only Whitechapel Jew whose incarceration fitted the timescale given by Anderson. Though his research was meticulous, Fido put forward the rather odd possibility that David Cohen was indeed 'Kosminski' and that the name was just a 'John Doe', or general sobriquet given to Jews whose names were difficult or impossible to pronounce.

Another case in point was suspect Severin Klosowski, also known as George Chapman, a serial poisoner hanged in 1903 for the murder of three of his wives. Klosowski was a barber-surgeon who, at the time of the murders, had a business in Cable Street, St George-in-the-East, and later, in 1890, in the cellar of the White Hart public house at the corner of Whitechapel High Street and George Yard. Again, it was the words of a prominent officer, this time Inspector Frederick Abberline, which brought Klosowski into the frame. In an interview in the *Pall Mall Gazette* the week before Klosowski's execution, Abberline spoke at length about him and his own suspicions while at the same time disagreeing with any notion that the murderer had died or was in an asylum:

there are a score of things which make one believe that Chapman
is the man; and you must understand that we have never believed
all those stories about Jack the Ripper being dead, or that he was a
lunatic, or anything of that kind. For instance, the date of the
arrival in England coincides with the beginning of the series of
murders in Whitechapel; there is a coincidence also in the fact that
the murders ceased in London when 'Chapman' went to America,
while similar murders began to be perpetrated in America after he
landed there. The fact that he studied medicine and surgery in
Russia before he came here is well established, and it is curious to
note that the first series of murders was the work of an expert
surgeon, while the recent poisoning cases were proved to be done
by a man with more than an elementary knowledge of medicine.
The story told by 'Chapman's' wife of the attempt to murder her
with a long knife while in America is not to be ignored.[16]

On the face of it, this interview appeared to suggest that
Abberline was all-out to cast Klosowski in the role of the Ripper. However, the following week, in response to great interest
in the story, Abberline was approached again, but this time he
said that Scotland Yard was 'really no wiser on the subject than
it was fifteen years ago'. He again dismissed the rumours surrounding the lunatic in the asylum and the Thames suicide:

'I know that it has been stated in several quarters that "Jack the
Ripper" was a man who died in a lunatic asylum a few years
ago, but there is nothing at all of a tangible nature to support
such a theory.'

Our representative called Mr Abberline's attention to a
statement made in a well-known Sunday paper, in which it was
made out that the author was a young medical student who
was found drowned in the Thames.

'Yes,' said Mr Abberline, 'I know all about that story. But what does it amount to? Simply this. Soon after the last murder in Whitechapel the body of a young doctor was found in the Thames, but there is absolutely nothing beyond the fact that he was found at that time to incriminate him. A report was made to the Home Office about the matter, but that it was "considered final and conclusive" is going altogether beyond the truth.'[17]

Abberline, perhaps as roundly qualified to talk about these murders as Anderson, Macnaghten, Swanson or anybody else, appeared to blatantly close the door on almost everything they said. Such anecdotal information, perhaps tainted by the passage of time or failing memories, shows how problematical such theorizing could be, and the continuing research into Aaron Kosminski as being the 'Kosminski' spoken of, as well as Druitt and Klosowski, shows the desire for clarity when addressing these important names. After all, they were named or hinted at by men in a position to know. Or, in the words of Chief Inspector John Littlechild when referring to Major Griffiths: 'He probably got his information from Anderson who only *"thought he knew"*.'

Littlechild, head of the Secret Branch from 1883 until his resignation ten years later, said those words at the end of a letter written to George Sims on 23 September 1913:

I was pleased to receive your letter which I shall put away in 'good company' to read again, perhaps some day when old age overtakes me and when to revive memories of the past may be a solace.

Knowing the great interest you take in all matters criminal, and abnormal, I am just going to inflict one more letter on you on the 'Ripper' subject. Letters as a rule are only a nuisance when they call for a reply but this does not need one. I will try and be brief.

I never heard of a Dr D. in connection with the Whitechapel murders but among the suspects, and to my mind a very likely one, was a Dr T. (which sounds much like D.) He was an American quack named Tumblety and was at one time a frequent visitor to London and on these occasions constantly brought under the notice of police, there being a large dossier concerning him at Scotland Yard. Although a 'Sycopathia Sexualis' subject he was not known as a 'Sadist' (which the murderer unquestionably was) but his feelings toward women were remarkable and bitter in the extreme, a fact on record. Tumblety was arrested at the time of the murders in connection with unnatural offences and charged at Marlborough Street, remanded on bail, jumped his bail, and got away to Boulogne. He shortly left Boulogne and was never heard of afterwards. It was believed he committed suicide but certain it is that from this time the 'Ripper' murders came to an end.[18]

The content of the letter took on a similar pattern to previous claims by police officials in that it was a blend of verifiable fact and peculiar inaccuracy. Littlechild was referring to Dr Francis Tumblety,[19] an eccentric character to say the least, flamboyant in his public appearances and yet, according to his acquaintances, possessed of a secretive nature in regard to his personal life. However, if one thing could be said of him, then that was that his life was rarely without controversy, often of his own making. As an adolescent, he had sold pornographic literature to canal-boat passengers, earning him a reputation of being uneducated and disreputable. He later set himself up as an herb doctor and travelled extensively, putting himself forward as an Irish Nationalist in an election campaign.[20] His abilities as a 'doctor' were called into question following the death of a patient. Tumbelty made many claims – that he was familiar with Abraham Lincoln and served in the American Civil War as a surgeon – although later he was implicated in the assassination of the president in 1865. Any proof of Tumblety's eminence often came in the form of documents of dubious provenance, and his grasp of reality was tenuous to say the least. He was later involved in a lawsuit against an acquaintance which was subsequently discredited, the acquaintance later suing Tumblety for sexual assault.

Tumblety was in London when the Whitechapel murders took place. With his penchant for attracting trouble, he was arrested on 7 November 1888 and charged with acts of gross indecency with several men. Apparently homosexual, or at least bisexual, he was also alleged to have an unhealthy mistrust of women, particularly of the 'unfortunate' class.

Jumping bail, he fled to France and thence to America, where his arrival was met with great interest, and he was soon being suggested as a suspect for the murders. In fact, Tumblety became a notorious celebrity in his home country and was literally all over the papers. He was given plenty of chances to answer his accusers and was interviewed by the *New York World*:

My guilt was very plain to the English mind. Someone had said that Jack the Ripper was an American, and everybody believed that statement. Then it is the universal belief among the lower classes that all Americans wear slouch hats; therefore, Jack the Ripper must wear a slouch hat. Now, I happened to have on a slouch hat, and this, together with the fact that I was an American, was enough for the police. It established my guilt beyond any question.[21]

In Littlechild's opinion 'the murderer undoubtedly was a sadist', and Tumblety wasn't one, but there were plenty of reasons why someone might have suspected him; perhaps the alleged bitter feelings towards women more than made up for the lack of sadistic tendencies, as well as the aforementioned plump file on him compiled by Scotland Yard, suggesting that the authorities must have held some store in his candidacy for the Ripper. Tumblety's 'psychopathia sexualis' was probably a reference to his homosexual proclivities as much as anything else but may have been seen by Littlechild as a root cause of sexual murder. The cessation of the crimes owing to Tumblety's 'suicide' was an unfortunate aberration, as Francis Tumblety died in 1903.

Again, the 'Littlechild Letter' fitted into the box filled by other anecdotal exchanges which were not always necessarily for public of official consumption (Anderson notwithstanding). As the nineteenth century gave way to the twentieth, and the Whitechapel murders began to recede in time, the task of collating this disparate and contradictory material became the main activity of those seeking to establish the murderer's identity, and as the police officers involved in the case began to pass away, that task was taken over by a growing band of armchair detectives keen to give 'Jack the Ripper' a name that everyone could see.

Naming Names

In 1923 William Le Queux published the book *Things I Know about Kings, Celebrities and Crooks*,[1] which contained a most original theory relating to Jack the Ripper. Le Queux was an Anglo-French freelance writer whose considerable literary output comprised of espionage and spy scares, as well as sensational gossip. He also claimed to be a member of the Crimes Club ('Our Society') and a good friend of George Sims. In *Things I Know*, he announced that 'the identity of Jack the Ripper has been disclosed and will be found for the first time disclosed in Chapter XVII'. Le Queux claimed to have been given a number of documents taken from the St Petersburg home of Grigori Rasputin, the so-called 'Mad Monk', who was murdered in 1916. The documents, typed in French, included a manuscript called 'Great Russian Criminals', in which Jack the Ripper was named as a Dr Alexander Pedachenko, assisted by a friend called Levistski and a young woman named Winberg. The motive for the murders was to show up the inadequacy of the British police force.

The story very much leaned on the characteristics of the then-favoured Ripper archetypes, the doctor *and* the foreigner, and the whereabouts of the documents he referred to have never been ascertained. What is also worth mentioning is that Rasputin had apparently never shown any interest in the Whitechapel murders during his lifetime and could not speak

French. The whole theory amounted to very little, and certainly, with no concrete proof to back it up, the premise smacked of Le Queux's penchant for sensation and gossip. And so Ripper theorizing entered into a new genre, that of producing a hypothesis based on anecdotal and esoteric material that might or might not have existed, whereby if one was to accept the theory put forward, one had to take the author's claims as true. One such theorist was Leonard Matters.

Matters was an Australian-born journalist and veteran of the Boer War who went on to become managing editor of the *Buenos Aires Herald*. Travelling widely as an international reporter, he later served as a Labour member of parliament for Kennington in London. Highly respected, he chose to write on the Ripper case in the *People* in 1926 following information he had gleaned whilst in Buenos Aires.[2] The source was an anonymous article written by an ex-student of one 'Dr Stanley', who had been summoned to the doctor's death bed, only to hear him confess to being Jack the Ripper. The story has it that Dr Stanley's son had contracted syphilis from Mary Jane Kelly on Boat Race night in 1886 and subsequently died of the disease. His enraged father, a brilliant London doctor, set about murdering Kelly and her friends as revenge before settling in South America in 1908. Matters's extended version of this theory was published in 1929 as *The Mystery of Jack the Ripper*.[3]

Although Matters had supposedly put a name to the Ripper, the story had little going for it in the way of reliable corroboration. Apart from the ex-student's article (published in a Spanish-language journal), the only other source to back this theory came from a 'Mrs North', who claimed to have known the doctor in 1888. It would be very easy to dismiss Matters's theory as yet another dubious anecdotal story, frustratingly backed up by material that could not be found, if it were not for an account published in an American newspaper twenty-five years earlier, when the actor John T. Sullivan claimed that Jack the Ripper was a physician who had developed a homicidal mania and had escaped from a private sanatorium in a London suburb, after which he fled to Buenos Aires.[4] Sullivan's suspect was 'Dr E' as opposed to a 'Dr S', but the similarity with Matters's story is intriguing nonetheless.

The Mystery of Jack the Ripper was the first full-length treatment of the Ripper case. It was divided into two sections titled 'Fact' and 'Theory' and, despite some reservations, is still considered the first important book on the subject. Having been written in the 1920s, Leonard Matters's book also allowed the reader some insight into the East End of that time from the on-the-spot descriptions of the murder sites. The most notable inclusion was Miller's Court, and in fact he was the last writer on the subject to see Mary Kelly's former home before it was demolished a mere three days after his visit in 1928. What was regrettable was that Matters would have had access to residents of the East End and others who would have been alive at the time of the murders and yet he chose not to take advantage of the availability of such oral history. His reasoning behind this was that he believed that such accounts would be riddled with inaccuracies and erroneous hearsay, despite the inevitable mistakes in his own account (as he invariably had to rely on secondary sources). Such stories would, of course, have proved fascinating years later and could have added important observations by significant witnesses and police officers. It is strange that none of the earliest commentators and authors on the crimes appear to have bothered to seek out these people, a great opportunity sadly lost.

Around the same time, another fascinating document was produced which appeared to fly in the face of the continuing trend of finding a motive for the crimes: a manuscript for an autobiography of one James Willoughby Carnac, which was, to all intents and purposes, the autobiography of Jack the Ripper.[5] In the manuscript, Carnac outlined his early life in north London, his motives and drives to murder in the autumn of 1888 and ultimately the reasons for the cessation of the crimes. The whole story does appear to be a work of fiction and, according to introductory notes, was written around 1929. Certain information in the manuscript regarding the murders was obviously part of the general feeling of the day, such as Martha Tabram's inclusion as a genuine Ripper victim, and some elements seemed to have been lifted from observations included in *The Mystery of Jack the Ripper*. Arguably, the writing of the Carnac autobiography may well have been influenced by the release of Matters's ground-breaking book, but what set this manuscript apart was the author's lack of real motive for committing the crimes; the killer was obviously of unsound mind, but there was no sense of revenge, or hatred of women, religious mania or otherwise. It was original because the killer committed his deeds because he felt compelled to do so, and coldly explained it all to the reader. Debate about the true authorship of the manuscript would begin when it came into the public domain eighty years after it was written, but as a work of Ripper *fiction*, at least, it was significant.[6]

Before the outbreak of the Second World War, two studies published within two years of each other attempted to change thinking regarding the identity of the Ripper by claiming that the murderer was female. This was not an entirely unique proposition as the suggestion that 'Jack' could have been 'Jill' had already been put forward by Sidney Godolphin Osbourne in 1888 and was also proposed by Surgeon Lawson Tait, who suggested that the killer might be a strong woman who worked as a slaughterhouse cleaner. She could, he suggested, have concealed her bloodstains by rolling up her skirt and walking through the streets covered by a heavy petticoat.[7]

The idea of the Whitechapel murderer as slaughterhouse worker was not picked up by Edwin T. Woodhall when he published *Jack the Ripper: Or When London Walked in Terror* in 1937.[8] As a former police officer, Woodhall felt he was well placed to give his sage views and unique insight into the murders, stating that he was not an 'author turned detective' like his contemporaries, but a 'detective turned author'.[9] Unfortunately, as an overview of the Ripper story, his effort had little merit.

Before the official files were accessible to researchers, no Ripper-based book was without significant errors. However, the severity of such errors varied. Woodhall's version claimed to be 'a true, honest, and as far as it is humanly possible – authentic account of the world-known "Jack the Ripper Mystery"?', before dating his introduction '1837'. Despite being an obvious mistake on the part of the typesetter, this did not bode well. Although Woodhall claimed to have referred to the memoirs of Anderson and Macnaghten, as well as Leonard Matters's book and numerous articles and newspaper accounts, one wonders whether he had actually read any of them. Non-existent witnesses were mentioned, Mary Kelly's name was initially given as 'Taylor', Martha Tabram's and Elizabeth Stride's injuries sounded like a compilation of those received by other victims, and Annie Chapman's head had been cut off and placed on her chest! It was no doubt written with a sensationalist market in mind.

Woodhall's own suspect for the Ripper crimes was Olga Tchkersoff, believed to be an immigrant from Russia whose sister, Vera, was lured by Mary Jane Kelly into a life of prostitution, later dying from the effects of an illegal abortion. Predictably, Tchkersoff avenges herself of her sister's death and other supposedly resulting misfortunes by murdering prostitutes, culminating in her ultimate quarry, Kelly. Whether Olga Tchkersoff actually existed is open to question and, as Woodhall claimed that his information came from a number of sources, the answer is probably that she did not, considering the author's alarming inability to get even well-reported contemporary facts correct. In fact, Woodhall seemed to have a thing about foreigners in general, but perhaps this was a sign of the times. It can be argued that perceptions of Jack the Ripper reflect the time periods from which they were generated, and in this instance Woodhall made a number of damning references to the immigrants of the time, describing them as 'the foreign scum of the earth' who were being 'dumped into the great cities of this country', conjuring up images of the neo-fascist sensibilities of Oswald Mosley, who was particularly active in the East End during the pre-war 1930s.[10] Woodhall would become virtually ignored by future researchers; in the forthright opinion of Richard Whittington-Egan, writing in 1975, Woodhall's book was 'badly written, shoddily researched, grossly inaccurate, it contributes nothing of importance'.[11]

Another attempt at pinning the identity of the Ripper upon a female suspect came with William Stewart's *Jack the Ripper: A New Theory*,[12] published in 1939. Stewart suggested that a woman trained as a midwife could have committed the murders. The argument was that a woman could go about the streets of the East End without arousing suspicion (after all, Jack the Ripper had universally been considered as male). A midwife could do so even if her clothes showed traces of blood, something that would not be unusual for someone in such a profession. The nature of the job would also require the requisite familiarity with human anatomy, especially those parts which the Ripper was believed to have extracted on two occasions. Another piece of reasoning behind the theory was based on several contemporary newspaper reports that Mary Kelly was pregnant at the time of her death, giving the killer midwife every reason to be at Miller's Court to undertake an illegal abortion.

Stewart also noted similarities between the *modus operandi* of the Ripper and that of Mary Pearcey, who was hanged after stabbing her lover's wife and child to death and cutting their throats in October 1890. With Pearcey, the notion that a woman was incapable of the thought processes and physical strength to commit such atrocities was dashed; even Melville Macnaghten commented that he had 'never seen a woman of stronger physique . . . her nerves were as ironcast as her body'.[13]

Like Woodhall, Stewart would go on to be maligned, this time as an 'uncaring fictioneer', and his book dismissed as 'one of the worst ever written on the subject'.[14] This is an unduly harsh condemnation. What Stewart did was to ask certain questions of the case; what sort of person could have roamed the East End at night without attracting suspicion, could wear bloodstained clothing without attracting suspicion, could have sufficient medical knowledge to carry out the murders and could have risked being found near the victim and yet have an alibi? In answer to these questions, Stewart went where this line of thought took him: the midwife. He was not necessarily looking for a name, as was becoming common in Ripper studies at that time, but a profession or occupation that could tie in with the execution of the crimes. The theory, however, fails because it hooks on to the notion that Mary Kelly was three months pregnant, a claim that was disproved many years later following the rediscovery of Dr Thomas Bond's post-mortem report.[15]

It could be argued that theorizing about the identity of Jack the Ripper has spawned three, perhaps four subsequent eras, each bringing with it differing perceptions and approaches from both the wider public and those who would study the crimes and times specifically. The first era produced the crimes them-selves, with the accompanying scramble for a motive. The second saw a move away from there to named individuals, pri-marily anecdotal by source, then anecdotal with supporting 'evidence' of an esoteric and often dubious nature. In 1959, Don-ald McCormick produced the next significant full-length study of the Ripper case, *The Identity of Jack the Ripper*,[16] a peculiar book for several reasons and one which could be seen as the final outing of the theorist scrabbling around with hitherto untraceable (or false) sources and strange foreign suspects who may or may not have actually existed.

McCormick reintroduced Dr Alexander Pedachenko as a sus-pect, and the motive behind the killings was a Tsarist plot to discredit the Metropolitan Police, a wholly successful conspir-acy which resulted in the resignation of Sir Charles Warren. The story was obviously a throwback to the one proposed by William Le Queux in 1923, but this time it was riddled with secret dossiers, obfuscating aliases and claims of counter-espionage. The sources for this theory were numerous and included the notes supposedly written in French by Rasputin. McCormick also claimed to have seen and taken notes from the three-volume 'Chronicle of Crime', handwritten by Dr Thomas Dutton. Briefly suspected of the Whitechapel murders in 1888, Dutton claimed that Jack the Ripper was 'a middle-aged doctor, a man whose mind had been embittered by the death of his son. The latter had suffered cruelly at the hands of a woman of the streets, and the father believed this to be the cause of his brilliant son's death,' which sounded very much like Leonard Matters's 'Dr Stanley'. McCormick said that Dr Dutton had made micro-photographs of the handwriting of Ripper correspondence and the writing on the wall in Goulston Street, but that Sir Charles Warren ordered the destruction of the prints of the latter. He also claimed that Dutton was a friend and adviser of Inspector Abberline. With no trace of Dr Dutton's writings to be found, it appeared that McCormick's book was wandering into the realms of pure invention, even in his examination of the events surrounding the murders themselves. Imagined conversations between witnesses or police officers littered the book, often lending an unintentionally comic air to the proceedings.

McCormick has also been accused of instigating several Ripper myths which would dog subsequent serious studies of the case. One of the most notable was perhaps his references to the 'Old Nichol Gang'. The 'Nichol', a notorious slum in Bethnal Green, no doubt had its criminal element, but evidence of a gang of that name has never been ascertained, and their presence in the East End in the 1880s has continued to surface in Ripper literature to the present day, all thanks to McCormick's fanciful writing. What is apparent is that McCormick's ideas stemmed from sources that probably didn't exist. His mysterious Russian doctor theory signalled the end of what was essentially a period of sporadic solutions fuelled by hearsay and the dubious recollections of sundry individuals, both in Britain and abroad. Like Edwin Woodhall's brush with quasi-racist rhetoric in the era of rising fascism in Europe, McCormick's theory reflected the developing 'Cold War' between East and West, brewing up a story that would put the most convoluted plot of any spy thriller to shame. Espionage was very much the rage in the late 1950s and early 1960s as a result of the changing political climate; the classy James Bond novels of Ian Fleming were well established and were soon to be joined by works by other popular writers of the genre such as John le Carré and Len Deighton. The Ripper crimes were now steadily becoming an international phenomenon, and it seemed that there was now a rapidly growing band of enthusiasts willing to lend their special knowledge and opinion to the fascination with solving what was by now considered to be the world's greatest crime mystery.

Ironically, as McCormick twisted and turned with his elaborate tale, the photographer, journalist and broadcaster Daniel Farson made an important discovery. While researching a series of television programmes for ATV in the UK entitled *Farson's Guide to the British*,[17] Farson had decided to devote some of his air-time to the mystery of Jack the Ripper. Often well connected, he had, purely by luck it seems, been introduced to Christobel McLaren, 2nd Baroness Aberconway, the daughter of Sir Melville Macnaghten, and she showed him the typed and handwritten transcriptions she had made of her late father's 1894 memoranda, which named the suspects Druitt, Kosminski and Ostrog. This artefact – now known as the 'Aberconway version' – was an important find to say the least and has since been considered as the initiation of serious post-war studies on the Ripper case. It must be remembered that for all the hint-dropping of Macnaghten, Anderson and Swanson *et al.*, the actual names of suspects were not included in anything that was to be published. Macnaghten's memoranda were for private and official use, and Swanson's marginalia were the private notation of a dear friend's autobiography. Now, by seeing the names Druitt, Ostrog and Kosminski for the first time, Farson was well placed to make these findings public on television.

Farson set his store by Macnaghten's first suspect, Druitt. It is no doubt likely that this information was familiar to other police officials of Macnaghten's day, for several hints had previously been made by various individuals that the Ripper had drowned in the Thames after the Mary Kelly murder. One of these claims was alleged to have been made as early as 1889 to Albert Bachert, the Mile End Vigilance Committee leader who had taken over from the eminent George Lusk that year. Bachert's story was that he had been advised to disband the Vigilance Committee owing to the fact that the Ripper's body had been found floating in the Thames at the end of 1888. It was quite possible that he was encouraged to do this merely to stop Bachert being a nuisance. However the story itself emanated once again from Donald McCormick and Dr Thomas Dutton's elusive 'Chronicle of Crime'.

When Farson's programme was broadcast, the name of the main suspect was given as 'M.J.D.' – this was in accordance with Baroness Aberconway's request not to make the full name public. As previously observed, it appeared that Macnaghten's notes had got a few biographical details wrong, for Druitt was thirty-one when he died, not forty-one as was stated. Nor was he a doctor, but a barrister. Whatever the plausibility of Druitt's candidacy for the Whitechapel murderer, he was certainly in keeping with a continuing trend of seeing Jack the Ripper as having emerged from the upper middle classes (such as the medical professions, for example), rather than from the poor underbelly of the East End slums or the rank environment of the lunatic asylum. It seems that Jack the Ripper was slowly going up in the world.

In literary terms, a new, improved era of 'Ripperology' began with two books issued within weeks of each other in 1965, Tom Cullen's *Autumn of Terror*[18] and Robin Odell's *Jack the Ripper in Fact and Fiction*.[19] With all respect to Odell, Cullen's book became the more significant and high-profile of the two, for here the theory of Montague John Druitt was expounded fully, and, more importantly, he was publicly named for the first time.

Although Daniel Farson was responsible for rediscovering Druitt, his own attempts to set his discoveries in print were significantly delayed, as he was by now busy running a popular pub on the Isle of Dogs as well as becoming quite a media personality in his own right. He was also hampered when a file of notes went missing, and his proclivity for the high life did not help matters either. So despite Farson's discovery and championing of Druitt as the Ripper, it was Cullen's now highly regarded book which placed Druitt well and truly in the public domain. And a popular suspect he turned out to be, not just with true crime aficionados, but also the public at large, no doubt helped by Farson's own public profile and his numerous subsequent newspaper articles on the subject. Tom Cullen changed Montague John Druitt from a tantalizing hint into the first important twentieth-century Ripper suspect who could be proved to have existed. In the 1960s he was considered by many to be the most convincing candidate so far, a status that was maintained for a good two decades.

Robin Odell's treatment of the Ripper case would have less far-reaching effects. Again, it was widely respected as giving an unsensational overview of the events of 1888 and even presented a survey of the fictional work inspired by the Whitechapel murders. Not to be outdone, Odell also put forward his own candidate for the crimes, this time a Jewish slaughterman or *shochet*. Without needing to name an individual, Odell believed the occupation was evidence enough, ticking the boxes of somebody local who could walk about in blood-soaked work clothes (thus avoiding suspicion) and who would also have a rudimentary, but sufficient, knowledge of anatomy to accomplish such visceral injuries. This rather rational and perhaps cautious theory won little support, even among experts on the Ripper case, but Odell's method was a sensible one. Like William Stewart, he looked at the case and went where the evidence took him and, as such, should be recognized as pursuing a logical solution at a time when naming a name would appear to be the minimum requirement.

In 1960 Colin Wilson, the best-selling author of the existentialist non-fiction book *The Outsider*, wrote a series of articles in the London *Evening Standard* entitled 'My Search for Jack the Ripper',[20] which kick-started his long-standing association with the field of 'Ripperology'. This term, coined several years later by Wilson himself, gave the study of Jack the Ripper a (not always favoured) definition.[21] The *Evening Standard* articles, which in spite of their brevity were at that time a pretty good résumé of the crimes, came to the attention of Dr Thomas Stowell, who, meeting Wilson over lunch, expounded his rather unique hypothesis that the Ripper was none other than Prince Albert Victor (Prince 'Eddy'), grandson of Queen Victoria, later Duke of Clarence and Avondale and heir presumptive to the throne. The theory was later mentioned in Wilson's *Encyclopaedia of Murder*, where the story of clairvoyant Robert Lees's 'eminent physician' was given consideration, as Stowell had presumably done in private:

> The weakness of the story lies in the certainty that the police would have taken pleasure in giving the widest publicity to the capture of Jack the Ripper. Perhaps it is to account for this discrepancy in the theory that the name of Queen Victoria is frequently brought into it. It is claimed that Mr Lees was twice

interviewed by the queen, who was greatly concerned about the Whitechapel murders. The story connected with Lees usually goes on to add either (a) that the doctor was the queen's physician, or (b) that Jack the Ripper was some relative of the Royal Family. [22]

Though not named in print on this occasion, the 'queen's physician' in 1888 was Sir William Gull.

Apparently, on the evening of the day he lunched with Stowell Wilson met diplomat and politician Sir Harold Nicolson and told him about the theory. The following year (1962), Philippe Jullian published his book *Edouard VII*, in which he thanked Nicolson 'for allowing me to delve into his works and for telling me a number of hitherto unpublished anecdotes'. What is interesting in this case is that Jullian's book said that

> Before he died, poor Clarence was a great anxiety to his family. He was quite characterless and would soon have fallen a prey to some intriguer or group of roues, of which his regiment was full. They indulged in every form of debauchery, and on one occasion the police discovered the Duke in a maison de rencontre of a particularly equivocal nature during a raid. Fifty years before, the same thing had happened to Lord Castlereagh, and he had committed suicide. The young man's evil reputation soon spread. The rumour gained ground that he was Jack the Ripper (others attributed the crimes committed in Whitechapel to the Duke of Bedford).[23]

According to Wilson, 'at least a dozen people had known about his theory since 1960',[24] showing that once again anecdotal passing of rumour and information was still going on at even this late juncture, harking back to the stories shared by old police colleagues and the well-connected members of smoky gentlemen's clubs. Then, after sitting on the story for a decade, Dr Stowell finally went public with an article published in the *Criminologist* in 1970 entitled 'Jack the Ripper – A Solution?'[25] Stowell set out his reasoning behind the notion that Prince Albert Victor was the Ripper without actually naming him. Originally calling his suspect 'X', he was apparently advised that such an alias was somewhat clichéd and reverted to 'S' instead.

In this version of the story, 'S' was suffering from syphilis, which had affected his brain to the point where he had completely lost his mind. He then embarked on a killing spree, but after the death of Catherine Eddowes he was detained, only to escape and commit the final murder of Mary Kelly. Stowell also hinted at confidential papers owned by Caroline Acland, daughter of Sir William Gull, which claimed that Prince Albert Victor died not from influenza in 1892 as was publicly stated, but from a 'softening of the brain' caused by syphilis. The fact that 'S' had knowledge of dressing deer not only explained the Ripper's alleged anatomical knowledge, but also pointed to the prince as being the suspect in question as he most certainly would have possessed such experience through his forays into game hunting.

Stowell's theory suggested that Sir William Gull was given the duty of following the prince on his sojourns in London and was therefore in a position to expose and then incarcerate him. This was the first time that Gull's name had been linked to the Whitechapel murders, echoing not just Colin Wilson's published comments about the killer possibly being the queen's physician, but also the Robert Lees story of the eminent London doctor. One has to weigh up whether Lees's story was actually true, but for argument's sake, if it was, then had that London doctor now been identified?

It was obvious that a public figure such as Prince Albert Victor would have had his movements carefully recorded by the Royal Court; anyone willing to destroy this new theory would not have had a difficult task in giving him an alibi. The matter was quickly attended to:

> Buckingham Palace is not officially reacting to the mischievous calumny that Albert Victor, the Duke of Clarence and Avondale and Earl of Athlone, was also Jack the Ripper. The idea that Edward VII's eldest son and, but for his early death of pneumonia aged 28, heir to the throne, should have bestially murdered five or six women of 'unfortunate' class in the East End is regarded as too ridiculous for comment.
>
> Nevertheless a loyalist on the staff at Buckingham Palace had engaged in some amateur detective work and come up with evidence on the Duke's behalf. Two women were murdered on September 30, 1888, in Berners Street [*sic*] and Mitre Square, and their murders were fully reported in *The Times* the following day.
>
> *The Times* of October 1 also carried a court circular from Balmoral, stating: 'Prince Henry of Battenberg, attended by a colonel clerk, joined Prince Albert Victor of Wales (the Duke of Clarence as he was to be) at Glen Muick in a drive which Mr Mckenzie had for black game.'
>
> Further, but less surely, he believes that the Duke was at Sandringham, celebrating his father's 47th birthday, on the occasion of the last murder of Marie Jeanette Kelly, in Miller's Court, on November 9, 1888. The court circular simply says that the then Prince of Wales celebrated his birthday with his family; but diary entries and other notes in the archives at Buckingham

Palace suggest that the Duke was in fact at Sandringham during the early days of November until November 11.[26]

Dr Stowell was interviewed for BBC Television's *24 Hours* current affairs programme,[27] where again he gave enough hints for people to assume that he spoke of Prince Albert Victor, again without naming him. Apart from Colin Wilson, others had to 'join the dots' to give 'S' his identity. In fact, Stowell went on record as denying that he had ever suggested that the prince was the Ripper when he wrote to *The Times* to make his feelings succinctly clear:

> I have at no time associated His Royal Highness the late Duke of Clarence, with the Whitechapel murderer or suggested that the murderer was of royal blood.
>
> It remains my opinion that he was a scion of a noble family.
>
> The particulars given in *The Times* of November 4 of the activities of His Highness in no way conflict with my views as to the identity of Jack the Ripper.[28]

But in the short time between the writing of this letter and its publication, Dr Stowell died. His son then read his collection of notes and, considering them to contain nothing of importance, burned them. He claimed that 'the case doesn't interest me particularly. It was before my time'.[29]

13.

Conspiracy

It was clear that the events of 1970 would herald a new approach to the riddle of Jack the Ripper. Mysteries have always been compelling and attractive to mankind, and, as nature abhors a vacuum, the empty space that was the Ripper's true identity must therefore be filled. From the first unsolved crimes, it was always necessary to create attributes for him, and invariably they would reflect the era in which they were made. During 1888, London appeared to be in fear of the new socialist and anarchist thinking that was being brought from overseas by the Eastern European immigrants, and thus initial suspicion would be placed upon foreigners, with the Jewish settlers of Whitechapel becoming early scapegoats. Perhaps a mistrust of Tsarist and subsequently post-revolutionary Russia helped furnish the mystery with a range of shadowy Russian suspects in the early to mid-twentieth century. By the onset of the 1970s, the upper classes were well in the frame, and there appeared to be a growing fascination with the perceived dubious proclivities of the privileged. Much of this could be seen as the start of a 'conspiracy culture'. It was during that decade that suspicions over the true events surrounding the death of President Kennedy would begin to take hold, stories about US government cover-ups of UFO incidents would gain ground, and even NASA's Apollo moon-landing programme would not escape the scrutiny of those who thought that everything was not as it seemed. The so-called 'peace and love' era of the late 1960s was quickly giving way to a more aggressive and questioning society.

In 1972, Michael Harrison's study of Prince Albert Victor, *Clarence: The Life of HRH the Duke of Clarence and Avondale (1864–1892)*,[1] attempted to exonerate the prince of the Ripper murders by re-emphasizing his whereabouts at the time. Appearing on BBC Television, Harrison explained that he could not accept that the Ripper was Prince Albert Victor, 'but I couldn't leave the reader high and dry, so what I did was find somebody who I thought was a likely candidate'.[2] Harrison's Ripper was James Kenneth Stephen, the prince's tutor, whose surname fitted more comfortably with Dr Stowell's suspect 'S'. He based his argument on the speculation that Prince Eddy and Stephen had become homosexual lovers during, or after, Eddy's time in Cambridge. He felt that some of Stephen's poetry suggested a hatred of women, with some even showing sadistic tendencies. According to Harrison, the relationship was broken off, and Stephen then killed prostitutes on dates which would appear significant to Eddy, such as birthdays of members of the Royal Family. In the same television interview in which Harrison appeared, Daniel Farson made a mockery of the theory, stating that 'you can make out a better case for Queen Victoria'. But an interesting letter to the *Sunday Times* in 1975 appeared to support the theory: Mary Hallam of Newbury wrote stating that her great-grandfather, a barrister, had long ago declared that the authorities knew that Stephen was the Ripper.[3]

Daniel Farson had now got round to publishing his own study of the case – simply titled *Jack the Ripper* – and predictably put forward his suspect, Montague Druitt.[4] Despite 'discovering' him, Farson had lagged behind, allowing Tom

Cullen to steal some of his thunder. Farson, however, was a media personality of some repute, and so Druitt began to gain the attention he probably deserved back in the 1960s, helped no doubt by Farson's frequent writings and interviews in national newspapers.

But it was BBC TV's 1973 series *Jack the Ripper*, a six-part documentary-drama which put fictional detectives Charlie Barlow and John Watt[5] into a modern-day investigation of the Ripper crimes,[6] which really began to hammer home the theory surrounding the royal household.

The 'investigation', in laying out the events of 1888, was remarkable in that the researchers were granted access to the official files and used the actual witness testimonies contained therein for the scripts when reconstructing scenes of the inquests. Much of this material was heard by the public for the first time, as most information before then had to be gleaned from contemporary press reports, which were not always accurate. These reports, with misheard or dubious information often being set down by otherwise dedicated journalists, produced errors that were invariably repeated for decades to come. Barlow and Watt's findings were channelled via the claims of Joseph Gorman Sickert, who, in the final episode,[7] sat in front of the camera smoking as he relayed a story apparently told to him by his father, the artist Walter Sickert. Prince Albert Victor was certainly part of it, but now the culpability for the murders was shifted elsewhere. Joseph's version of the story goes thus:

> When Eddy, the Duke of Clarence, was twenty his mother thought it would be a good idea if he met an artist and writers as well as just usual people who made up court circles at the time. She arranged for him to meet the painter Walter Sickert,

whose family had been painters to her own Royal Court in
Denmark – at the time, Walter Sickert lived in the Cleveland
Street area, and when Prince Eddy went there during his vac-
ations at Cambridge he was passed off as Sickert's younger
brother and was known as 'Mr S'. He also met a close friend of
Sickert's, a girl called Anne Crook, who worked in a tobacco shop
at no. 20. She actually lived at no. 6 Cleveland Street. She was very
beautiful and in fact she looked very much like Eddy's mother.

Eddy fell in love with her, and she became pregnant, and
there was also some sort of a wedding ceremony at St Saviour's
private chapel in 1888. The two lovers, Clarence and Anne Elizabeth, were parted after a police raid on a party in Cleveland
Street, and Anne Elizabeth was in Guy's Hospital for 156 days
before she had been put into a smaller hospital at 367 Fulham
Road. She was supposed to be mentally ill. She was kept in the
Fulham Road hospital until her death in 1921. The servant girl
also disappeared at the same time. Her name was Mary Kelly.
The little girl Alice Margaret was then looked after by old Walter Sickert with the help of various local friends.

Now one day, when she was about seven years old, in 1892, a
woman friend was taking her for a walk along Drury Lane
when a carriage ran the girl down. The driver of the carriage
was recognized as John Netley, a man who had been used as an
outside coachman by Clarence on his visits to Sickert, a man
who knew the story of the lovers and the child and their Irish
servant girl, Mary Kelly.

The girl, Alice Margaret, was fortunate; after a spell in
Charing Cross hospital she recovered from her injuries. Mary
Kelly was not so lucky. She was of course a Catholic girl. She
was known by the nuns of the convent in nearby [?] Place. She
went first of all to an assistant convent which was in the
East End.

What happened then was that various people behind the government and the royal household were very worried indeed about the possibility of the news getting out, that the heir presumptive to the throne of England was married and had a child and that the child had been born of a Catholic mother. You have to remember that it was a time when the possibility of revolution was thought to be a very real one and that the problems and violence surrounding Ireland – it was decided that Mary Kelly would have to be silenced.

The operation was undertaken by the driver, John Netley, and the royal physician, Sir William Gull. To conceal the dangerous motive behind Mary Kelly's death and the enquiries they were making for her, she was killed as the last of five women in a way that made it look like the random work of a madman. The child, however, survived – she was protected by Walter Sickert and had two sons by him. The first one was Charles, who disappeared at the age of two, and I am the other son.

The prince appeared to be vindicated, no doubt because his alibi for the murders had been firmly established. However, the 'scion of a noble family' was still the source of so much trouble. Now Sir William Gull was firmly in the frame, not merely as the guardian and protector of a homicidal prince, but now fulfilling Robert Lees's story of the 'eminent London doctor' by actually being Jack the Ripper himself. But even before this episode could be broadcast, the first glimmers of doubt were beginning to show. One newspaper columnist, having done his homework, mentioned the inconvenient matter of Sir William Gull's health, namely the strokes he suffered in 1887, which caused partial paralysis and prompted his early retirement from general practice. In fact, by 1888 Gull's health was so poor that 'this would surely not have allowed him to launch into a series of grisly murders, with or without help'.[8]

With interest in a 'royal conspiracy' in the ascendant, City of London Police officer Donald Rumbelow put his considerable knowledge of the Ripper mystery into print with *The Complete Jack the Ripper*.[9] Rumbelow, as a serving police officer, had used his professional acumen to further knowledge of the Ripper case by rescuing material from the City Police's rather ad hoc archives – rescuing being the operative word, as the archives were not necessarily organized, and often material would be lying around ready for the refuse collectors. In this way, Rumbelow discovered a large cache of letters to the City Police and, perhaps more significantly, mortuary photographs of Catherine Eddowes and the police photograph of Mary Kelly in Miller's Court. Through his interest in the subject, he had met many of the movers and shakers in the field and was well placed to commit himself to a factual and unsensational overview of the subject. *The Complete Jack the Ripper*, in an age where theories were becoming more convoluted and outlandish, was a breath of fresh air, a factual account of the Ripper crimes, placed within their historical context, with an overview of the suspects without moulding the narrative to put forward any one theory in particular.

Similarly, Richard Whittington-Egan produced *A Casebook on Jack the Ripper*,[10] which, as well as attempting to redress the balance of fact over fiction, looked at the theories up to 1975 with a critical mind and made several important assertions in an attempt to dispel some of the more enduring errors. He also introduced rarely discussed ideas, such as the occult theories pertaining to Roslyn D'Onston Stephenson, whose prominence as a suspect would later find new supporters. However, Whittington-Egan was circumspect on the subject of suspects and, unable to draw any solid conclusions after some considerable analysis, said, 'I find no case to answer against any of the accused. They are dismissed. The verdict must remain undisturbed. Some person or persons unknown.'

But naming Jack the Ripper was still the order of the day. By 1975, *East London Advertiser* journalist Stephen Knight was busy finalizing his own contribution to the steadily growing canon of Ripper literature. Knight was sent by the newspaper to interview Joseph Gorman Sickert about his royal cover-up story and found his subject so persuasive that he decided to undertake further research of his own. The results were published the following year in *Jack the Ripper: The Final Solution*,[11] a book that would see phenomenal worldwide success and truly nail the 'royal conspiracy theory' into popular culture.

The Final Solution invariably took Sickert's story as its central foundation. However, Knight had been busy examining other elements of the case that he believed dovetailed with the basic premise. He was able to consult the official files at the Public Record Office before they were legitimately accessible to the public and made several valuable discoveries, including naming Israel Schwartz as the man who saw the alleged attack on Elizabeth Stride in Berner Street a mere fifteen minutes before her body was discovered. But what Knight also brought to the story was a new level of intrigue and conspiracy, alleging the involvement of the Freemasons and that the clues to that complicity were plainly evident in the events of 1888.

According to this amended version of Sickert's tale, the murders were committed by Sir William Gull, a Freemason, in compliance with ancient Masonic execution rituals, specifically in the cutting of the throat and the throwing of the 'heart and vitals' over the shoulder of the corpse. This latter detail resembled mutilations in the murders of Chapman and

Eddowes. The victims were killed in a coach (driven by John Netley) after being rendered incapable by being fed grapes laced with laudanum; Knight was obviously keen to emphasize the detail of the grapes, therefore adding to their mystery and undoubtedly giving this confusing and controversial element of the Elizabeth Stride murder a relevance and even importance that was perhaps unwarranted. The bodies were then deposited where they were eventually found, which Knight claims explained the lack of blood present at the murder sites, notably in the case of Mary Ann Nichols in Buck's Row. The erroneous reporting of carefully arranged coins and other objects at the site of Annie Chapman's murder also prompted Knight to suggest that they were placed there as part of Masonic ritual.

Other members of the Freemasons were also involved with organizing the operation – Sir Charles Warren, Lord Salisbury, Robert Anderson – and in fact Warren's involvement was particularly important in light of the events surrounding the discovery of the writing on the wall in Goulston Street. Knight directed the reader's attention to the spelling of the word 'Juwes' and made the assertion that the 'Juwes' were Jubelo, Jubela and Jubelum, the three assassins of Hiram Abiff, chief architect of King Solomon's temple in Masonic lore. The graffiti was a hidden clue, and Warren, upon his arrival at the scene, realized this immediately.[12] Not wanting any suspicion to rest upon his esoteric society, he had it removed forthwith.

The involvement of Mary Kelly was expanded to make her a key player in the whole story, suggesting a blackmail attempt on the government, with three friends complicit in the plot and conversant with the Annie Crook/Prince Eddy affair: Mary Ann Nichols, Annie Chapman and Elizabeth Stride. Kelly had sent the blackmail threat via Walter Sickert, who was compelled to send it on to the relevant authorities. Knight also suggested that Catherine Eddowes, not part of the plot, was murdered by mistake, for when she was released from Bishopsgate police station on the morning of her murder, she had given a false name, 'Mary Ann Kelly'. With Mary *Jane* Kelly as the ultimate quarry, this was supposed to explain the brutality of Eddowes's injuries, as she was erroneously believed to be the woman most deserving of the Masonic slaughter.

The theory took a major knock in 1978 when Joseph Gorman Sickert claimed in the press that the whole story was 'a hoax . . . I made it all up'. He would later retract this denial, saying that he had only cried 'hoax' because of his resentment of Knight's assertions that his father, Walter Sickert, was being implicated in the murders themselves:

> I want to clear the name of my father. I didn't think that much harm would come from it at the time because I thought the story was just going to appear in a local paper. As far as I am concerned Jack can go back to the Ripperologists.[13]

However, it did not need Sickert's fluctuating opinions to prove this particular story as false, and over the years numerous pieces of information surfaced that essentially proved the theory to be untenable. Apart from Sir William Gull's poor health, it was also observed that no documentary evidence existed to prove that he was ever a Freemason, and the same went for Robert Anderson and Lord Salisbury, who, it was said, had apparently masterminded the entire Masonic clean-up operation. Further doubt on the Masonic links to the murders surfaced when it was noted that 'Juwes' had not been a term used in Freemasonry and that Jubelo, Jubela and Jubelum were known as 'the ruffians', and even that term had fallen out of use in English Freemasonry seventy years before the Whitechapel murders. Where Knight got these notions of Masonic lore is anybody's guess. Researcher Simon Wood also worked hard to find out the truth regarding this story, unearthing records which would have undoubtedly been known of by Knight and perhaps passed on as they interfered with the integrity of the theory. Wood raised doubts about the existence of the Cleveland Street addresses at the time of the events which sparked the cover-up in the first place, as well as the truth about Annie Crook's religion; according to infirmary records, she was Protestant, not Catholic.[14]

But this drama had staying power, no doubt assisted by the burgeoning interest in conspiracy theories. The high-profile Watergate scandal had shown the world a disastrously deceitful side to government, and in Britain the mysterious disappearance of Lord Lucan in 1974 (following the murder of his children's nanny) suggested that the upper classes were, in theory at least, capable of shocking acts of violence. The popularity of such ideas has been given many origins, from the 'search for meaning' to the projection of the unacceptable side of human behaviour upon the conspirators. It also suggests a belief that events which have far-reaching effects are invariably the result of man-made decisions, rather than a chance series of incidents. With the Ripper being such an unknown quantity, the 'search for meaning' and the desire to allocate identity and blame to some person or persons no doubt contributed to the popularity of Sickert's story and Knight's theories.

In 1991, Melvyn Fairclough's *The Ripper and the Royals*[15] gave the conspiracy theorists another bite of the cherry, drawing upon further evidence supplied by Sickert. This evidence came in the form of three diaries allegedly written between

1896 and 1915 by Inspector Frederick Abberline. Abberline had long been considered as an important linchpin in the Ripper case, and new revelations by this most esteemed police officer would no doubt be worth their weight in gold. The diaries, however, were in the possession of Sickert and were not mentioned in Stephen Knight's book, although whether Knight was unaware of their existence or just passed on the opportunity of consulting them was not clear. Sickert contributed a brief foreword to Fairclough's book, in which he stated that he wanted to set the record straight about his father's involvement, commenting that this element had not been fairly portrayed by Stephen Knight. The diaries implicated Lord Randolph Churchill (father of Winston), coachman John Netley and Frederico Albericci as the main conspirators, with Sir William Gull carrying out the murders.

Drawing on such 'evidence', the story had grown into one of utter corruption in high places, going so far as to suggest that Prince Eddy did not die of influenza in 1892, but was taken out of circulation, specifically that he was incarcerated in Glamis Castle, where he died in 1933.[16] The scandal had even wider implications with the claim that Eddy's brother, as George V, had been deliberately and surreptitiously put to death by his physician with the consent of Queen Mary to stop him making a confession as he lay dying. Daniel Farson, in review, was moved to write: 'Phew! This is fun if taken as a send-up of Ripperology but I have the awful suspicion that Fairclough believes every word that Sickert told him.'[17]

Alas, the 'Abberline diaries' were no doubt forgeries, putting Joseph Gorman Sickert's reputation even further into disrepute. There were several glaring errors in them, notably on one page where the author had put Abberline's initials the wrong way round. Also, details regarding the victims appeared to have been lifted from articles which had appeared in *True Detective* magazine two years previously[18] and carried mistakes. The handwriting wasn't even Abberline's. Fairclough's book also published an alleged letter from actor and artist Harry Jonas confirming that Sickert had met with Peter Sutcliffe – the infamous 'Yorkshire Ripper'[19] – in the mid-1970s and discussed the events of 1888 with him. The handwriting was distinctive and appeared practically identical to that on the diaries, suggesting very strongly that Sickert had written both.

Sickert maintained his belief in his story until his death in 2003. Despite the fact that much of the tale has been negated by careful research, one must weigh up the possibility that there might have been no smoke without fire. This does not mean to say that there was any involvement in the Whitechapel murders by the government or royalty whatsoever, but all the individuals named in it did exist. Some of Sickert's less sensational claims might have been true, but embellished by his father in the telling. It is regrettable that this most colourful of characters got swept away with it all and wilfully helped perpetuate the developing saga until, just like Lyttleton Forbes Winslow many years before, he somehow felt compelled to doctor and fabricate evidence to justify himself.

On a final note, one of the present authors, while conducting a Jack the Ripper walking tour in 2010, was approached by one of the attendees who rather apologetically imparted a most curious tale. The woman claimed that her great-grandmother, who died in 1969 aged almost 100, had been a resident of Buck's Row at the time of the murders. Following the death of Mary Ann Nichols, residents spoke of a horse and carriage that had been seen in the neighbourhood on the night of the murder. Significantly, the coach bore a coat of arms. What is interesting about this story is that the source was somebody who was a young woman at the time of the murders and who died before the royal theories were made public, and one must make the following conclusions. If the story is true, it is noteworthy; it reflects variously held beliefs that Jack the Ripper was not from the East End slums, but from the upper classes, or it supports the idea that the victims were not murdered where they were found; in its extremest interpretation, it even gives credence to the Sickert/Knight theory of 'the highest in the land'. There is also the possibility (or indeed probability) that the tale is a 'Chinese whisper' passed on to future generations by a former resident of a Ripper murder site, which by osmosis has become infused with elements of the royal conspiracy theory. Alternatively, it may be a total fabrication. Nonetheless, it demonstrates how popular this form of the story has become and that, even in the twenty-first century, the Ripper story will never be free of anecdotal claims and gossip. It is almost a matter of 'ownership', where anybody can have their little piece of the Ripper legend or can claim to know about something that others do not. Each published theory would come to make the declaration that the mystery had been solved once and for all, effectively wiping out what had come before – until the next one.

14.

A Crisis of Identity

In April 1982, Bruce Paley published an article in *True Crime* magazine[1] which put forward Joseph Barnett, Mary Kelly's former lover, as Jack the Ripper. This was an interesting proposition, not just for the theory itself, but because responsibility for the murders had been laid at the feet of somebody who had been *directly* involved in the first place. Paley had been working on the idea of Barnett as the Ripper for some time, and a fiction novel[2] had also been published, putting Mary Kelly's former lover forward as the killer. Paley's premise, later expanded in a well-received book,[3] suggested that Barnett killed prostitutes to scare Mary Kelly from working the streets. When this failed, he killed her, making it look like a Ripper murder, and with the motive for his deeds now extinguished, he moved on to a quiet life in Shadwell. A significant development in theorizing was made apparent in the book, for Paley used recently developed criminal profiling methods to present Barnett as his suspect and was convinced that he fitted many of the criteria. Nevertheless, with his close association with Mary Kelly, Barnett had been questioned thoroughly following the murder and had been well and truly exonerated. Another writer, Paul Harrison, who was also convinced of Joseph Barnett's guilt, had previously produced his own theory in print,[4] but not only did Harrison publish his theory without any acknowledgement to Paley's ideas from the 1980s, but he extended his theory into a book-length treatment entirely using the *wrong* Joseph Barnett. In his search to find Joseph Barnett in the records, he settled on a different Barnett as Mary Kelly's lover. This one lived from 1860 to 1927, whereas later research found that the real Barnett lived from 1858 to 1926.

The early 1980s were a period of relative inactivity in a field that had attracted considerable recent interest, but it was merely the calm before the storm. After all, the centenary of the Whitechapel murders was fast approaching, and this would bring with it media coverage without precedent, producing some of the most valuable discoveries in the case.[5] By 1986 numerous authors had already begun to put together their individual contributions to the literary output of the period. In August of that year, John Morrison, a former lorry driver from Leytonstone, made a rather unique contribution to the Ripper theory bank. Morrison had his own ideas about the identity of Jack the Ripper and claimed to have been researching the case since he had lost his job in 1982. Apparently, like a modern-day Stuart Cumberland or Robert Lees, it all came to him in a dream:

> I dreamt I was in court. They were trying Jack the Ripper. Lord Hailsham was the judge. He called for the evidence – and they produced a *Guinness Book of Records*. Next morning I went along to the library and looked up the *Guinness Book*. And there it was! James Kelly was listed as the longest-ever escapee from Broadmoor. He had murdered his wife in Liverpool and been declared insane.[6]

He then went on to propose the theory that James Kelly had had an affair with Mary Jane Kelly (who took his surname) in Liverpool and was so infatuated with her that he killed his wife. Mary deserted him after carrying his child, which James considered 'vile treachery', and he made his way to the East End, where he murdered ten prostitutes in his hunt for Mary Kelly. Each time he asked them their names and then murdered them to silence them. But Morrison's story was riddled with dubious sources, including an alleged book written by the mistress of Inspector Joseph Chandler, which, although disguised as fiction, set out the story. Morrison's ideas received a considerable amount of media coverage, particularly in the local press, and he was in and out of the newspapers for a good two years after his original claims were published. James Kelly would be reconsidered as a suspect several years later, when James Tully, using considerably better sources, made him a more promising prospect.[7]

In early June 1883, James Kelly married Sarah Bridler, his landlady's daughter, but shortly after the marriage he became increasingly mentally unstable. Furious quarrels with his wife and mother-in-law ensued, climaxing in him fatally stabbing Sarah in the neck with a pocket knife. Kelly was convicted of murder and sentenced to death, but a new Criminal Lunacy Act led to his undergoing further mental examination by specialists, and they concluded he was mentally disturbed. His sentence was commuted to life imprisonment, and he was sent to Broadmoor. In January 1888 he escaped and was later seen in east London. At the end of the year, he went to France, returning to England at some point before going to New York in 1892. He continued to travel extensively in America, periodically returning to Britain and eventually, tired of running and in ill-health, he presented himself at Broadmoor, where he stayed until his death in 1927. The case against Kelly as the Ripper was that he did not appear to have been dangerous to any women other than his wife, and there was no evidence that he was actually in London at the time of the murders.[8]

The run-up to the 1988 centenary saw a quick surge of new works. Authors such as Martin Fido, Martin Howells, Keith Skinner, Terrence Sharkey and Melvin Harris made their Ripper debuts at this time and were joined by such members of the old guard as Colin Wilson, Robin Odell and paranormal researcher Peter Underwood. Donald Rumbelow's 1975 book was also given a timely reprint. Many of these efforts made a point of putting forward a suspect, introducing the wider public to as-yet ignored candidates like Aaron Kosminski and David Cohen (Fido) and Roslyn D'Onston Stephenson (Harris).[9]

Ironically, the centenary year saw only *one* new Ripper book published, Paul Begg's *The Uncensored Facts*,[10] an attempt to lay down the story of the Whitechapel murders in as factual a way as possible, taking advantage of the material from the Scotland Yard and Home Office files that had now been made available for general consultation at the Public Record Office. By this time, several important discoveries had been made which should have put the study of the Whitechapel murders on to a level historic footing. The first of these new revelations came in the form of the copy of Robert Anderson's 1910 memoirs *The Lighter Side of My Official Life*, which had once belonged to Chief Inspector Donald Swanson and contained the marginalia relating to Anderson's suspect, who Swanson said was 'Kosminski'. Swanson's copy of the memoirs had been passed on to his daughter and on her death (about 1980) the book came into the possession of Jim Swanson, her nephew.[11]

Kosminski, of course, was not a new name. He was included in Melville Macnaghten's memoranda of 1894, along with Druitt, although it was the latter who found favour with the theorists after the discovery of the document in 1959. But here was a previously named suspect who was now mentioned once again by one of the most senior officials in the case and consequently could not be ignored. Jim Swanson managed to get the notes published in the *Daily Telegraph*,[12] although the accompanying article hardly hit the heights of sensationalism. It referenced Martin Fido's research and included comment by Donald Rumbelow, but the whole tone appeared to be one of caution. In the UK, London Weekend Television's *Crime Monthly* series, featuring investigations into crimes past and present, took on the Ripper. With a distinct sense of 'owner-ship', *Crime Monthly*, and in particular its presenter Paul Ross, claimed to have unmasked Jack the Ripper at last.[13] Right up to the eleventh hour, Ross was tight-lipped: 'All I can say is that the man we think was the killer was arrested as a suspect at the time, but he is not a famous suspect.'[14] Nor was he a new one. In a classic case of the media presenting previously known facts as if they were some form of esoteric investigative secret known only to them, *Crime Monthly* named its suspect – Kosminski.

The ever popular game of 'whodunnit?' was properly addressed in *The Secret Identity of Jack the Ripper*, another TV special, introduced by the actor Peter Ustinov and featuring a panel of experts from various relevant fields.[15] As well as appearances by authorities Colin Wilson, Daniel Farson, Don-ald Rumbelow and Martin Fido, the studio panel consisted of William Waddell, curator of Scotland Yard's Black Museum, forensic pathologist William Eckert, Anne Mallalieu QC and Roy Hazlewood and John Douglas of the FBI. The latter pair brought with them their 'state of the art' criminal profile of the Whitechapel murderer, something that had been created especially for the programme. This study, created using psy-chological profiling techniques developed over many years dealing with serial murderers, was seen as a ground-breaking tool in the attempt to identify Jack the Ripper.

In short, it stated that the Whitechapel murderer was a male. He was of white race in view of the fact that white was the predominant race at the crime scene locations, and that generally crimes such as these are intraracial. He would have been between twenty-eight and thirty-six years of age, did not look out of the ordinary and was probably unmarried. He came from a family where he was raised by a domineering mother and weak, passive or absent father. In all likelihood, his mother drank heavily and enjoyed the company of many men. As a result, he failed to receive consistent care and contact with stable adult role models. His anger would have become internalized, and in his younger years he would have expressed his pent-up destructive emotions by creating fires and torturing small animals, seeking an employment where he could work alone and experience his destructive fantasies such as butcher, mortician's helper, medical examiner's assistant or hospital attendant. He would have had some type of physical abnormality, although not severe, but he would have perceived this as being psychologically crippling. He would have been seen as being quiet, a loner, shy, slightly withdrawn, obedient and neat and orderly in appearance. He lived or worked in the Whitechapel area. The first homicide would have been in close proximity to either his home or workplace. Finally, prior to each homicide, the subject would be in a local pub, drinking spirits, which would lower his inhibitions, and would be observed walking all over the Whitechapel area during the early-evening hours. He did not specifically seek a certain look in a woman; however, it was by no accident that he killed prostitutes.

Altogether it was a rather austere presentation, serving the

Ripper with the gravitas a serious criminal case no doubt deserved, but the real thrust of the proceedings was to get these esteemed experts in crime history, law, forensics and murder investigation to pick a likely candidate to be the Ripper. They had five suspects to choose from: Roslyn D'Onston Stephenson, Montague Druitt, Prince Albert Victor, Sir William Gull and 'Kosminski', and each suspect was put forward with reasons for their candidacy. But the results of the investigation were rather interesting; each member of the panel independently chose 'Kosminski', albeit for differing reasons. A studio audience vote was, perhaps, less surprising, with the most votes going to Sir William Gull and Prince Albert Victor, proof that the royal conspiracy theory had bitten very deep into the public consciousness.

Another name that had been lingering on the outskirts of Ripper theories for many years was finally put in the frame as a *bona fide* suspect himself: Walter Sickert. Jean Overton Fuller's *Sickert and the Ripper Crimes*[16] took its central idea from claims made by Ms Fuller that Sickert's friend Florence Pash had told her that Sickert had seen all the victims, presumably at the murder sites. By this time, the story that Walter Sickert was somehow 'Ripper obsessed' had done the rounds many times. Stephen Knight's theory went as far as saying that there were many references to the murders in Sickert's paintings, despite there being scant evidence to support such claims, although Sickert subsequently did a painting of an interior called *Jack the Ripper's Bedroom*, the only example. Perhaps the genesis of this belief was that he had once told a story that a room in which he had lodged in Mornington Crescent, north-west London, could boast the Ripper as a former occupant (according to the landlady), but Jean Overton Fuller's theory, in keeping with earliest traditions of suspect-based

Ripperology, was derived from hearsay and inventive thinking, as well as further unsubstantiated material which nobody else ever saw. It could be fair to say that the notion of Walter Sickert as the Ripper was a hangover from the 'royal conspiracy' theory. Most of the major players in the story had been exonerated of any involvement by careful research since the publication of Stephen Knight's book, perhaps leaving Sickert as a last-gasp attempt at implicating somebody with friends in high places.

With that concept worryingly in mind, the field wholeheartedly welcomed the arrival of *The Jack the Ripper A-Z*, an illustrated encyclopedia which attempted to set out as much information about the Whitechapel murders as possible in an easy to reference format.[17] Its authors, Paul Begg, Martin Fido and Keith Skinner, were by now well respected in the field, and in his foreword Donald Rumbelow described it as 'the anchor of future Jack the Ripper studies'. In the ensuing years, new research and a sudden glut of new suspects would ensure several updates, but most theories, no matter how unlikely, were included. Many of the dubious claims of early twentieth-century authors were given the caution they no doubt deserved, and the by-now popular royal cover-up theories were no exception. Perhaps in a polite attempt to put these spiralling ideas to rest once and for all, the *A-Z* politely stated in reference to Joseph Gorman Sickert that 'it is to be regretted that overall extreme caution is recommended in examining any story emanating from or otherwise associated with Mr Sickert'.

Then in 1991, a discovery was made which sent tremors through the world of Ripper studies, breaking the boundaries of that relatively specific research field to become a controversial international media event of its own. The background story of what became known as the 'Maybrick Diary' made the events surrounding Joseph Sickert's eccentric claims of royal conspiracies seem tame by comparison. It is without doubt one of the most highly controversial affairs in a field that thought it had heard it all. In fact, so tortuous and contentious were the multifarious events surrounding the 'diary' that they generated an independent study of their own.[18]

In 1991, unemployed Liverpudlian Michael Barrett was given a journal by a close friend, Tony Devereaux, in a pub and told to 'do something with it'. The journal appeared to be an old photo album with numerous pages cut out at the beginning. The remaining pages were written upon, detailing a peculiar series of events which culminated in the confession: 'I give my name that all know of me, so history do tell, what love can do to a gentle man born. Yours truly Jack the Ripper. Dated this third day of May 1889.' Barrett, apparently intrigued, attempted to discover the identity of its author and finally came across James Maybrick, a Liverpool cotton merchant who had been poisoned by his wife in 1889 and for which she endured a long prison sentence. It was a prominent criminal case in its time, presided over by Justice Stephen, father of sometime Ripper suspect James Kenneth. The 'diary' (as it shall be called hereafter) suggested that Maybrick had perpetrated the Whitechapel murders in a fit of insane rage as a response to his wife's perceived infidelities, all fuelled by an uncontrollable addiction to arsenic. Further research revealed specific information in the diary which confirmed his identification, from the pet names of Maybrick's two children to their residence at Battlecrease House in Aigburth, Liverpool. Unsure of how to progress, Barrett took the diary to a literary agency, and, excited about the prospect of a publishing scoop, they set wheels in motion to have the diary published.

That is the original story behind the discovery of the May-brick Diary, put as simply as possible. However, before anybody would commit to publicizing it, it had to be tested for authenticity. And this is where the whole story becomes *very* complicated. In the months that followed, experts in ink and paper dating, handwriting, criminal psychology and, of course, 'Ripperologists' would pore over the text and conduct numerous debates over the veracity of the document. Publishing rights were bought by Smith Gryphon (with author Shirley Harrison commissioned to write the book)[19] and Paul Feldman, a businessman who had been partly responsible for bringing the 1990 movie *The Krays* to the screen, acquired video rights. The stage was set for a war unprecedented in such a small arena. Complicating matters was the discovery of a pocket watch, the interior of which was engraved with the initials of the five 'canonical' victims of Jack the Ripper, the words 'I am Jack' and the supposed signature of James Maybrick himself. This too went for testing with seemingly more consistently favourable results showing that it was contemporary with the 1880s.

Following earlier hints in the press, the proper media eruption took place on 23 April 1993, when it seemed that all the national papers were plastered with headlines about the 'new' discovery. The alleged diaries of notorious historical characters had become a sore point for journalists following the press attention on the so-called Hitler Diaries in 1983, a publishing *faux pas* of gargantuan proportions[20]. Despite giving tremendous publicity to the Maybrick Diary, the press was guarded, and the *Observer* even went as far as to call the document 'bogus' from the outset.[21]

The unfurling saga of the Maybrick Diary generated a series of disasters for many concerned, as well as litigation, accusations of foul play, threats of violence and, in one case, suspected murder. Press attention kept the controversy afloat, though a film based on the Maybrick story contained within the diary was planned, but after tests on the diary proved inconclusive, its backers pulled out. Paul Feldman, who had become a staunch supporter of the diary, eventually produced a video documentary which told the story of the diary and the resulting investigation. In one sequence, a round table of experts including Colin Wilson, Donald Rumbelow, Paul Begg, Martin Fido and Martin Howells, as well as Feldman and Shirley Harrison, are shown in debate, with Messrs Begg and Fido particularly in full swing. Feldman himself, passionately committed to the idea that Maybrick was indeed the Ripper, was later involved in a notoriously angry confrontation with diary sceptic Melvin Harris at a book launch party.

Regrettably for those clinging on to the notion that the diary was at least promising, Michael Barrett would later drop the bombshell that he had forged it, putting the story back into the headlines. He subsequently retracted his statement, but matters took another twist when Anne Graham (Barrett's estranged wife) also claimed that the diary had been in her family for many decades, further adding confusion and disagreement to the already bubbling pot. Barrett later said that his claim of forgery was merely to 'get at' Anne, as the two were going through an acrimonious divorce at the time. Subsequently, it has become impossible to go into any real depth about the diary without getting drawn into a myriad of claims and counter-claims, and Maybrick's candidacy as the Ripper is still hotly debated twenty years on.

What the Maybrick Diary presented to the avid researcher was a rarity; usually a theorist would find a suspect and use the facts to build a case, or use the facts to direct them to a suspect.

But, as with Macnaghten's memoranda or Swanson's marginalia, the theory presented *itself* to the researcher. Name and motive were already in place, and the difficulty lay in making sure that all the information added up. Unfortunately, in situations such as this, it never completely does, and with the Maybrick Diary we had the opinions of experts divided over the provenance and date of creation of the document offset with the more positive deductions surrounding the watch.

As the Maybrick debacle ground on, a slew of new studies on the Whitechapel murders emerged. A. P. Wolf produced *Jack the Myth*,[22] a work which attempted to demolish what the author saw as damaging assumptions served to a gullible public by the old guard of 'Ripperology', with Colin Wilson receiving a large proportion of the author's ire. In the process, Elizabeth Stride was removed from the 'canonical' five victims (her lover Michael Kidney was the culprit in this case) and Thomas Cutbush, the suspect mooted by the *Sun* but exonerated by the Macnaghten memoranda in 1894, was held responsible for the other Ripper crimes. A. P. Wolf importantly set no store by the old canards of the Ripper story, and his approach could be seen as ground-breaking, regardless of whether one agreed with his suspect theory. It showed a willingness, all too lacking in studies of the Whitechapel murders at that time, to deconstruct the case and not to get too precious about the established thoughts of other commentators, which had become set in stone and taken for granted over the years: hence Wilson's place in the firing line.

The same could be said for Philip Sugden's highly respected book *The Complete History of Jack the Ripper*.[23] Sugden was not actually a true-crime enthusiast who had spent years studying the Ripper, but a historian who had turned his attention to the Whitechapel murders and felt that the subject had become shrouded in myth and unreliable documentation and, as a result, resolved to cast a critical eye over the events of 1888 to produce a truly unbiased account of the crimes and times. In this, he was hugely successful, and the book is still lauded as possibly the best account of the murders to date. Although some have said that the book might discreetly lean towards Severin Klosowski as the killer, 'the best of a bad lot' in Sugden's view, as an unsensational account it was enormously successful.

Sugden's book also contained some quite cutting criticism of the way Ripper studies had been going previously. Several years later he very critically wrote of the average Ripperologist that 'First he decides who he wants Jack the Ripper to be. And then he plunders the sources for anything that will invest his candidate with a veneer of credibility.' Few people outside the field at that time took Ripperology seriously – it was considered akin to the study of UFOs, the Bermuda Triangle and other oddities; during the rush of books on the subject in 1987, one journalist was moved to write:

> Not until you read the dispassionate inquest testimony and compare it with the pathetic heaps of rags and flesh in the faded police photographs, are you brought face to face with the messy, stinking reality of what the Ripper did. These latest books prefer to titillate. They dip their pens in the blood of the five mutilated women as lovingly as the slaughterer's thin-bladed knife.[24]

Sugden attempted to bring Ripperology out of the 'fringe' and give it academic kudos. However, his criticism was in some ways undeserved, as there were many Ripper authors before him who had been trying to do exactly that.

A new and important suspect, in the form of the previously unconsidered figure of Francis Tumblety, re-emerged courtesy of Suffolk police officer Stewart Evans's acquisition of Chief Inspector John Littlechild's 1913 letter to George Sims. As we know, Tumblety ultimately fled to America, where he was considered a celebrity and a possible Ripper suspect, albeit a curious one, and it is odd considering his profile in the USA at that time, that he was never given any attention later. Subsequent research led to the publication of *The Lodger: The Arrest and Escape of Jack the Ripper*,[25] which, along with a great amount of detail on Tumblety's life, also highlighted several facts that could well link him with the Ripper murders: apparently he had a dislike of women; he had once boasted of his collection of uteri, linking him perhaps with the American doctor mentioned by Wynne Baxter at the Annie Chapman inquest; the possibility that he was a mysterious American lodger who had left some bloodstained shirts in his room in Batty Street in the East End after the double murder. There were, of course, as with any suspect theory, frustrating discrepancies.

The considerable media attention afforded Maybrick and Tumblety re-energized interest in the Ripper story; serious television documentaries began to appear with greater regularity, and more books would be published which presented new suspects, including contemporary witness George Hutchinson, taking a lead from Bruce Paley by naming a significant witness in the original case.[26] Paul Feldman was able to give his own lengthy account of the Maybrick investigation, truly nailing his colours to the mast, convinced that Maybrick was indeed the author of the diary and therefore undoubtedly Jack the Ripper,[27] and James Tully gave us James Kelly's less unorthodox candidacy for the Ripper crimes.

The 1990s saw the emergence of a number of periodicals

such as *Ripperana* (1992),[28] *Ripperologist* (1994)[29] and *Ripper Notes* (1999),[30] containing articles written by researchers and experts on the case. Some touched on Victorian social history and other famous crimes, but they were vital to the development of the study of the Ripper crimes. The articles were often studious and well researched and gave authors the perfect platform to develop new theories and, importantly, present new and often ground-breaking information to their peers. Such periodicals, published by enthusiasts, would not prove limiting to the researcher, and ideas could be freely shared and peer-reviewed, bringing the often derided study of the Whitechapel murders and their social milieu into a respectable, academic arena. An even wider audience was available to the internet website *Casebook: Jack the Ripper*,[31] started by Stephen P. Ryder in 1996. It was not a gimmicky site, but a resource that grew quickly, offering the browser access to impartial information about theories, victims, letters, documents and Victorian London, and it soon picked up international awards and accolades. Its mission statement was clear:

> In the past 110 years, the name 'Jack the Ripper' has become synonymous with evil and misogyny, eliciting images of foggy nights and gas-lit streets in the minds of millions worldwide. The mass media and entertainment industries are largely responsible for the popularity of the subject, but they are also to blame for many of the myths and misconceptions which have crept in among the facts of the case. Sloppy research performed by those motivated by personal dreams of fame and greed has only added to the mire. Though this situation has recently been aided by the valiant efforts of a handful of diligent researchers, the myths persist, the lies are repeated, and the facts of the case remain hidden beneath a cloud of confu-

sion. It is our hope that the information provided by *Casebook: Jack the Ripper* will help scatter this cloud and, perhaps, finally allow a glimpse into that most elusive aspect of the mystery: the truth.

By the time *Casebook* arrived, 'Ripperology' was a veritable minefield – even in its early days, the website held the equivalent of 8,900 pages of text and over 450 photographs and illustrations. Rare documents from the early days of Ripper studies were transcribed in full, relevant chapters from the memoirs of police officers and others became available at the click of a mouse. A band of dauntless transcribers saw to it that *Casebook* now contained a library of contemporary and relevant press reports from around the world, and all of it word-searchable. As if these resources were not important enough to the budding researcher and theorist, a message board, or forum, was added, where enthusiasts could discuss the case in a medium that was more direct than post and cheaper than telephone. Suddenly, anybody with even so much as a passing interest in the Ripper could communicate easily and, as in the periodicals, new information and theories could be shared among a like-minded 'community'. The website would be used by students studying social history as well as the casual, curious surfer and would be a concept much emulated in the field.[32]

In 1999, author M. J. Trow proposed a new suspect, philanthropist and brewing heir Frederick Charrington. Despite his family connection, he was a teetotal extremist who often picketed pubs and music halls. He conducted tent-meeting crusades in the East End and built a huge mission hall, where he distributed free teas to the poor, and in 1887 started a campaign against prostitution, noting down the identities of clients visiting brothels and threatening to reveal their names. It was widely known that the disreputable lodging house keepers who permitted prostitution on their premises were more afraid of Charrington than of the police, and one house even had his portrait on the wall so that they could recognize him should he turn up unannounced. Trow's theory presented Charrington as the Ripper, citing his disapproval of prostitution as a main motive and suggesting that his suspect was merely 'street cleaning'. What was important about this proposition is that Trow did not believe that Charrington was the Ripper in the slightest. In a presentation to the Cloak and Dagger club and later in a print article[33], Trow said that Frederick Charrington was 'a good man doing a difficult job at a difficult time and no more Jack the Ripper than I am'. What Trow had done was pick a person and use facts and supposition to put them in the frame – the whole exercise was intended as a valuable demonstration of the ease with which an innocent man might be framed as Jack the Ripper, effectively summing up the activities of most theorists of the preceding hundred years.

The internet radically changed the world of 'Ripperology', granting access to information at the tap of a keyboard and supplying information that previously would have taken researchers months of legwork and expense to accumulate. By the end of the millennium, more information found its way to the researcher, when all the surviving information retained in the Scotland Yard and Home Office files of the Public Record Office were made truly accessible to all and Stewart Evans and Keith Skinner produced *The Ultimate Jack the Ripper Source Book*.[34] The result of many years of transcribing the documents first-hand, it gave everybody the chance to go back to basics, see the words of the official reports made by policemen, politicians and others, to hear their thoughts and get as rounded an account of their investigation as possible. With the surviving official records now on the bookshelves, that thrust towards the importance of contemporary facts was given a much-needed boost, showing the world that the Ripper story was not beholden to the world of cranks and sensation seekers, but could now be considered as an important field of study for the true crime enthusiast, the social historian and the academic alike.

The Appliance of Science

The artist Walter Sickert had been skirting the fringes of culpability for the Whitechapel murders for decades until American crime novelist Patricia Cornwell decided to follow her criminologist nose and declare him to be the Ripper. Cornwell's wealth, success and high profile ensured that her investigation into this marginal player would gain enormous coverage. In fact, it probably became the most publicized example of Ripper sleuthing ever.

In a move that would become repeated by others in the following years, Cornwell undertook her own investigation, using modern investigative methods and the help of several experts in the field of forensics. She had been struck by the imagery of a number of Sickert's paintings which depicted women often as though they were dead or even mutilated. Cornwell believed that Sickert fitted the psychological profile of a sex killer, the trigger being a childhood operation to treat a fistula in his penis, resulting in deformity and impotence. The clues to his guilt were in the paintings, but Cornwell was able to go further than most. Not only was she able to finance DNA testing on Ripper letters kept at the Public Record Office (with the intention of finding matches on known Sickert correspondence), but she also began buying the paintings.

Tests on the letters drew a blank, with no matches found in the nuclear DNA. But then testing was done for mitochondrial

DNA (mtDNA), which proved more positive. Unfortunately, mtDNA is no guarantee of proof. Stephen P. Ryder, in his *Casebook* dissertation on Cornwell's theory, stated simply that:

> Finding an mtDNA match between two samples does not mean that one person left both, but that only a certain percentage of the population could have left both . . .
>
> In this case, the mtDNA 'sequences' found indicate, according to Cornwell, that only 1% of the population of the U. K. could have left the DNA found on those Ripper letters, and that the person who left DNA on Sickert's correspondence was a member of that 1% population. (Other DNA experts, when asked to comment on this analysis, state that the actual percentage could range anywhere between 10% and 0.1% of the contemporary population). In 1901 there were nearly 40 million people in the United Kingdom. That means that Sickert, if we assume it is his mtDNA that was found, and that Cornwell's figure of 1% is correct, was one of approximately 400,000 people whose mtDNA shared those same sequences.[1]

Such odds were hardly conclusive of one man's guilt, and Cornwell's theory was slowly pulled apart by sceptics, often savagely, and with no small amount of personal rancour, which Cornwell most certainly did not deserve. It was noted that there was no proof that Sickert had ever had an operation for a penile fistula, though there was the possibility that he had suffered from an anal fistula. What's more, Walter Sickert was certainly not impotent or sexually backward; if anything, he was known for being rather promiscuous. In other words, he was not sexually scarred and incapable, and thus this reason for him killing prostitutes need not have entered the equation. Critics also stated that there was no evidence to suggest that

Sickert was in London at the time of the murders. Cornwell hit back with the claim that there was no evidence to suggest he *wasn't*. Unfortunately there was: several pieces of evidence quoted by Sickert's biographer Matthew Sturgess put the art- ist in France from late August until the beginning of October 1888.[2]

Obviously there was more to Cornwell's theory, and she eventually published her investigation in *Portrait of a Killer*,[3] a huge seller, which was not perhaps surprising considering the combination of crime fiction's most successful novelist and the world's greatest crime mystery. An inevitable documen- tary also appeared on BBC television, with Cornwell shown at the heart of the investigative process, surveying the East End streets, joining the forensic teams as they worked and flying round the world in her pursuit of the 'real' Jack the Ripper. She didn't mind getting her hands dirty either, handling a range of rather intimidating knives and cutting up large slabs of offal in order to demonstrate which kind of weapon could have been used to inflict the injuries on the Ripper victims. Donald Rumbelow was not convinced and not too happy either. The unfortunate by-product of naming a prominent individual as Jack the Ripper had manifested itself in the van- dalism of graves, notably those of Sir William Gull at Thorpe-le-Soken in Essex and James Maybrick in Liverpool. Rumbelow argued that

> Out there, there is an element that is going to believe this non-
> sense that Sickert was the Ripper. Some lunatic will go in the
> Tate or somewhere else and slash a canvas because he was
> Jack the Ripper. This is the sort of thing – this is the sort of
> nonsense – which actually triggers this behaviour and there is
> this element out there who'll believe it.[4]

Patricia Cornwell's belief in Sickert as the Whitechapel murderer was, in her own words 'a given', and there was some merit in her attempt to drag Sickert's candidacy away from his royal conspiracy connections, making him a suspect in his own right, investigated separately from the information and misinformation that had gone before via Joseph Sickert, Stephen Knight and Melvyn Fairclough. But then the other players in the original story had been effectively exonerated, leaving Sickert as a 'last man standing'.

The research behind *Portrait of a Killer* coincided with the early appearances of the American TV show *CSI: Crime Scene Investigation*,[5] which followed the fictional investigations of a team of Las Vegas forensic scientists as they unravelled the circumstances behind mysterious and unusual deaths and other crimes using state of the art technology. It essentially brought the deductive reasoning of popular fictional detectives into the twenty-first century, and its slick production values revived interest in crime investigation drama in much the same way as *The X-Files* had inspired a resurgence of fascination for the paranormal in the 1990s.[6]

Also, satellite broadcasting had come into its own, offering literally hundreds of TV channels worldwide, many of which specialized in particular themes. Following on from Patricia Cornwell's 'forensics-heavy' investigation, a trend in Ripper theorizing would gradually become apparent, chiefly manifesting itself in documentaries. Previously, these films had covered known information, often just relying on a retelling of the Whitechapel murders story with relevant reconstructions, graphics and comment from experts in the field. The sudden interest in forensic science as a vehicle for entertainment would see an increase in documentaries which would appear to show the presenter as investigator, perhaps earnestly sifting through evidence, claiming to have 'reopened the case' and coming up with their 'definitive' solution. Invariably, this 'evidence' would be known to keen students of the case already, but the fact that TV treatments of the case had to appeal to a wider audience meant that very often the material was cited as being new or exclusive.

Another good example of the growing interest in solving the Ripper mystery using now obligatory modern methods came with the claims of a former police officer, Trevor Marriott: 'Mr Marriott, who worked on many murder investigations during his career in the police, has subjected the facts to forensic dissection and has used proven modern investigative techniques to attempt to solve the mystery.'[7]

Like many theories, Marriott's attempt to name the Ripper was full of holes. Settling on the notion that the killer was a merchant seaman, he undertook research into finding correlations between ships berthed at the London docks and the nights of the Ripper murders, which threw up several possibilities. Although inconsistent records did not permit Marriott to name a definitive individual, his suspicion rested upon Carl Feigenbaum, who was executed in 1896 for the murder of Juliana Hoffman in New York and who had confessed to his lawyer that he was Jack the Ripper. The investigation also attempted to dispel some long-held beliefs; it was always assumed that the murderer removed the victims' organs at the scene of crime, whereas Marriott, convinced that this could not have been so owing to the time frames available, claimed that the organs were removed by somebody while the corpses were lying outside the mortuary. The difficulty involved in tracing these organs and removing them under very tight circumstances was investigated thoroughly by Marriott, who consulted with pathologists and even attended dissections of corpses to demonstrate his point. If anything, he was thorough in his pursuit of the truth in that respect. But his early decision to look into the idea of a merchant seaman as a suspect came from his belief that nobody had looked at the case from this angle before; it was a mistaken belief, for, as we have seen, seamen and workers at the docks and riversides, owing to their ease of transit and often disreputable characteristics, had been very much in the frame from the earliest days of the investigation. Edward Knight Larkins tried repeatedly to direct the police to a number of individuals who may have been on boats berthed at the docks at the time of the murders, and even Queen Victoria had suggested searching the boats in her telegram to the government following Mary Kelly's murder.

Trevor Marriott, as a former detective,[8] also tried to use his investigative experience to go back to the original case and work from a modern police perspective. Not only was he branching into the now-obligatory world of 'cold case' investigation, but he was also deconstructing the evidence to find new interpretations of it. One significant notion was that the bloody apron piece in Goulston Street was not deposited by the murderer of Catherine Eddowes, but by Eddowes herself after using it as a makeshift sanitary towel. With claims like this, expounded in books, internet forums and, later, lecture tours, Marriott attempted to challenge preconceived ideas of the Whitechapel murders and their investigation. Once again, a theorist would claim some form of 'ownership' of the case.

A recurring theme in the new methodology behind Ripper theorizing was 'profiling'. The FBI character profile of 1988 had by now been joined by visual and geographical profiling, the latter pioneered by British investigative psychologist David Canter, who declared: 'Criminals reveal who they are and where they live not just from how they commit their crimes, but also from the locations they choose.'[9] These methods were used in a documentary[10] which eventually put together the *face* of Jack the Ripper, apparently based on *thirteen* contemporary witness statements. The resulting image received considerable publicity, mainly because it resembled Lord Lucan or Queen vocalist Freddie Mercury, which partially took the sting out of the enterprise for those not fully conversant with the content of the original broadcast. Nonetheless, the claims of the investigators were evidence that the concept of 'ownership' of the identity of the Ripper was still going strong, almost as if nobody else had ever tried:

> Laura Richards, head of analysis for Scotland Yard's Violent Crime Command, analysed evidence from the case using modern police techniques and has been able to form the most accurate portrait of the Ripper ever put together.
>
> She said: 'For the first time we are able to understand the kind of person Jack the Ripper was. We can name the street where he probably lived; and we can see what he looked like; and we can explain, finally, why this killer escaped justice.[11]

The project did not name a name – it probably did not intend to – but according to Laura Richards he was somebody from the lower classes, poorly educated and what he did was by choice, reacting to events that had shaped him early in his life. The geographical profiling techniques suggested that the Ripper lived in the Flower and Dean Street area of Spitalfields, confirming his status as a poor, local man.

Another theorist who chanced his arm at identifying the murderer during this period was M. J. Trow. Trow had written a number of books on true crime, as well as historical biographies and crime fiction,[12] and his *The Many Faces of Jack the*

Ripper used an interesting exercise whereby he listed all of the main suspects and rated them with marks for eligibility.[13] Following a challenge from his publisher,[14] Trow began to look into a potential suspect, one that had not been considered before, and settled on Whitechapel workhouse mortuary attendant Robert Mann. Using the FBI profile, as well as geographical and offender profiling techniques as a key, Trow noted that Mann worked in a job that gave him access to dead bodies, where perhaps he could glean information about anatomy and surgical procedure and, as victims Tabram, Nichols, Chapman and McKenzie had ended up in his mortuary, gloat over his handiwork. Mann was born in the immediate area and, as an inmate of the Whitechapel Union workhouse, was well placed geographically to commit the murders. Trow stated that Alice McKenzie was the last true Ripper victim and that her injuries were significantly less violent because Mann was weak and terminally ill. A book was produced,[15] outlining the case in full, as well as a TV documentary tie-in,[16] as was becoming customary.

But there were problems with the hypothesis, and it was on the internet that the greatest dissenters made their voices heard, calling Mann a 'non-starter' and picking out significant flaws and inaccuracies, which were later acknowledged by Trow himself. In answering his critics, he was apologetic, but felt that some of the criticism was unfounded:

> I repeat I cannot prove that the strange, enigmatic mortuary attendant was definitely Jack the Ripper. All I can say is that he is closer than most other possibles and, at the very least, a starter! [17]

The case of Robert Mann's candidacy as the Ripper showed how much a blanket media promotion could bend a 'proposition' into a 'solution'. The title of the book treatment of the theory, *Quest for a Killer*, basically described what it was, the author's search for the identity of Jack the Ripper. The television documentary called itself *Killer Revealed*, suggesting that the quest had actually come good and the mystery was solved. And herein lay the very marked distinction between the way publishing and television had come to treat the theorist. Whilst publishing always has its eye on the next 'best-seller', it does have the capacity to recognize the merit of serious books like the *A to Z* and *Ultimate Sourcebook*; it appears that television has a harder time coming to terms with this concept and should realize that it *can* get away with just telling the story. It rarely seems to be interested in maybes and conjecture, preferring a theorist to put their cards on the table (or putting the cards on the table for them) to ensure that yet another Ripper scoop will pull in the biggest audience.

The present authors had direct experience of this when they wrote *Jack the Ripper: The Definitive Story*, a two-part documentary for Channel 5 in the UK.[18] The idea was to produce a lengthy treatment covering the entire story of the Whitechapel murders without suspect bias, the unique selling point being extensive computer-generated imagery (CGI)[19] of the crime scenes merged with live action; the audience would at last get to see the events surrounding the murders portrayed in an accurate setting. However, it became a continual struggle to get the commissioning editors to understand that you could tell the real story and provide information about suspects without choosing one in particular, and that it would still make valid television. We chose to concentrate on the contemporary suspects Druitt, Tumblety, Kosminski and Klosowski (George Chapman) and attempted to give them an equal hearing. In the end, the involvement of an independent script editor and some choice editing pushed Kosminski to the fore, and subsequently the documentary was accused of promoting Aaron Kosminski as the chief suspect, much to our dismay. The publishing world was much more forgiving, and the book which resulted from work done on the documentary was allowed to remain impartial, concentrating on the story, crime locations and the local geography of Whitechapel and Spitalfields. That said, the working title of the book, *Jack the Ripper: Crime Scene Investigation*, was enthusiastically seized upon by the publishers, who saw a good opportunity to tap into the continuing popularity of the American crime series, finally calling the book *Jack the Ripper: CSI Whitechapel*.[20]

Attempting to completely document the theories and suspects which have appeared in the first two decades of the twenty-first century is an onerous task. In fact, it is an impossible one. Perhaps the main reason for this is the exploitation of technology – self-publishing using internet-based processes and retail outlets[21] has become increasingly popular for those authors and researchers with a theory to sell when conventional publishing routes have proved fruitless. The downside of this is that there is little or no 'filter', and anybody with even the most wayward theory can put it into the public arena. Similarly, without recourse to proofreaders and editors, some publications lack a basic grasp of grammar and, worse still, can be little more than 'cut-and-paste' rehashes of material purloined directly from internet dissertations or Wikipedia.

The upside of the new methods of output is that much great research is shared, especially in dedicated Ripper publications and message boards. Part of this comes when a theory is posited on a forum, making it immediately open to peer-review; with so many being able to join the debate, facts are wheeled out, obscure material is brought to the attention of all, and more research is instigated to either prove or disprove the argument. What becomes apparent is the breadth of study undertaken by contributors, and many appear to concentrate on various aspects of the case; the police, the local geography, the victims, specific suspects and more, all combining to make 'Ripperology' a vast and formidable subject for study. Some may not necessarily specify an area of interest but perhaps a concept; whereas as some hold rigidly to the contemporary official files as source material, others feel that these important documents are there to be questioned, leading some to believe that not all the statements given by police or witnesses can be relied upon. The urge to analyse these sources in such a way is perhaps understandable; however, it can become counterproductive. It is generally agreed that newspaper reports of the time could not always be relied upon to get the facts right, thanks to mistranscriptions or the overzealous reporting of some journalists, but to declare that the only remaining information we have to confirm any events in the Ripper case is also highly flawed leaves us with nothing concrete whatsoever to go on. The concept of a single killer is also up for grabs, with accusations of press and police complicity in creating the man-monster that was Jack the Ripper when, in all probability, there was no such individual and the murders were wholly, or at least in part, unrelated. Eleven true Ripper victims? Five? Three? What does one believe?

Electronic 'Ripperology' still produces its theorists, and the sheer weight of information and opinion that can be shared in any twenty-four hours makes for a veritable minefield. But among this information overload is plenty worth noting, and two examples of suspect-based research have proven very interesting, seeing as they choose to re-examine contemporary figures in the case. The first is that of Charles Le Grand, a criminal of long standing who posed as a private investigator at the time of the Whitechapel murders and who, along with partner J. W. Batchelor, figured prominently during the investigation surrounding the murder of Elizabeth Stride. Employed by the Mile End Vigilance Committee and also working alongside a number of newspapers, Le Grand and Batchelor interviewed the Berner Street fruiterer Matthew Packer and were believed to be responsible for the story that a grapestalk was found at the murder scene. The police were not impressed by Le Grand's meddling. He was first considered as a suspect in 1998,[22] and since then articles about him and his candidacy have appeared in the main Ripper periodicals.[23] Researcher and writer Tom Wescott, very much responsible for building a thorough picture of the often confusing events surrounding the Berner Street murder and the people involved, was one of several looking into the life and activities of this most enigmatic and colourful suspect, and a colossal amount of information has been posted on the message boards as a result, making interesting links and dispelling a few myths into the bargain.

Another suspect drawn from key players in the Ripper story is Charles Cross, the first person to discover the body of Mary Ann Nichols. Several researchers felt that he was a good contender for the Nichols murder as he was found by Robert Paul standing by the corpse in Buck's Row.[24] Not only that, he gave his name as 'Cross' (his stepfather's name) when his birth name, the one he used at all other times, was Lechmere. This was seen by his accusers as evidence of creating a smokescreen to hide his obvious guilt. From here the theory would expand, suggesting that Cross had every reason to travel near the various murder sites, thus potentially making him truly Jack the Ripper. Christer Holmgren and Edward Stow became the two most vocal supporters of this theory,[25] even going so far as to publicize it as part of a memorial presentation about the Bethnal Green Tube disaster, where some of Cross's descendants died.[26] The discussion really took shape on internet message boards, and as more joined the debate, more angles were explored, with one poster adamantly believing that Cross had killed Nichols before Paul arrived, only to then mutilate her after Paul went off looking for a policeman. Almost every report has it that the two men left together and that they were still together when they met PC Jonas Mizen, but this poster would have none of it, leading to some interminable pedantic debates over report wording. But such is the way of things where internet Ripper studies are concerned.

What the activities surrounding Le Grand's and Cross's appearances as suspects show us is that neither of these suspects have had full-length accounts published about them, and yet many thousands of words have been typed – in dedicated Ripper periodicals and most notably cyberspace – already. It is as though these theories are doomed for the moment to float on the ether, which is a pity, as both Le Grand and Cross can be considered as far better choices than some other suspects which have been proposed. The efforts that have gone into researching these previously little-known individuals is waiting for a lengthy, less fragmented treatment and as such would be warmly anticipated.

In his overview of almost every person ever accused of being Jack the Ripper,[27] C. J. Morley listed nearly 300 names, from obscure individuals accused at the time to the more covered suspects, to celebrities whose alleged guilt flies in the face of reason: Inspector Abberline, King Leopold II of the Belgians, Arthur Conan Doyle, Canon Samuel Barnett, Dr Thomas Barnardo, Joseph Merrick (the 'Elephant Man'),

Edward VII, Lewis Carroll, William Gladstone and Lord Randolph Churchill. Not named in Morley's book, but demonstrating how deeply the suspect barrel can be scraped, are Vincent Van Gogh and Queen Victoria!

A century and a quarter after the Whitechapel murderer left the world looking for an answer, a truly definitive solution is still not forthcoming, despite the assurances of theorists and the media. Nor is it likely to be, and thus the international game of 'hunt the Ripper', this veritable 'pin the tail on the donkey', will continue unabated. But there is one other element that contributes to the longevity of fascination with the story: because he is an unknown quantity, still lacking a firm motive or identity, Jack the Ripper can become anything we wish him to be. He has become the stuff of folklore, a myth, a legend.

And you can't kill off a legend.

PART THREE

Mythologies

Genesis of the Ripper

On the corner of Commercial Street and Fournier Street, opposite the old Spitalfields market and with Nicholas Hawksmoor's boxy but beautiful Christ Church on the adjacent corner, sits the Ten Bells pub. The current building dates from 1845, but records show that there has been a pub here since at least 1753, and almost certainly earlier. There are a number of alleged minor connections between it and Jack the Ripper, mainly claims that the victims drank there, although the only two references to that being the case come from probably unreliable press reports following the deaths of Annie Chapman and Mary Kelly. But much of the pub is essentially as it was in 1888 when it is very probable that, owing to their proclivities towards heavy drinking, all the victims of Jack the Ripper might well have been familiar with its comforts. Other places which would have had worthier associations with the victims were the Britannia and the Queen's Head, both nearby, but the former has been demolished and the latter closed down, and thus it falls on the Ten Bells to become the focus of attention in this respect. The centenary of the Ripper murders fell in 1988, 'the year of the Ripper' as it was described by the *Guardian*'s Deborah Cameron,[1] in what can be seen as an opening salvo of a skirmish in which a group calling themselves Action Against the Ripper Centenary (AARC) played a prominent part, receiving a high profile throughout 1987–8 and featuring repeatedly in the national and local press. Very soon the rather nebulous 'centenary' came together in the Ten Bells.

In early 1975 the pub had closed for a £15,000 refurbishment and when it reopened on 30 April 1975 it had also received a name change: it was now called 'the Jack the Ripper'.[2] Basically a themed pub, the vogue for which never really took off in the UK,[3] the Jack the Ripper was decked out with relevant memorabilia and promised its new clientele 'plush decor' with an accent on the Ripper. This revamp caused little stir at the time; however, the upcoming centenary promised a boost in trade and the sale of souvenirs, including, most bizarrely, a teapot and a drink called the 'Ripper Tipple'. It was a parade upon which the feminist AARC was determined to rain, its members campaigning to have the pub's name changed. As AARC spokesperson Kelly Ellenborne stated, it was 'outrageous that anybody should be using the historical and horrific murder of women as a tourist attraction to make money'. The then tenants, Yvonne and Ernie Ostrowski, responded by pointing out that 'The fascination is not with the murders but with the mystery that surrounds them.'[4]

Both were right. Both were wrong. The trouble is that nobody was celebrating or commemorating a man who murdered women. They were essentially commemorating the centenary of a fictional creation, one that for many was no more real than Dracula, Sweeney Todd or Sherlock Holmes.

By 1988 Jack the Ripper had well and truly become the stuff of myth and legend: the popular image had become one of gin palaces, foggy streets and dark alleys with alluring but seedy women struck down by a gentleman murderer wearing a top hat and cape, holding a black bag and perhaps blessed with a surgeon's skill. Surrounding this iconography were a police force helpless in their attempts to catch him, always one step behind, and a terrified, unwitting public, trapped in the middle as an increasingly exasperated press screamed out the horrible details. But the creation of a mythical Jack is not a purely twentieth-century concept; in fact, the Whitechapel murderer was most definitely taking on such a legendary status during that period in 1888 when the crimes were still ongoing.

To all intents and purposes, the mysterious 'Leather Apron', suggested in the first week of September 1888, was the original mythical killer. Before the Whitechapel murderer had even been given his more famous, lasting sobriquet, the sensational newspaper descriptions of the character seared terrible images into the minds of the public, and so well known did he become that he was the title character in one of the earliest pieces of Ripper literature, *Leather Apron or the Horrors of Whitechapel*, published in December 1888.[5] 'Leather Apron' also became effectively one of the earliest issues in the case to be talked of overseas. With reference to the murder of Mary Ann Nichols, one American newspaper imaginatively said that:

> The crime, committed last Friday night, has shocked the whole of England, and is generally charged to a short, thickset, half crazy creature, with fiendish black eyes, and known as 'Leather Apron.' He frequented the dark alleys, and like a veritable imp haunted the gloom of the halls and passage ways of Whitechapel, and lived by robbing the female Arabs who roamed the streets after nightfall. Of powerful muscle, carrying a knife which he brandished over his victims, the London murder fiend was too terrible an assailant for the victim that cowered beneath the glitter of cold steel.[6]

A number of prostitutes attempted to assist the press in locating him. Two took a reporter to the corner of Commercial Street and Wentworth Street, where the mysterious man was often allegedly seen, adding: 'it would be necessary to look into all the shadows, as if he was there he would surely be out of sight'.[7] But did 'Leather Apron' exist outside of the East End rumour mill or the pages of the sensational press? It is arguable that he did not,[8] for it seems that at one point anybody seen acting suspiciously became 'Leather Apron' and was swiftly spoken of and reported, giving the newspapers plenty to shock their readership with. The arrest of John Pizer, who made an appearance at Annie Chapman's inquest to clear his name, did little to quell the fear on the streets. Pizer declared, on being accused of being 'Leather Apron', that he was not and that he did not know of any such man,[9] but Sergeant William Thick, who arrested him on 10 September, was reported as saying 'almost positively' that Pizer was indeed 'Leather Apron'.[10]

The 'Leather Apron' scare demonstrated that the late nineteenth-century Londoner and pressman alike were extremely susceptible to a form of mass hysteria and showed that, even at that early stage, the image of the Whitechapel murderer was being shaped into whatever form felt suitable at that time. With the East End (and indeed London as a whole) reeling from the fear of 'midnight terrors' and 'man-monsters' during those early weeks of September, it would perhaps be fitting to mention that, by that time, a well-received stage rendition of Robert Louis Stevenson's 1886 tale *The Strange Case of Dr Jekyll and Mr Hyde* had been playing at London's Lyceum Theatre for a month. Stevenson's story is well known: the mild-mannered doctor changing into the bestial Mr Hyde was as much a comment on the double standards of the professional classes

Stevenson saw around him as it was gothic horror. It would be a story retold in many forms in the ensuing century.

The star of that Lyceum production was Richard Mansfield, an American actor who had impressed theatre-goers and critics alike with his uncanny on-stage transformations from Jekyll to Hyde, successfully achieved by lighting effects and sheer physical performance. With the onset of the Whitechapel murders, comparisons would soon be made:

> The Whitechapel murder has taken a turn of most ghastly romance. Those whose sensations were not handicapped while they read it by a haunting idea that 'the strange case of Dr Jekyll and Mr Hyde' was a performance at least as grotesque as it was grim will remember how the horrible Hyde in one of his transformations, butchered a woman just for the fun of the thing. That is an effective passage in the book, and those whom it thrilled with a pleasing terror will snatch fearful joy from the story of 'Leather Apron'.[11]

The man-monster idea was taking hold, leading one letter-writer to go so far as to suggest a solution to the mystery based on the 'dual personality' concept in the story:

> MEANWHILE, writes an eccentric correspondent, you, and every one of the papers, have missed the obvious solution of the Whitechapel mystery. The murderer is a Mr Hyde, who seeks in the repose and comparative respectability of Dr Jekyll security from the crimes he commits in his baser shape. Of course, the lively imaginations of your readers will at once supply certain means of identification for the Dr Jekyll whose Mr Hyde seems daily growing in ferocious intensity.[12]

It has been said that the production closed down as a result of dwindling audiences, forcing Mansfield into bankruptcy, all because of the Whitechapel murders and the fear they generated. Audiences did decline as a result of the considerable fears on the streets, but although the play did indeed close at the end of September, it was successfully resurrected in repertory theatre only a week later.

If the Whitechapel murders did affect the size of theatre audiences and the profits of small shopkeepers, it did allow some of a more maverick persuasion to make a profit, sometimes in very questionable taste. One enterprising pavement artist attracted a large crowd by drawing his own interpretation of the Mitre Square murder on the pavement in Whitechapel Road, making a respectable sum of money as a result. His cartoon was described as 'certainly a masterpiece of sanguinary ghastliness. What it lacked in delineation and unity it made up for in disgusting details, and there was a constant struggle among the crowds in the street to get a view of it.'[13]

A more disturbing manifestation of an attempt to give form to the events unfolding in the East End – and make money from it – came with a grotesque waxworks exhibition. The proprietor was Thomas Barry who, along with his daughter, ran a live entertainment venue from 107 Whitechapel Road, only a few hundred yards from Buck's Row.[14] Next door at no. 106, on the corner with Thomas Street, Barry created a wax museum which generated great interest and outrage in equal measure:

During the past few days a highly-coloured representation of the George Yard and Buck's Row murders – painted on canvas – have been hung in front of the building, in addition to which there were placards notifying that life size wax models of the murdered women could be seen within. The pictures have caused large crowds to assemble on the pavement in front of the shop. This morning, however, another picture was added to the rest. It was a representation of the murder in Hanbury street. The prominent feature of the pictures was that they were plentifully besmeared with red paint – this of course representing wounds and blood. Notices were also posted up that a life-size waxwork figure of Annie 'Sivens' [*sic*] could be seen within. After the inquest at the Working Lads' Institute had been adjourned a large crowd seized them and tore them down. Considerable confusion followed, and order was only restored by the appearance of an inspector of police and two constables. A man attired in workman's clothes and who appeared to be somewhat the worse for drink then addressed the crowd. He said – 'I suppose you are all English-men and women here; then do you think it right that that picture (continued the orator, pointing to the one representing the murder in Hanbury street) should be exhibited in the pub-lic streets before the poor woman's body is hardly cold.' Cries of 'No, no, we don't' greeted this remark, and another scene of excitement followed. The crowd, however, was quickly dis-persed by the police before the showman's property was further damaged.[15]

Such shows were described as 'sinks of iniquity',[16] with one observer stating that 'to what extent it may influence the East-enders deleteriously, by fostering a morbid interest in crime and criminals, can of course only be a matter of conjec-ture; but it seems a pity that such a debasing exhibition should constitute one of the principal amusements available to the population of a poverty-stricken neighbourhood'.[17]

The controversy surrounding Barry's waxworks[18] was

understandable and a reflection of what would happen exactly a century later when the AARC focused their attention upon the Ten Bells and other events of 1988. One could suppose that the opening of such an exhibition (which included waxworks of other famous murders) was no different from Madame Tussauds's Chamber of Horrors or more modern creations such as the London Dungeon, where onlookers can enjoy a grisly spectacle safe in the knowledge that they are not actually threatened by what they are witnessing. But in 1888 that was most certainly not the case, and the fact that Barry was adding exhibits to the show with each new Whitechapel murder must surely have added to the public outrage. A very real killer was still at large, no woman felt she was safe, and Thomas Barry was shoving it in their faces, at a profit.

Nobody in their right mind would really wish to come across a horrifically mutilated body, however such tableaux allow the spectator to obtain some small, visceral entertainment from something which is essentially taboo.

The use of Jack the Ripper as entertainment would be something that would increase dramatically as the decades passed. The mythical Jack we know today was still a long way from forming, but elements of that mythology would introduce themselves as the 'autumn of terror' progressed. Descriptions of men seen with the victims shortly before their deaths had no bearing on the image of Jack that is so ubiquitous today. Witnesses like Elizabeth Long (Hanbury Street), Joseph Lawende (Mitre Square), Israel Schwartz and PC William Smith (Berner Street) might well have clapped eyes on the murderer, but their descriptions were pretty sober and bore no resemblance to the cloak-and-dagger image that perseveres. The first element of that popular iconography came after the murder of Elizabeth Stride, namely 'the black bag'.

In *The Times* of 1 October 1888 two witnesses were described as seeing men with such an item. The first was Fanny Mortimer, the resident of 36 Berner Street who, standing at her front door on the morning of the Stride murder, saw Leon Goldstein pass, carrying a black shiny bag which, it was later discovered, contained nothing more sinister than empty cigarette boxes. A second, more suspicious, encounter with a man with a black bag was made by Albert Bachert, who would later become chairman of the Mile End Vigilance Committee:

> I was in the Three Nuns Hotel, Aldgate, on Saturday night, when a man got into conversation with me. He asked me questions which now appear to me to have some bearing upon the recent murders. He wanted to know whether I knew what sort of loose women used the public bar at that house, when they usually left the street outside, and where they were in the habit of going. He asked further questions, and from his manner seemed to be up to no good purpose. He appeared to be a shabby genteel sort of man, and was dressed in black clothes. He wore a black felt hat and carried a black bag. We came out together at closing time (12 o'clock), and I left him outside Aldgate Railway Station.[19]

In the ensuing panic generated by the double murder, it was now a dangerous thing to be in possession of a shiny black bag. Around the country, totally innocent bystanders were being targeted for violence simply because they carried one, as this example from Birmingham demonstrates:

> The hue and cry after the Whitechapel fiend has exercised an almost irresistible influence over the minds of innumerable men and youths in all parts of the country. A feverish desire to

run him to earth goads them on to be ever on the alert for a 'dark man with a black bag.' Under these circumstances the danger of carrying a black bag is very great. It resulted in the attention of the police being called to a suspect in Birmingham during the week. Late on Tuesday night a commercial traveller with a small black bag was hurrying down Stephenson Place to catch a train, when he was pounced upon by a strongly-built man. The suddenness of the attack took the possessor of the bag by surprise, and wishing to escape from the rather tight grip his assailant had of his throat, he began to struggle violently. The unknown retaliated and shrieked for help, but before the police arrived the pair were wriggling on the pavement. The strife having ended, the gentleman wished the constable to arrest his assailant for assaulting him, while the latter requested the policeman to lock the unfortunate owner of the black bag up for being the Whitechapel murderer.[20]

The suspicion upon owners of such bags continued well after Mary Kelly's murder, and the pictorial cover of the *Illustrated Police News* of 17 November 1888 contained no fewer than three illustrations of encounters with men holding them.

As the Whitechapel murders progressed, the killer was already developing his mythical status: as 'Leather Apron' he was a by-word for terror; he had already exerted an early influence on what was considered entertainment; and he was tentatively beginning to acquire visual characteristics that would later refuse to go away. All he needed now was a name that would stick, and that came soon and easily enough in the form of the 'Dear Boss' letter and 'Saucy Jacky' postcard, received by the Central News agency on 27 September and 1 October 1888 respectively. Immediately after the double murder, it is assumed that the police gave the go-ahead for the content of these missives to be released to the press.

The effect of these communications is a given. The excitement generated by their publication has been well documented, even though elements within the press and police felt that they were bogus. Melville Macnaghten, Robert Anderson and John Littlechild were convinced that a journalistic deception was responsible, and Littlechild, in his letter to George R. Sims in 1913, said that 'it was generally believed at the Yard that Tom Bullen [*sic*] of the Central News was the originator, but it is probable Moore, who was his chief, was the inventor. It was a smart piece of journalistic work.' The *Star* reporter Frederick Best has also been credited with the creation of the original Jack the Ripper letters,[21] but whoever did write the 'Dear Boss' letter perhaps unwittingly created a name that resonated at the time and continues to do so.

As the popular form of 'John', the name 'Jack' already had built-in associations with legendary characters from folklore and popular history: Jack-o'-Lantern, Jolly Jack Tar, Jack the Giant Killer and Spring-heeled Jack. 'Ripper' is self-explanatory. It was catchy, spoke volumes for the vicious intent and anti-heroic cockiness of the alleged author and would soon overtake the cumbersome 'Leather Apron' as the ideal name for this already most infamous of killers. 'Jack the Ripper' was a 'Jack-the-Lad' from a world of nightmares.

Throughout the lull of October of 1888, the myths surrounding the Ripper began to grow. The fear of the unknown was beginning to take its toll, and as a dense fog descended over London for much of that month[22] imaginations began to run riot. The murder of Catherine Eddowes, or specifically its location, Mitre Square, became a focus for supernatural supposition in *The Curse upon Mitre Square*, a lurid piece of fiction written by J. F. Brewer and published soon after the 'double event'.[23] Tapping into the late-Victorian fascination for superstition and gothic horror, it claimed that the site of Catherine Eddowes's murder was haunted by the ghost of Brother Martin, a monk of the former Priory of the Holy Trinity, Aldgate. The Priory had stood on the site until its dissolution in 1538, after which the buildings were sold off and subsequently demolished. Brother Martin had, according to the legend, murdered a woman at the altar steps in a fashion not unlike that of the Ripper:

> The monk had seized the woman by the throat; a dozen times he gashed the face; the knife descended with lightning rapidity – pools of blood deluged the altar steps. With a demon's fury, the monk then threw down the corpse and trod it out of very recognition. He spat upon the mutilated face, and, with his remaining strength, he ripped the body open and cast the entrails round about.

The monk then plunged the knife into his own heart after realizing that he had killed his own sister.

As preposterous as the idea of a malevolent, unavenged spirit being guilty of the Whitechapel murders is, such a story was no doubt devoured with great interest by literate Victorians, and it attached a mythology not just to the murder of Catherine Eddowes, but to the very place where it occurred. In Brewer's words; 'woe to anybody who would live on that spot; woe to him, who remained there at night and out of reach of help!'

The day before the shocking events that inspired Brewer's histrionics, the satirical magazine *Punch* published a poem entitled 'The Nemesis of Neglect', a lengthy verse which espoused the wrongs of the slums and how failure to right such wrongs had resulted in the visitation of awful crime.[24] The final verse was particularly evocative:

> Dank roofs, dark entries, closely-clustered walls,
> Murder-inviting nooks, death-reeking gutters,
> A boding voice from your foul chaos calls,
> When will men heed the warning that it utters?
> There floats a phantom on the slum's foul air,
> Shaping, to eyes which have the gift of seeing,
> Into the Spectre of that loathly lair.
> Face it – for vain is fleeing!
> Red-handed, ruthless, furtive, unerect,
> 'Tis murderous Crime – the Nemesis of Neglect!

The poem was accompanied by a most evocative illustration; it depicted a translucent phantom floating through a slum alley, large knife drawn, staring out like some form of supernatural predator, its eyes piercing and its jaw hanging loose in a horrifying gape. The left hand was extended out with the bony fingers posed into a claw. On its forehead was the word 'CRIME'. This illustration was without doubt the most striking image from those fearful times – a perfect embodiment of the Whitechapel 'fiend', a product of hell. This was echoed in descriptions in other limbs of the sensationalist press:

A nameless reprobate – half beast, half man – is at large, who is daily gratifying his murderous instincts on the most miserable and defenceless classes of the community ... The ghoul-like creature who stalks through the streets of London, stalking down his victim like a Pawnee Indian, is simply drunk with blood, and he will have more.

Here then was not a man but a creature of the night, conjuring images of ghouls or vampires to inflame the superstitious Victorian imagination. It was reports like the one above that caused Mary Burridge of Blackfriars to collapse in a fit and die. Elizabeth Sodo was another possible casualty – suffering depression and having become increasingly distressed and agitated by the reporting of the murders, she hanged herself from the stairwell at her home in Hanbury Street on the morning of 11 October.[25]

Following the murder of Mary Kelly, the 17 November edition of the *Penny Illustrated Paper*, which had included the depictions of men with black bags, unwittingly contributed to the most notable iconography of the mythical Ripper. The illustrator had obviously been influenced by George Hutchinson's description of the gentleman seen with Mary on the morning of her murder:

Description age about 34 or 35. height 5ft6 complexion pale, dark eyes and eye lashes slight moustache, curled up each end, and hair dark, very surley looking dress long dark coat, collar and cuffs trimmed astracan. And a dark jacket under. Light waistcoat dark trousers dark felt hat turned down in the middle. Button boots and gaiters with white buttons. Wore a very thick gold chain white linen collar. Black tie with horse shoe pin. Respectable appearance walked very sharp.[26]

Whereas some illustrators attempted to show the man as described, the version in the *Penny Illustrated Paper* revealed a certain amount of artistic licence; it showed Mary Kelly entering 13 Miller's Court with a 'gentleman' tall enough to be looking down on her. He was sporting a distinguished moustache, suggesting grandeur but, more importantly, he wore a top hat, a long coat and was carrying a bag. This was the first depiction of Jack the Ripper in the iconic form that so many recognize today. The following year, clairvoyant Stuart Cumberland's *Mirror* article did pretty much the same thing, and the accompanying illustration, showing a head-and-shoulders portrait of a 'toff', with delicate features and a 'chimney-pot hat', suggested again that the Whitechapel murderer was not of the poorer class, but from a more privileged background. Lyttleton Forbes Winslow, that disgraced theorist, said as much in his letter to the press in September 1888.[27] A correspondent from the *Evening News* went visiting lodging houses and interviewed some of the lodgers, one of whom believed that 'the murderer was a "toff" and deserved to get off' just for clearing the streets of prostitutes.[28] The idea had not gained much currency at the time, but the concept of the upper classes visiting the East End, or 'slumming', as it was known, was very in vogue:

> The most intense amusement has been caused among all classes of the London world by the arrest of Sir George Arthur on suspicion of being the Whitechapel murderer. Sir George is a young baronet holding a captaincy in the regiment of Royal Horse Guards, and is a member of most of the leading clubs in town. He is also a well-known amateur actor, and was a great friend of the late Prince Leopold.
>
> Since the past few weeks the old mania for 'slumming' in Whitechapel has become fashionable again. Every night scores of young men who have never been to the East end in their lives prowl around the neighbourhood in which the murders were committed, talking with the frightened women and pushing their way into overcrowded lodging houses.[29]

By the time the Whitechapel murders had run their course, the attributes of a mythical Jack the Ripper had already begun to form. These attributes, which would lie dormant for decades, suggested not a deranged lunatic or crazed butcher, nor a volatile sailor or homicidal syphilitic, but a sinister, calculating and almost gentrified stalker. With developing overtones of the supernatural, Jack was becoming a 'character', already poised for exploitation, set against a backdrop that verged on the apocalyptic:

Horror ran throughout the land. Men spoke of it with bated breath, and pale lipped women shuddered as they read the dreadful details. People afar off smelt blood, and the superstitious said that the skies had been of a deeper red that autumn.[30]

17.

The Lodger and Other Stories

The idea that Jack the Ripper was a solitary man who lodged in the East End and kept himself to himself had a number of contemporary points of reference. The strange case of the 'Batty Street Lodger', where a mysterious tenant left a blood-stained shirt for his landlady to clean, only never to return to his lodgings, was one. Lyttleton Forbes Winslow's suspect, G. Wentworth Bell Smith, with his obsession with religious tracts and peculiar overnight excursions, was another. A third was Nicolai Wassili (or Vassili or Vasilyef), a suspect suggested by Richard K. Fox, a journalist with the *National Police Gazette*.

According to Fox, Wassili was a financially self-sufficient member of the fanatical 'Shorn' sect which condemned sexual relations, yet had a faction which devoted itself to violence. After the Russian Orthodox Church attempted to suppress the sect, Wassili went into exile in Paris and there attempted to continue his work by trying to convert prostitutes, largely unsuccessfully. Apparently, he became infatuated with a young woman who rejected his attentions and, reeling from this rebuff, he chose to 'save' prostitutes by killing them, committing five murders in the space of a fortnight. He was subsequently put into an asylum in 1872 but on his release in January 1888 he declared his intention of going to London. Wassili had actually been mentioned in the international press during the period of the murders,[1] apparently lodged among the underclass of the East End and pored over religious tracts in his rooms before scouring the streets for the 'fallen'. He was known as 'the Avenger'.[2]

As the daughter of a French barrister, Marie Belloc may well have been familiar with the Wassili case. In January 1911, under the pen-name of Mrs Belloc-Lowndes (she had by then married Frederick Lowndes), she published a story in *McLure's Magazine*[3] entitled 'The Lodger'. Despite having shades of G. Wentworth Bell Smith and not a little of Nicolai Wassili, the idea for the story actually came from a chance encounter at a dinner where Marie was told by a lady sitting next to her about a mysterious lodger they had had many years before, his behaviour generating suspicion that he may have had some-thing to do with the Whitechapel murders. She later turned the tale into a novel, published in 1913, which helped turn the Ripper story into a classic melodrama which would subsequent-ly provide a rich vein of fictional interpretation, particularly in film.

'The Lodger' tells the story of Mr and Mrs Bunting, who own a house in Marylebone Road and who, at the start of the story, are suffering grave financial problems. However, their fortunes appear to change when they take on a new lodger, the enigmatic Mr Sleuth, who pays them handsomely for the use of their upstairs rooms. By this time, a series of horrific murders have taken place across London, the killer leaving a 'calling card' at each one and calling himself 'the Avenger'. Despite the peculiar nature of their new tenant, the Buntings are happy in their new-found security. Mr Sleuth spends his time poring over and reciting from the Bible and a concord-ance, particularly on issues of drink and women, for which he has an obvious distaste. Most notable is his habit of leaving the house in the early hours of the morning and creeping back in before the Buntings have risen. It predictably transpires that Mr Sleuth is indeed 'the Avenger', casting a strange influence over the household.

The story is loaded with melodrama and borrows heavily from the real events of 1888: the name of the local detective who visits the household frequently is Joe Chandler, which also happened to be the name of the first police officer at the scene of Annie Chapman's murder. 'The Avenger' commits a double murder, and the newspapers report on the potential use of bloodhounds. Mrs Bunting's occasional 'turns' suggest, as the lodger continues to maintain an increasingly malevolent hold over the home, that there are perhaps darker forces at work.

What is worthy of note is the description given of Mr Sleuth on his first appearance at the door of the Buntings' home:

> On the top of the three steps which led up to the door, there stood the long, lanky figure of a man, clad in an Inverness cape and an old-fashioned top hat. He waited a few seconds blinking at her, perhaps dazzled by the light of the gas in the passage. Mrs Bunting's trained perception told her at once that this man, odd as he looked, was a gentleman, belonging by birth to the class with whom her former employment had brought her in contact.

He also possesses a bag to which he seems attached to the point of paranoia. It is a classic description of the mythical Jack the Ripper, set in print decades before it would become the standard.

As a rapidly developing symbol of fear, the Ripper provided a rich vein to tap into for film-makers and the story of 'The Lodger' would become a most exploitable tale for them. His first appearance on celluloid was in a nightmare sequence in Paul Leni's expressionist *Waxworks* (or *Das Wachsfigurenkabinett*).[4] His appearance was a peripheral one, but the character was blessed with a disturbing presence, marking him out as an emerging motif of unease and psychological dread. But it was that master of suspense Alfred Hitchcock who first brought 'The Lodger' to the screen in his first directorial outing, aged only twenty-six.[5] The film was subtitled *A Story of the London Fog*, drawing heavily on the original storyline and starred matinee idol Ivor Novello in the title role. It was filled with gloomy set-pieces of London locations, shrouded in foggy darkness save for the hint of dim street lighting, close-ups of faces expressing terror and, of course, the overpoweringly sinister portrayal of the lodger himself. His first appearance became a truly iconic image: Mrs Bunting opens the door of her home to reveal the figure of a man dressed in a long coat and tall hat and carrying a bag, with the swirling menace of a London fog in the background.

Expressionist cinema had another crack at the Ripper story in 1928 with Georg Pabst's *Die Büchse der Pandora* or *Pandora's Box*.[6] This was essentially a remake of *Lulu*, a morality tale which had its roots in a play first penned by Frank Wedekind in 1893 and which was subsequently filmed in 1917 and 1923. Lulu was a 'good-time girl' or vamp whose loose living would culminate in a final encounter with a man considered to be the epitome of evil, namely Jack the Ripper. Her resulting death is represented as some sort of 'wages of sin'. *Lulu* would later go on to be a popular production, even being made into a successful musical, and variations on its story have become the most filmed fictional treatment of the Ripper story.

Similarly, so successful was the impact of *The Lodger* and the brooding menace it created that the film was remade numerous times – and with variations in content – over the ensuing decades: Novello reprised his role in *The Phantom Fiend* (1932), which was followed in 1944 by *The Lodger, Room to Let* (1950) and *Man in the Attic* (1954) with Jack Palance. The frequency of these movies indicated a growing schism between myth and reality, as screenwriters began to mould Jack the Ripper, or variations of him, into a horror genre character, something which transformed the Whitechapel murderer into a character of fiction. The same had happened with Dracula: Bram Stoker's vampire count, created in 1897, *was* fiction of course, an amalgam of various influences, predominantly Eastern European vampire legends and ancient superstitions about shape-shifters such as werewolves. But beginning with Bela Lugosi's definitive portrayal of the sinister aristocratic bloodsucker in the 1930s, later reinforced by Christopher Lee's numerous films thereafter, the movie industry very quickly produced an iconic visual interpretation of him that became set in stone. The same would happen to Jack the Ripper in the eponymously titled 1959 film by Robert S. Baker.[7]

Jack the Ripper was essentially a reinterpreted version of the 'Dr Stanley' theory put forward by Leonard Matters thirty years earlier. The Ripper kills prostitutes in revenge for the death of his son, who contracted venereal disease from one woman in particular. As the Ripper approaches each victim, he asks, 'Are you Mary Clarke?' Visually, he is the archetype of all subsequent Ripper depictions: silhouetted in the gloom as a tall, aristocratic gentleman wearing a top hat and cloak and carrying a black Gladstone bag. In a sensational trailer for the film, London was described as 'a city torn apart by fear and hate as the mob howled for the blood of the human monster Scotland Yard could never catch!'

So Jack the Ripper, the horror 'superstar', was born, complete with foggy claustrophobic period settings, glamorous victims and theatrical violence. The visual image of the murderer was well and truly in place, and it would be hard to find any depictions of the Ripper after this film was released which did not conform to that type. One could argue that screenwriter Jimmy Sangster and wardrobe supervisor Jack Verity created the ultimate 'Jack the Ripper'.

Now a media icon, the Ripper was deemed a suitable subject for other popular art forms, notably popular music. In the early 1960s, David 'Screaming' Lord Sutch released 'Jack the Ripper', a lolloping chunk of British rhythm and blues, which was little more than a novelty song, made even more absurd by Sutch's public appearances when performing it. Clad in the now accepted garb of the 'toff', wielding a black bag and knife, Sutch would scream out the lyrics to his audience, occasionally pushing his grotesquely made-up face towards an unsuspecting female member of the audience at just the right moment to unlock the still-underlying fear of the Whitechapel murderer. The song would often be the finale of his stage show, giving him the opportunity to present a performance that wasn't just grisly, but tipped over the edge into what could be considered bad taste. Not only would he portray a staged evisceration during the song, but he would also produce a fake severed head with real offal hanging from it, which he would then wave in the faces of the girls in the front row. If the venue was large enough he would throw larger pieces of offal into the audience; 'that always sent them running for the exits like rabbits,' said Sutch in his autobiography.[8] The song would be re-released several times over the years (including a disco version in 1977) and would later be one of many songs using the Ripper as a theme, including those by Link Wray (1959), Judas Priest (1976), Thin Lizzy (1980), Morrissey (1992), Nick Cave and the Bad Seeds (1992) and the White Stripes (2004), among others.

The 1960s had obviously seen a resurgence of interest in Jack the Ripper; Tom Cullen's and Robin Odell's respected books had been published almost simultaneously.[9] While they concentrated on giving the true story of the Whitechapel murders, fictional Jack was soon to meet his fictional nemesis in the form of Arthur Conan Doyle's eminent detective Sherlock Holmes in the film *A Study in Terror*.[10] Considered to be an underrated piece of Ripper cinema, it was not only the first film to pit Holmes against the Whitechapel fiend, but was also the first to bring the names of the real victims to the movie-going public. In fact all the major victims were included, and even Emma Smith made an appearance. With *A Study in Terror*, Jack the Ripper moved into the realms of a chronologically versatile fictional character and would later be seen crossing boundaries of time and even space. Paramount's cult sci-fi series *Star Trek* gave the Ripper a place in the wider universe when he became entangled with the crew of the USS *Enterprise* in 1967.[11]

The episode 'Wolf in the Fold'[12] was written by Robert Bloch, a writer notable for penning *Psycho*, which formed the basis of Alfred Hitchcock's most famous film, released in 1960. But he had also written a short story called 'Yours Truly, Jack the Ripper' in 1943, which essentially dealt with the concept that the Ripper was still alive and willing to kill again almost sixty years after his initial reign of terror.[13] By bringing Jack the Ripper into the realms of science fiction in *Star Trek*, Bloch did something that, with hindsight, is quite profound. The plot centres around the existence of 'Beratis', 'Kesla' and 'Redjac', all names for an ancient entity that has intense hatred for the life of women. The *Enterprise* computer tells the crew that

Beratis (of Rigel IV), and Kesla (of Deneb II) are names given to the unknown identities of serial killers on those planets. The computer suggests that Redjac may have been responsible for other killings on Earth, namely seven women in Shanghai in 1932 and five similar murders in Kiev in 1974. It also reports eight murders of women in the Martian Colonies in 2105 and ten on Alpha Eridani II in 2156. But importantly, Redjac (as 'Red Jack') was Jack the Ripper on Earth in 1888.

What is fascinating about this concept is that Bloch, not content with suggesting that the Ripper was still around in the 1940s, puts forth the notion that Jack the Ripper, as a collective equivalent of violence and fear, has *always* been around and always will be. One of the many reasons the Ripper legend persists is that no matter how many people try to name him or explain him, he remains almost an 'entity', the lurker in the shadows, the sum of all our dread and anxieties, a universal embodiment of fear, past, present and future.[14]

Science fiction can often be that cerebral, whereas horror, especially in the movie genre, can often be happy to go for the more base instincts. This would explain how the Ripper was treated by later film-makers, spurred on by the relaxation of censorship in the late 1960s. Mainstream films now pushed the boundaries of what was considered acceptable content, particularly in the areas of sex and violence. Movies such as *A Clockwork Orange* (1971), *Straw Dogs* (1971), *The Exorcist* (1973) and others created great controversy, and the British horror genre, spearheaded by Hammer Films, was now competing against productions that could outdo them in terms of sensationalism. Hammer adjusted its output accordingly.

In 1971, they combined two great Victorian gothic characters, the Ripper and Mr Hyde, to produce the camp and sexualized *Dr Jekyll and Sister Hyde*.[15] In a bizarre twist on Robert Louis

Stevenson's 1886 story, Dr Jekyll discovers the elixir of life, for which he requires female hormones taken from cadavers initially supplied by the grave robbers Burke and Hare. Regular experimentation with the resulting potion causes Jekyll to not only become Hyde, but also to change gender. Having to murder young girls to ensure a regular supply of hormones, Jekyll abhors his actions, but Mrs Hyde begins to enjoy it and, struggling to stabilize his personality (and gender), Jekyll goes all out to commit one last murder. The film could be seen as the apotheosis of bad Ripper mythology, throwing into the pot nearly every crass preconception associated with it, especially with the appearance of a poster which reads:

WANTED! IN CONNECTION WITH THE WHITECHAPEL MURDERS. Police wish to interview a person described by various witnesses as A TALL MAN WEARING A TALL HAT AND A DARK CLOAK.

Enough said.

The same year saw the release of Hammer's *Hands of the Ripper*, an altogether different movie, which employed yet another new twist;[16] the Ripper's daughter commits the murders as a result of mental traumas acquired after witnessing the killing of her mother by her father as a child. A wholly more sensible film than Hammer's offering, it still revelled in its licence to depict gore, despite the promise of more mature themes, as a psychiatrist attempts to find the causes of the daughter's behaviour. Here are shades of the 'Jill the Ripper' idea favoured by Conan Doyle, Lord Godolphin Osborne, William Stewart and Edwin Woodhall; however, the story behind the killer's motivation stands alone.

As the Ripper enjoyed a sudden increase in public profile in the mid-1970s BBC TV's *The Two Ronnies*, a popular comedy show featuring Ronnie Barker and Ronnie Corbett, screened a short mini-series entitled 'The Phantom Raspberry Blower of Old London Town'.[17] It was written by Spike Milligan and Barker (credited as 'a gentleman') and was an obvious parody of the Ripper scare of 1888. In this case, however, the miscreant would merely utter flatulent noises (or 'raspberries'), which would leave his victims in a shocked stupor. The whole idea was as much a spoof on the perceived prudish sensibilities of Victorian society as it was a Ripper farce. The eponymous villain was seen as the top-hatted 'gentleman' and the skit was filled with set-pieces from the now-established Ripper mythology, particularly London fog. In one episode cliffhanger, the Prince of Wales is considered as the phantom after a terrible realization by his own mother, the queen. 'The Phantom Raspberry Blower', by parodying the popular myths surrounding the mystery of the Whitechapel murders, showed just how 'Jack the Ripper' had become so distanced from reality that it could even be turned into comedy of the silliest kind without any problem.

Perhaps the honour of the most famous modern filmed accounts of the Whitechapel murders must fall to the 1988 two-part TV series *Jack the Ripper* and the movie blockbuster *From Hell*, both of which seem to have attempted to redress the story with some much needed drama and gravitas. The former,[18] starring Michael Caine as Inspector Frederick Abberline and Lewis Collins as George Godley, was a joint effort between Thames Television in the UK and Lorimar in the United States. The big-budget production was promoted as a retelling of the Whitechapel murders story in which the name of the Ripper would be revealed. Such deductions were allegedly aided by direct information from the files of Scotland Yard and the Home Office. Several endings were to be filmed, so that even the cast would not know the result until the screening.

Unfortunately, what eventually transpired was merely a rehash of the continually popular 'royal conspiracy', which for students and researchers into the case was a theory that had been put to bed. It was the second outing of this particular plot (the first being 1979's eminently enjoyable Sherlock Holmes picture *Murder by Decree*, featuring Christopher Plummer and James Mason as Holmes and Watson)[19] and featured a capable cast which included Armand Assante, Ray McAnally, Susan George, Jane Seymour, with Lysette Anthony starring as a typically pretty Mary Kelly. Several previously ignored characters from the Ripper legend also featured – Robert Lees, George Lusk and even the actor Richard Mansfield had major parts to play in the story. Despite becoming a subsequent favourite for many 'Ripperologists', it was rather a disappointment, occasionally marred by a tacky script and some choice overacting. Lusk was portrayed as a bellowing revolutionary, Lees was a gibbering aesthete, and Michael Caine's alcoholic Abberline often launched into vocal histrionics without the support of decent lines. Despite impressive viewer ratings, critics were none too impressed. One contemporary commentator described it as 'particularly embarrassing'. Poor old Michael Caine and numerous other stars must have wondered what they had let themselves in for in this made-for-Americans western-style mauling of the story.'[20] Time has been kind to the series, however. Many students of the Ripper crimes say it is their favourite, some even declaring that seeing it in their youth first ignited their interest in the subject.

From Hell, released in 2001,[21] trod familiar ground, the 'royal conspiracy', but was influenced by a graphic novel of the same name by Alan Moore and Eddie Campbell.[22] With its name derived from the chilling opening of the 'Lusk Letter', it was much more than just a rehash of Stephen Knight's theory. This take on the 'highest in the land' story was laced with adult themes of sex and graphic violence, and deep significance was given to the mythologies of London itself, wonderfully demonstrated during an epic journey around the capital by Gull and his coachman, John Netley. Influenced by the studies of London 'psychogeography' by writers such as Iain Sinclair and Peter Ackroyd, this lengthy sequence took inspiration from ancient pagan rites, old legends and ley-lines, turning the very fabric of London into an instrument of occult intent. The resulting murders meant more to Gull than just saving the face of the Royal Family. Eddie Campbell's visuals ably complemented the gritty nature of the work, with an attention to detail in both the characters and places. But *From Hell* was too complex to be done any justice by the movie industry. There was just too much in it. Moore's graphic novel would have to be greatly simplified (and toned down) to be a success on the big screen, an unfortunate necessity, as the original story was loaded with concepts that would have expanded the film beyond the jaded royal cover-up plot.

Despite the work that went into the visual quality of the movie and the all-star cast of Johnny Depp, Robbie Coltrane, Ian Holm and Heather Graham, it was really just a big-budget rehash of the Michael Caine series with better production values and a more disturbing undercurrent – and significantly more gore. Johnny Depp's Inspector Abberline was now depicted not as a drunk, but as an opium addict afflicted with psychic visions, which seemingly combined him with contemporary clairvoyant Robert Lees. Depp's ethereal take on the good inspector no doubt compensated for the screenplay's trimming of the mystical themes in the original graphic novel.

Ian Holm's William Gull also helped to chivvy along the darker mythologies of Jack the Ripper, atmospherically summed up by the line 'One day men will look back and say I gave birth to the twentieth century.'

It is telling that the most recent foray of the Ripper on celluloid – at the time of writing – should hark back to the earliest days in the medium, with a reworking of 'The Lodger'. A film of that name was released in 2009, starring Alfred Molina as Joe Chandler,[23] an altogether modern interpretation of Mrs Belloc-Lowndes's classic, with plenty of references to the original story, but this time featuring the activities of a Ripper 'copycat'. With this interpretation of what could be considered a well-worn tale suggesting that 'Jack the movie star' had come full circle, it would be down to television to reinvent the Ripper drama, a feat it achieved with no little success. Looking at the crimes from a fresh dramatic angle, ITV in the UK screened a three-part drama series called *Whitechapel*,[24] a story pitting the wits of a new inspector against a serial killer who was quite literally emulating the Ripper, including murder sites, dates of the crimes and injuries. It was a wholly enjoyable affair and gave plenty of nods to the real Ripper case, but productively kept fact and fiction separate. Progressive and modern-thinking Inspector Chandler, with much to prove, is thrown into the ring with a hardened group of detectives whose cynicism and lack of 'political correctness' threaten to undermine their professional relationship. When the horrific murder of a community police officer throws up few leads, Inspector Chandler battles against the set ways of his colleagues until a Ripper tour guide comes forward to explain that the killer has copied Jack the Ripper's first murder and that they should expect more.

All the characters from the series were named after real

personalities from the events of 1888, and so we have Joseph Chandler, Mary Bousfield, Frances Coles, James Kent and Edward Buchan, to name but a few. Buchan is the tour guide and 'Ripperologist' who helps the police in the case using his deep knowledge of true crime, which comes good despite an initially hostile reaction. Some of the scenes were actually filmed in the East End, and throughout the drama we await the next discovery, each one an echo of the original crimes, such as the arrival of a kidney in the post and the discovery of an earlier murder bearing the hallmark of Martha Tabram's death.

Whitechapel was successful enough to spawn several sequels, each one dealing with cases that emulated famous East End crimes, such as the activities of infamous gangsters the Kray Twins and the Ratcliffe Highway murders of 1811. Though this could be seen as stretching the concept a little too far, the original series worked for several reasons. The characters were well defined, and the interplay between the different stereotypes (uptight inspector, rough and ready detectives and the eccentric Ripperologist) created a unique chemistry. The concept also did not insult the intelligence of its audience; the trick of keeping fact and fiction separate was exceptionally well executed, giving the seasoned Ripper student plenty of inward chuckles as in-jokes presented themselves and allowing the less informed viewer the dignity of not having to be spoonfed hackneyed iconography and spurious claims of a solution to the original murders in order to ensure they enjoyed the offering. In the words of Andrew Billen in *The Times* following the airing of episode two of the first series, 'Slowly, the show is making Ripperologists of us all, as Jack's "canonical" murders are separated from the ones he actually committed. It is all in the worst possible taste and bloody good fun.'[25]

METROPOLITAN POLICE.

Fac-simile of Letter and Post Card received by Central News Agency.

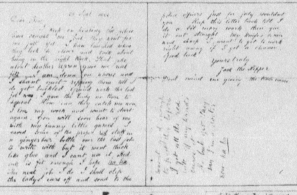

Any person recognising the handwriting is requested to communicate with the nearest Police Station.

Metropolitan Police Office,
3rd October, 1888.

Printed by M°Corquodale & Co. Limited, "The Armory," Southwark.

18. Police poster featuring the 'Dear Boss' letter and 'Saucy Jacky' postcard, circulated in October 1888: one of many such handbills that were circulated at the time to encourage assistance from the public.

19. Sir Charles Warren, chief commissioner of the Metropolitan Police, 1886–8.

20. Dr Robert Anderson, newly appointed assistant commissioner at the time of the Whitechapel murders.

21. Inspector Frederick Abberline: a sketch from *Toby* magazine. No confirmed photograph of this important officer has yet been located.

22. Chief Inspector Donald Swanson in later years. His important role in 1888 was to oversee the reports and investigations into the murders.

23. Sergeant William Thick, taken from an H-division group shot. Known as 'Johnny Upright', he was described as 'a holy terror to the local lawbreakers'.

24. Sir Melville Macnaghten, who became assistant chief constable of the Metropolitan Police CID in 1889.

25. Police photograph of early suspect Jacob Isenschmid, known by some as 'the mad pork butcher'.

26. Roslyn D'Onston Stephenson, an early theorist and latter-day suspect.

27. 'Dr' Francis Tumblety. This interesting character was suspected of the crimes at the time and was a prominent figure in the American press, but his prominence as a police suspect did not come until the early 1990s.

28. Montague John Druitt. His body was found in the Thames on the last day of 1888 and was seemingly favoured by Melville Macnaghten as the Ripper.

29. Sir William Gull, physician-in-ordinary to Queen Victoria and a linchpin of the 'royal conspiracy' theory.

30. Prince Albert Victor, first suggested as a potential suspect in 1970.

31. Artist Walter Sickert. Although implicated in the 'royal conspiracy', Sickert has also been put forward as the Ripper in several other theories.

32. Sketch of Mary Kelly leading her murderer into her room at
13 Miller's Court, from the *Penny Illustrated Paper*, 17 November 1888.
The earliest depiction of the iconic Ripper.

33. A still from Hitchcock's 1927 classic film *The Lodger*: an image laden
with Ripper iconography – tall hat, cloak, black bag and fog.

In response, BBC TV's *Ripper Street* again approaches the crimes from an original perspective. Despite the rather odd title, the series is set in April 1889, the year after the original murders are deemed to have ended. When more women are murdered on the streets of Whitechapel, the police begin to wonder if the killer has returned. The plot centres on the characters of Inspector Edmund Reid (Matthew McFadyen) and his sidekick Sergeant Bennett Drake (Jerome Flynn), each episode presenting them with a stand-alone crime to test their powers of investigation. A gritty production which also deals with heavier themes such as bare-knuckle boxing, early pornography and prostitution, the series features cameos from other real characters in addition to Reid, such as George Lusk and Commissioner James Monro. Like *Whitechapel* before it, it was a slow burner, with critics warming to it as characters were allowed to develop. In the *Guardian* Sam Wollaston was guarded in his opinion of yet another Ripper-based offering, saying, 'It would be easy to be negative about *Ripper Street*. Do we really need more on a story that's been not just done to death, but then carved up, and had its insides torn out?' but concluded his review stating, 'the script is real, alive and human. It's beautifully performed, and beautiful to look at – stylish, and stylised. The bare-knuckle fight scenes are brutal and memorable. It's proper, character-based crime drama, gripping, and yes – I'm afraid – ripping as well.'[26] What Wollaston nearly failed to recognize was that *Ripper Street*, and *Whitechapel* before it, may well have instigated a new era of fictional interpretations of the Jack the Ripper story: smaller productions with tangential stories which television is perfect to project, bereft of the trappings of Hollywood gimmickry, the writing focusing on real characters rather than stereotypes and jaded interpretations of Ripper mythologies that, in terms of drama, passed their shelf-life decades ago. It remains to be seen if this stays the case as more series of both productions are commissioned.

As true crime stories go, no other offers such a blank canvas of creativity for the entertainment world as Jack the Ripper, even though, in the words of Denis Miekle, 'the screen image of Jack the Ripper has undergone no great revision in the 75 years between Hitchcock's "The Lodger" and the Hughes Brothers' "From Hell" '.[27] As well as the rich stream of film and television, every year amateur theatre companies perform their own interpretations of the story, some using drama, others using song. Musical interpretations are popular, with some performed on stage, or professionally recorded for distribution like any other release. Artists create vivid renderings of the victims, street scenes and, of course, Jack himself, using traditional methods, computer-generated imagery, installations or conceptual art. The moving picture may have the most influence and exposure, generating new impressions and reinforcing established ones, but one thing is certain: it is a subject that will continue to inspire indefinitely. In the same way that the mystery attracts theorists attempting to put a name to the killer, so it attracts those who wish to interpret the story in their own creative way, unencumbered by facts and figures, limits of conjecture or the burden of proof.

But it is a theme that is not for everybody.

18.

A Question of Taste

Because Jack the Ripper has been seized upon so enthusiastically by the public as an entertainment form of some magnitude, it is often forgotten that the story of the Whitechapel murders is a very real one. The women who were dramatically put to death by his knife had family, brothers, sisters, sons and daughters, and their descendants vary from knowing of their historic lineage to having no idea whatsoever. Some of those that do know have chosen to embrace that lineage, whereas others have kept it to themselves. The man himself may be buried in some unmarked grave, once mourned by family or friends, who perhaps had no idea of his true nature. His descendants may go about their daily lives in the twenty-first century, sharing his surname or DNA, yet blissfully unaware of the terrible family secret that in all probability will remain as such for ever.

The lack of a culpable perpetrator and the passage of time have seen to it that the reality of those fearful nights has become dulled, and we have become anaesthetized to the suffering and brutality which form the backbone of the Jack the Ripper mystery. But as the world seemingly relishes the escapism and visceral entertainment frequently offered by the Ripper story, there are those who refuse to accept that the brutal murder of East End prostitutes can be anything other than a shocking episode reflecting the all-too-real concept of 'man's inhumanity to man'. It is a wholly understandable belief.

It is interesting to note that for many decades after the murders the general approach to the subject of Jack the Ripper was not particularly bound up in controversy. Newspaper articles tended to focus on the overriding mystery, devoid of the sensationalism which preceded and, in a different way, would follow later. As we have seen, the early movie depictions of the Ripper tended to sidestep the reality, often portraying Ripper-like characters such as Mrs Belloc-Lowndes's lodger 'Mr Sleuth' without actually saying that they were the very real Whitechapel murderer. The 1959 film *Jack the Ripper* could be seen as being responsible for pushing Jack into the role of super-villain, complete with costume, murdering the real victims and inspiring a fear that really did exist in 1888. It appeared that the Whitechapel murders were at last being used for entertainment in a new and blatant way, inviting the audience to actually enjoy a grisly spectacle that actually happened and within the memory of some who still lived. In the original theatre trailer for the film, the voice over exclaimed:

> Now you'll see the sensational story from the files of Scotland Yard revealed in all its shocking scope! Girls the Ripper marked for death caught in the grip of uncontrolled hysteria! The wild gay nights of the turbulent City, shadowed by the blood lust of the most terrifying killer of all time!

As the twentieth century rolled on, 'the Ripper' became a generic label for any serial murderers who exhibited the viciousness of the original. The earliest was Peter Kurten, the 'Dusseldorf Ripper', who killed women, men and children out of a yearning for revenge on a society that had given him nothing but hardship and indignity. He wanted to outrage and was motivated by the urge to shock and appal through his gruesome acts of bloodletting. He gained sadistic sexual pleasure from his crimes and even wrote letters to the authorities, so intoxicated was he by the Ripper legend. Kurten was sentenced to death and was said to have been gratified when he was told that he may be able to hear, for a tiny moment, the sound of his blood gushing from the stump of his neck after his beheading by guillotine; 'That would be the pleasure to end all pleasures,' he said.[1] Interestingly, a rarely seen film about Peter Kurten, 1964's *The Vampire of Dusseldorf*, was criticized for turning him into some sort of anti-hero whilst all but ignoring the real impact of his murders, a situation that had been de rigueur in the Ripper movie genre for years.

Twenty-eight-year-old RAF cadet Gordon Cummins strangled and mutilated women during the blackouts in London during the Blitz, using a variety of implements, from a razor blade to a can opener. Cummins preyed on vulnerable, lonely women during the difficult days of the Second World War, and the papers blessed him with the familiar-sounding sobriquet of the 'Blackout Ripper'. Again, in London in the early 1960s, the Thames Towpath murders saw the strangulation and sexual abuse of women by an uncaught killer dubbed 'Jack the Stripper' on account of his habit of removing the clothes of his victims before seemingly performing sexual acts on the bodies.

In 1978 the murder and disembowelment of a nine-year-old girl outside the Russian mining village of Shakhty was the first in a series of shocking murders of children (and some adults) which took place around the provincial city of Rostov. The perpetrator was Andrei Chikatilo, whose subsequent slayings often featured disembowelment, organ extraction and, in some cases, cannibalism. Brought to trial in 1992, the 'Rostov Ripper' confessed to fifty-five killings, making him one of the worst serial murderers of all time.

Back in the United Kingdom, concern had been growing about the proliferation of sexual violence aimed at women during the 1970s. This was a seemingly long-overdue reassessment of the subject: sexual assaults by the 'Rapist of Tottenham' and the activities of the 'Cambridge Rapist'[2] were still a recent memory; lurid films with titles such as *Violation of the Bitch* and *Barbed Wire Dolls*[3] kept the idea of women as ripe for sexual and violent exploitation in the movie theatres. The final straw came with the murders committed by the infamous 'Yorkshire Ripper'.

October 1975 had seen the first in a series of brutal attacks and killings by Peter Sutcliffe, a lorry driver from Yorkshire, which for the next half-decade held the north of England in a state of terror. Many of the victims were prostitutes – Sutcliffe was particularly drawn to kill prostitutes apparently on the instruction of inner voices – and, as in 1888, they would have been vulnerable targets, but as the murder spree progressed it was apparent that no woman was safe on the streets of West Yorkshire. He was soon being referred to as 'the Ripper', a name that obviously had echoes of the distant past and suggested that fears associated with the original murderer had not abated. There were also several parallels between this case and the 1888 Ripper apart from the choice of prostitutes as victims. The West Yorkshire police were criticized for their apparent inability to catch the killer. Also, in 1978, letters signed 'Jack the Ripper' were sent to the police and the Manchester offices of the *Daily Mirror*, the phrasing of which were chillingly familiar, and, in an embrace of the modern age, the police also received a cassette recording. However, all these were eventually revealed to be hoaxes.[4]

Perhaps it took the very real case of Peter Sutcliffe to spark a reassessment of the original Ripper crimes, shrouded as they now were by fiction and mythology and invariably passed off as entertainment. Inspired by the events in Yorkshire and the publicity surrounding the discovery of Sutcliffe's thirteenth victim in November 1980, various action groups began to galvanize themselves into a nationwide campaign to declare that enough was enough and, as one spokesperson put it, 'to put across the message that violence against women is commonplace, and condoned by current attitudes, bolstered by the law'.[5]

The growth of such groups would take on considerable impetus as the centenary of the Whitechapel murders approached. In the meantime, Tower Hamlets, the London borough which contained Whitechapel and Spitalfields, made a proposition that, considering the approaching storm, was none too wise. In 1986, looking for an emblem to represent the Stepney Neighbourhood Committee, the council proposed to use a local landmark or personality in the design; ideas included the Whitechapel Bell Foundry (where 'Big Ben' was cast), the London Hospital or a fashion theme reflecting the East End rag trade. Strangely, Ronald Kray, half of the notorious gangster twins, and Jack the Ripper were also proposed. The idea of using Kray or – especially – the Ripper as a 'mascot' for a borough council sounds ludicrous to say the least, and a local spokesperson was reported as saying 'the themes listed are what's famous and infamous about Stepney. It's likely the neighbourhood committee will opt for a less controversial choice.'[6] It seems the spokesperson's guarded comments were the order of the day and neither Jack nor Ron made the final design. What the growing protestors made of this is unclear, but was Jack the Ripper really so iconic as to be accepted as an emblem for local government?

The protesters may have missed that peculiar Ripper

reference, but they certainly did not miss the centenary of the Whitechapel murders, which effectively started in 1987 with the publication of many books on the subject. Notably it was the press, once responsible for building up Jack the Ripper in the first place, that seemed dead set on demolishing the monster they had created in 1888. Choosing to review these books en masse, critics such as Christopher Hudson in the *Evening Standard* were obviously suffering from 'Ripper indigestion' already and could scarcely contain their contempt for the revived interest in the murders.

The authors themselves also came in for considerable derision, often being denounced as ghoulish fanatics or obsessives. Writing in the *Sunday Times*, Stephen Pile was certainly not backward in coming forward:

> More utter nonsense has been written about Jack the Ripper than any other figure, real or imagined. Next year marks the centenary of this total pervert and we shall never hear the end of it.
>
> The only real evidence they have got after 99 years of non-stop sleuthing is some bit of blood-stained pinny found three streets away and now lost. If you suggest that this might belong to someone else who simply cut a finger slicing jellied eels or whatever they eat in the East End, you are howled down as a dolt . . .
>
> From the start authors have manipulated the complete absence of any known facts to engineer sensational conclusions. And so a highly profitable industry was born.

With one eye on the promised Michael Caine mini-series, due to be broadcast in late 1988, Pile concluded: 'I do hope that Thames settles the question for ever because it means that all books on the subject can be shredded instantly and Ripperologists will have to find a proper job.'[7]

The release of the *Jack the Ripper* computer game in 1987 was fuel to the fire of journalists like Stephen Pile and also attracted some significant ire from the increasingly vocal protesters. The game (intended for the popular ZX Spectrum home computer) created outrage the moment it was released. It also established a precedent, being the first computer game to be given a British Board of Film Classification certificate. *Jack the Ripper* showed images of mutilated women – some with their legs apart and breasts exposed – and though the graphics were not as visually life-like as on today's computer games, they were deemed shocking enough to make the BBFC give an '18' rating. The idea behind the game was simple enough – you are accused of being the Ripper and must prove your innocence whilst solving the mystery of the killer's identity. Interestingly, the game was actually devised by women. One of the female creators was Marianne Scarlett, self-styled 'headmistress' of the 'Women of St Bride's' in Ireland, a bizarre 'school' where women over eighteen could live out a fantasy nineteenth-century life. She was unrepentant about the nature of her creation:

> As far as we're concerned this is a classic tale of a battle between good and evil set in Victorian London. In an age which doubts the existence of good and evil, we wished to present evil in a form so terrible and so real that no one could mistake it.[8]

The legend of Jack the Ripper was attracting the eccentric, perhaps, but with journalists attacking even those authors who were attempting for the most part to work responsibly around the case, the Ripper and all that surrounded him were now being tarred with the same 'tasteless' brush. But it was the Jack the Ripper pub that would feel the earliest effects of growing outrage at the centenary 'celebrations'. It is significant to note how attitudes had changed since 1975, when Bobby Wayman and Mickey Taheney opened their joint pub venture. The Ten Bells had been going through a downturn in fortunes – meths drinkers and petty thieves would use its chaotic upstairs rooms[9] – and it was in need of a serious revamp. Financing the refit themselves, Wayman and Taheney opened the Jack the Ripper to a small fanfare of jocular publicity. The *East London Advertiser* obliged with the necessary complimentary write-up, laced with the obligatory puns:

> New East End nightspot looks all set to be a rip-roaring success!
> It's got: Top-pop music plus DJ all night, every night; pretty barmaids; plush decor – with the accent on the pub's connections with the real Jack the Ripper.[10]

The redesigned interior was sumptuous, having been given an 'olde worlde atmosphere'. The walls were decorated with numerous photographs, documents and contemporary newspaper illustrations. Outside, a sign-written board listed the names of the victims from Tabram to Kelly, and the whole ensemble was finished off with the swing signs, depicting the essential top-hatted Ripper silhouetted in the London fog. As part of the opening promotions in May 1975, a local amateur dramatic group, touring a production called *Hunt the Ripper – or the Whitechapel Horror Show*, performed at the pub. According to press reviews, the highlight was when 'actress Lynne Suffolk, playing the part of a tart balances a pint of beer on her head wearing only bra and panties'.[11] Such frivolous treatment of the fates of the Whitechapel murder victims seems bizarre today, but it could be seen as a sign of the times. Some would say that the 1970s suffered a form of moral vacuum which by the centenary of 1988 had more or less been filled by the burgeoning popularity of 'political correctness'.

In 1987 it was the decision of Jack the Ripper managers Ernie and Yvonne Ostrowski to mark the centenary by selling T-shirts, postcards and even a blood-red drink called the 'Ripper Tipple' that sparked the backlash. These plans were immediately seized on by the group Women Against Violence Against Women (WAVAW), along with splinter group Action Against the Ripper Centenary (AARC), with members spending a great deal of time around Christmas 1987 collecting signatures for a petition to have the pub's name changed. Despite the managers' assurances that their 'celebration' was not intended to be tasteless, the campaigners found hefty support and, with pressure mounting, Truman's (who owned the pub and who were only a year away from closing down) had the name changed back to its original Ten Bells, just before the anniversary of the first Ripper murders. Although the pub still continued to display and sell its memorabilia, the anti-Ripper lobbyists appeared to have won their first battle.

Naturally, most of the publicity would be reserved for the autumn of 1988, when landmark dates would be crossed and media attention would be at its height. It would become a struggle between those who saw the murders as historical events which needed to be put into context responsibly and those who saw them as a vile piece of history that had no place in the enlightened late twentieth century. In the middle were those who still believed in mythical Jack.

Deborah Cameron's *Guardian* article, cited earlier, talked of the threat of sexualized murder in society:

The hopeless obsessive quest to unmask Jack the Ripper deflects our attention from what should be obvious: the extreme desires and fantasies which animate sexual killers are shared to some extent by a great many men, growing up as they do in a culture which promotes them, not least by its portrayal of murderers as heroes. If we want to do something about sexual murder, it's the culture and its attitudes that need to change.

This was what the WAVAW and AARC wanted to make understood, and the Ripper centenary came along at the right time to push home the message. The AARC particularly received a high profile throughout 1988 and was featured repeatedly in the national and local press. They were extremely forthright in their condemnation of the whole media circus, admittedly to the point where they seemed to be 'man-bashing' at times. The proposed release of Screaming Lord Sutch's 'Jack the Ripper' single in 1987, apparently to coincide with the centenary, sent Anne McMurdie, chief spokesperson for the ARRC, into a fit of rage, especially when it was discovered that a promotional video was to be shot in Whitechapel:

I am disgusted that Lord Sutch and his record company should even consider releasing something of such bad taste. It is simply endorsing male violence against women, further glorifying the Ripper who has become some sort of folk hero. As to filming it all on the original site, well that just shows no sensitivity at all to women. I am completely horrified and think it is sick. This is just men jumping on the bandwagon and trying to make money out of something that was an obscene event and should not be remembered fondly . . . We will do anything we can to have these, and all the books, posters and T-shirts also being produced by other money-grabbing men, banned.[12]

A protest march against male violence and the Ripper centenary (planned for September 1988 and running from Bethnal Green to the Ten Bells) was promoted in the *East London Advertiser*, which promptly got into a contretemps with the AARC by publishing a twelve-part series on the Ripper crimes.[13] As a result of these prominent articles, the *Advertiser* came under fire from the protestors:

> By printing the mortuary photograph of Polly Nichols and recounting explicit details of the mutilation she suffered, you are using the sexual murder of women to entertain and titillate your readership . . . when will journalists realise that they are contributing to the mass industry of glamorising a murderer?[14]

The photograph in question was one of several of the victims that had been recently rediscovered, allowing the public to see for the first time the faces of Mary Ann Nichols, Annie Chapman and Elizabeth Stride, as well as a second crime-scene image of Mary Kelly. The decision to publish these new images in the local and national press was a controversial one. One reader made her opinion very clear in the *Hackney Gazette*:

> I do not wish to see photographs of murdered women and cannot understand how their publication can be seen as anything but bad taste. Is it necessary to drag up 100-year-old male violence with such relish?[15]

The *Gazette*'s response was predictably polite:

> Our article neither glorified the crime nor dragged up male violence with relish – at least not on purpose. What the feature

attempted to do was publicise new evidence which coincided with the 100th anniversary of the Ripper murders.[16]

The demonstration, organized by the AARC, took place on Saturday 24 September 1988 and attracted considerable publicity. The *Hackney Gazette* stated that 'people who run guided tours of the murder scenes, writers who glorify the killings and people who think it's just an interesting story were the targets'. The focus of the 300-strong march was the Ten Bells pub, which, despite having been forced to change its name earlier in the year, was still exhibiting its Ripper memorabilia inside. The local press displayed headlines such as 'Women slam Ripper moneymakers' and 'Up in arms'.[17]

The AARC still found itself challenging long-held attitudes to the Ripper in December when the White Chapel Theatre Company staged a musical about the murders at a venue in Whitechapel Road. Objecting to songs such as 'The Ripper's Going to Get You (If You Don't Watch Out)', the busy protesters held a demonstration outside the theatre, issuing leaflets to the cast and audience saying that such entertainment 'adds glamour and mystique to these events. It serves to obscure the truth and is insulting'.[18]

What protesters were saying was effectively true: such frivolous depictions did indeed convert brutal murder into pantomime and mere 'harmless fun'. During the height of the centenary, East End prostitutes, who walked the same streets as their predecessors a hundred years before, claimed that some of their clients were requesting to be taken to the Ripper murder sites for sex. Despite finding these requests abhorrent, they duly capitalized on the situation and charged double. They did not mind having their photographs taken by tourists in return for money either![19]

Following the lead set by Madame Tussauds's 'Chamber of Horrors' back in 1980, the London Dungeon in Tooley Street, by London Bridge, opened its 'Jack the Ripper Experience' in 1993. Whereas there had been no protests in the Tussaud's case, this new, even gorier exhibit became the focus of attention for the Campaign Against Pornography (CAP), again demonstrating how times and attitudes had changed during the preceding decade. Their stance was identical to that of the WAVAW and AARC groups during the centenary, attacking the organizers of the exhibition for what they felt was the trivializing of sexual violence as entertainment and titillation. The London Dungeon's marketing manager was hard pressed to come back with a convincing argument:

> We have given careful consideration as to whether it should be a rose-tinted picture or a realistic one. We think we have done it in an unglamorous way. There's obviously an element of entertainment, but we believe there are many lessons to be learned from such horrific crimes.[20]

'Unglamorous' it most certainly was, and the Dungeon's graphic waxwork portrayals of the Ripper's freshly killed victims made for a particularly disturbing spectacle. What didn't help was the gift shop 'Ripper Mania', which sold T-shirts, mugs, hats and other merchandise emblazoned with a sinister man wielding a bloodstained knife. The snack bar was even named 'Ripper's Rapid Snacks', serving the 'Ripper steak sandwich', providing further evidence to the dissenters that the London Dungeon had gone too far.

Such was the confusion of principles which presented themselves to anybody who wanted to dip their toes into the controversial world of Jack the Ripper. The protest groups were attempting to change strongly ingrained ideas about violence against women, using these *particular* murders as a well-publicized fulcrum for raising awareness. But the creation of the mythical Jack had already preceded the centenary activities by many decades, and he was part of folklore as much as anything. Despite the few changes that resulted in their actions, groups like the AARC, WAVAW and Reclaim the Night would never be completely successful in their attempts to turn the world against the mythology of the Ripper. It would need to be something more considered and less 'rapid-response' to achieve that aim.

The 'Jack the Ripper and the East End' exhibition at the Museum in Docklands in 2008 reflected a welcome change in approach to the study of the Whitechapel murders which had been developing gradually since the centenary furore. For so long the Ripper story had been dominated by the media in increasingly outlandish movies, irresponsible populist journalism and the popular imagination of those who were merely content to soak up what that media spoon-fed them. The case of Jack the Ripper, as a subject, was bigger, more wide-ranging and more deserving of a proper evaluation than it had so far been allowed. Through the work of dedicated researchers, it had become a platform for studies into late Victorian social history, the history of law enforcement, immigration, culture and any number of related factors. It was the effect the murders had on these issues that made 'Ripperology' such an appealing area for research, something lost on the average tabloid-reader or movie-goer. And thus, in a world dominated by 'amateur' historians and crime enthusiasts, the Ripper came under the close scrutiny of academics, perhaps a little late in the game, but nonetheless giving the field a sheen of respectability that so many genuine authors had attempted to bestow upon it for decades.

The Jack the Ripper conferences in Britain and America had been bringing together like-minded enthusiasts from around the world since 1996, and London's own 'Cloak and Dagger Club'[21] had done likewise, both presenting guest speakers on a range of topics relating to the case. The internet, via *Casebook: Jack the Ripper* and other websites, had turned 'Ripperology' into a fast-paced research field which often threw new light on not just the case itself, but the events that were the cause and result of the murders. The world of academia duly took notice.[22]

The Museum in Docklands exhibition was therefore a product of that shift. Using artefacts from the Museum of London's own collection as well as original documents from the National Archives and private collectors, it produced an extremely impartial overview of the period and the crimes themselves. As well as items which demonstrated factors in the lives of East End dwellers at the time, the exhibition included notable paraphernalia from the Ripper case – original police statements, Ripper letters (including the 'Dear Boss' letter) and objects belonging to key figures in the investigation. The Macnaghten memoranda and the Maybrick Diary were present, as was Walter Sickert's painting *Jack the Ripper's Bedroom*, but the exhibition did not push any suspects.

Here was a genuine attempt to put the murders into their historical context to the point of being described by one reviewer as 'The History of the East End (by stealth)', as well as an attempt to dispel the wider myths, fictions and misconceptions. A series of lectures was undertaken, featuring established Ripper authors as well as East End historians, writers and academics. All the Whitechapel murder victims were represented, from Emma Smith to Frances Coles, and the final exhibit, a separate area where visitors could view the mortuary photographs through small windows (complete with warning), attempted at least to avoid the crass sensationalism of exhibits like the London Dungeon. Of course, on that score, there was a certain amount of protest from feminist groups; despite the unsensational, perhaps conciliatory nature of the project, it did not quite please everyone:

> I'd rather I hadn't looked at the cigarette card style, sepia photos of the victims that are displayed at the end of the exhibition. Each one is lined up along a starkly lit, white circular wall that forms a sort of round, mini-gallery. There is a warning on the outside, that some may find the crime scene photos disturbing. They certainly are images I could have done without putting into my head, and now they are an addition to all the other horrors that men inflict on women that I know far too much about. As I walked round the photos, with the name of each woman underneath, like some sort of ghoulish roll call, it felt like a memorial; an unfitting memorial. It made me think that perhaps we do need somewhere to remember our dead, to remember all our sisters fallen in a struggle that has been going on for far too long. But this place is not in a museum exhibition dedicated to one of their killers.
>
> When I left, I felt rather sullied, and found myself wondering what I'd been part of.[23]

The book published to accompany the exhibition[24] was a handsome, full-colour affair, featuring essays by a number of academics on different aspects of the case, a companion perhaps to *Jack the Ripper: Media, Culture, Diversity*, a similar, less glossy offering from the previous year.[25] Both took a fresh stance from an academic viewpoint, one that is instantly recognizable as being different from that of the conventional

'Ripperologist'. In fact the Ripper exhibition tie-in book actually had very little about Jack the Ripper in it, preferring to concentrate on analysis of the more tangential subject matter that the Ripper case often throws up. Despite this, one thing was very telling; this may have been a robust and thoughtful look at the subject, but it still needed the man with the top hat in the fog on its cover to deliver the message.

Looking back at the events of 1988, the field's most publicly turbulent era, it is strange to imagine how much anger Jack the Ripper provoked in people. Today, opinion seems more circumspect, although it is certain there are still those who, if given the right opportunity, will be happy to dive headlong into the fray and remind us all that, by giving the murders attention, we are glorifying sexual violence, trivializing the lives of the women who died and ignoring real issues. As that now seems to be a rare occurrence, perhaps academia has finally saved 'Ripperology' from being filed away with other subjects in the box marked 'lunatic fringe'.

Murderland Revisited

Should one feel disposed to walk the streets of Whitechapel and Spitalfields on any given night, at any time of the year, one will invariably pass a guided Jack the Ripper walk. Within a minute of passing the group of avid listeners, it is very likely that you will encounter another, or be caught in the path of a large crowd of chattering students being led to the next site of interest by their guide. Sometimes, Mitre Square is packed with tour groups and Goulston Street can have so many that the only way to continue is to walk in the road. Each guide is in the flow of their narrative, the passer-by catching small soundbites of royal conspiracy, descriptions of mutilation or the name of a familiar suspect. What is apparent is that these guided walks are massively popular and do good business; they are truly a phenomenon and are the biggest manifest-ation of the continuing fascination with Jack the Ripper today.

The concept of visiting the Ripper's murder sites is not a new idea; in fact, it is as old as the murders themselves. In the aftermath of each crime, hundreds of curiosity seekers would assemble at the scene of the latest tragedy to see for them-selves the dreadful places, perhaps to catch a glimpse of congealed blood between the flagstones or to find out the lat-est news and gossip. Following each subsequent murder, crowds would gather at the most recent location and all the other murder sites that had gone before. As if to prove that such curiosity knew no bounds, following the murder in the back yard of 29 Hanbury Street residents of neighbouring properties would profit by 'renting' out the windows that overlooked the yard to anybody willing to pay a penny to see the place where Annie Chapman met her end at the hands of 'Leather Apron', as he was then known.

No other murder case has so much emphasis on 'place' as the Ripper crimes. Some of the names of the murder sites, such as Buck's Row and Mitre Square, are almost as well known as the names of the women who died there. Only 10 Rillington Place, the slum house in London's Ladbroke Grove where serial murderer John Christie executed hapless women, has as much infamy. But the house, and Rillington Place itself, are gone. The streets where the bodies of the victims of Jack the Ripper once lay are still there, much altered, but still accessible to the curious. The fascination with Ripper's London began with the first press descriptions of the murder sites and continues unabated today.

In 1890 the *Pall Mall Budget* published a lengthy article entitled 'Murderland Revisited',[1] a piece conducted in the form of a journalist's self-guided walk. Many newspaper reports contained detailed descriptions of the murder sites as the murders were happening, giving the reader a sense of the 'scene of crime', but this particular report was retrospective in tone and could be seen as one of the first documented examples of exploring the Ripper's territory in the aftermath of the murders. Although he did not visit Dorset Street, the writer went to Buck's Row, George Yard, Hanbury Street, Mitre Square, Berner Street and Castle Alley. As well as describing these places in terms of their visual appearance and atmosphere, the author mentioned incidents that occurred during his visits and a little of how the events of two years before had instigated changes, or not, as the case may be. But the *Pall Mall Budget* journalist was not alone in his perambulations, for within a short time, the residents of Buck's Row became so frustrated by the undeservedly mean reputation of the street that was perpetuated by the continual visits from curiosity seekers that they petitioned to have the name changed. The Metropolitan Board of Works originally could see no reason to do so, but eventually capitulated and on 25 October 1892 renamed the thoroughfare Durward Street.[2] It remains the only name change directly influenced by the notoriety of the murders.

The year after the *Pall Mall Budget* article was published Canadian journalist Kathleen Blake Watkins was sent to London and ventured into Whitechapel to visit the Ripper sites, leaving a grim account of her experiences there. Hanbury Street was described as 'a foul, stinking neighbourhood where the children are stunted little creatures with vicious faces' and Miller's Court was accessed via 'an arch reeking with filth'.[3] There she met 'Lottie', the current occupant of Mary Kelly's old room, who had trouble speaking owing to the broken nose her husband had recently given her. Watkins's passing mention of black stains on the wall of room 13 suggested that Mary Kelly's bloodstains were still evident after three years. Fifteen years later, a group of distinguished gentlemen from the Crimes Club were taken around the murder sites by Dr Frederick Gordon Brown, accompanied by three detectives; among the attendees were the noted coroner Samuel Ingleby Oddie, writer and critic John Churton Collins and one Arthur Conan Doyle. Together, they made up what could questionably be regarded as the first *organized* Ripper tour.[4]

By the late 1950s and 1960s, Ripper authors were still fortunate enough to be able to speak to elderly members of the public who remembered the murders or who could recall their parents talking about them. Authors like Daniel Farson and Tom Cullen were often offered to be taken to the sites by these residents, as if they too realized the importance of the locations in the story. Farson, a noted photojournalist as well as writer and broadcaster, seemed particularly taken with the area and took photographs which would ultimately appear in some of his books. At the end of 'Autumn of Terror', Cullen produced his own brief equivalent of 'Murderland Revisited', creating a highly evocative view of a 1960s Spitalfields still seemingly under the Ripper's pall:

> It is wandering around the area at night, when the garment factories are empty and the loading bays at Spitalfields Market have shut down, that one feels the presence of Jack the Ripper. At night Commercial Street is now so silent and deserted that in passing Christ Church one fancies that one can hear the death-watch beetles gnawing away at the fabric of this, Nicholas Hawksmoor's most noble spire. On the corner is the Ten Bells pub where Mary Kelly used to stop by for a quick gin. Standing outside as a customer pushes through the saloon bar door, one listens for the ghostly laughter of Mary Kelly and her sisters in trade. But no, the Ten Bells at night is now quite sedate. Its customers are respectable working-class types who linger long over a pint of beer. An air of stagnation hangs over the entire district. Somehow one feels that Spitalfields is cursed, that this is unhallowed ground.[5]

With the old residents of the East End slowly passing away, 1970 saw the advent of the true organized Ripper tour. Keith Baverstock, an Australian liaison officer for a travel agency who was interested in the more unusual sights of London, created several different tours which aimed to take the walker away from the more hackneyed London tourist destinations and even included one devoted to unusual public conveniences. Baverstock's project eventually became London Walks, and the Jack the Ripper tour was his first walk, taking place in August 1970:

> 'The head had nearly been cut off, and the body had been disembowelled. And I don't know if anybody here is squeamish, but certain parts of the female anatomy had been removed,' the guide said with relish, yesterday afternoon. The crowd of about 30 pressed happily closer, anxious to have their flesh made to creep. This was that most curious of English Sunday afternoon entertainments, a trip for tourists around Whitechapel in the bloodstained footprints of Jack the Ripper, fee 5s, children under 10 free. Footfalls echoed uneasily in the memory, hurrying footfalls of a tall man in a dark cloak wearing a top hat, carrying a black bag, and hiding something long and glinting silver beneath his cloak.[6]

Baverstock also took visitors to Rillington Place, which would remain standing for one more year. Whether these crime-based tours attracted criticism is not clear, but the following year Baverstock was reported as saying that his tours were not morbid and that he would never conduct tours around more modern cases.[7] This declaration demonstrated a peculiar dichotomy in that most murders, particularly recent ones, or those where the perpetrators were caught, were 'out of bounds' and yet Jack the Ripper was considered acceptable. The mythology of Jack the Ripper had pretty much won over, and he was now folklore, harmless fun from the world of foggy Victorian melodrama.

Those curious members of the public who had chosen to take Keith Baverstock's Ripper walks in the early 1970s would be the last to see many of the locations as they once were. Slum clearance programmes had seen to it that in a very brief period of time George Yard Buildings, 29 Hanbury Street, parts of Mitre Square and Durward Street had disappeared, and the redevelopment of the East End was seen as being a major threat to the success of Jack the Ripper tours. Guides began to find it increasingly difficult to 'recapture that sense of melodrama on a site overshadowed by a multi-storey car park or concrete office block'.[8] London Walks had by that time been joined by London Unlimited; however, such was the pessimistic outlook that the latter was forced to close. The *Daily Telegraph* joined eighty tourists on their last tour in August 1974, believing it had attended 'the last Ripper ramble'.

But the draw of Jack the Ripper meant that there was still a story to be told, and a good one at that. Unperturbed by the disappearance of key locations, surviving tour companies continued their walks, and throughout the early to mid-1980s the industry began to grow. Companies like City Walks and Footsteps realized that a Ripper walk was essential to their business. Often starting at Whitechapel Underground station, many of the tours would take in the less central locations such as Durward Street and nearby Wood's Buildings. The former Buck's Row was at this time entirely derelict, and the overpowering gloom of the area complemented the public desire to be 'spooked' by the ambience of the Ripper's London. Wood's Buildings, a narrow, urine-soaked alley, was the perfect atmospheric place to recount the activities of the prostitutes, as well as supplying customers with the appropriate menace.

Jack the Ripper tours came under a fair amount of flak during the centenary protests, but one imagines that the centenary itself would have contributed so significantly to the success of these walks that the industry would have been too strong for the protestors to take down. So many people really did want to visit the East End and hear the Ripper story in its original context, or at least an atmospheric and entertaining version of it, and so a cycle of supply and demand was instigated. By the end of the 1980s enough companies were operating to make the continual night-time presence of such large groups of tourists a cause for concern. Spitalfields, which for so long had been run down and neglected, had begun to undergo a change, as the old Georgian houses of Fournier Street, Wilkes Street and Princelet Street were slowly being bought by wealthy professionals, the new owners gradually restoring the houses to their former glory. The rejuvenation of Spitalfields as a place to live, rather than just a place to toil, was gradual at first, but the incoming residents of this once maligned and neglected area of London would make their opinions heard and pose a potential threat to the Ripper tour industry.

The centenary furore did little to quash the abiding fascination with Ripper's London. The guided walks were flourishing and steadily gaining publicity. Tabloid journalism was enamoured of the concept of supposed Ripper experts taking hordes of excitable tourists around the East End and was quick to inject long-held fears into the proceedings, playing into the hands of those who believed (rather irrationally, considering the passing of a century) that, if the Ripper was never caught, then he must still be at large! 'It's not until you actually stand on the murder spot and hear the story once more, that you start to shiver and wonder if you should take a cab home . . .'[8]

And therein lay the success of the Ripper tour. These guided walks would promote the fact that the participant was 'walking in the footsteps of the Ripper' or 'on the trail of the

Ripper', perhaps following the scent as detectives would have done back in 1888. In other words, everybody had an opportunity of succeeding where Scotland Yard had failed. And visiting the murder sites, regardless of the changes, was part of that 'ongoing investigation'. It is as though the practically non-existent scene-of-crime analysis of the Victorian police had left unfinished business and that visitors need to see these places to fully understand the context of the crimes. Of course, another obvious reason for the interest in the Ripper's haunts is the fact that they are so accessible. Most of his victims were found in publicly accessible places, and even now, if one is so disposed, one can stand on the very spots where Nichols, Chapman, Eddowes and Kelly met their terrible fates. And many who visit the East End on these guided walks also want atmosphere, the essence instilled into the Ripper story by so many books and films, but with the changes to the area it is not always a promise that is easy to live up to.

This emphasis on 'sense of place' could be considered as making these Ripper tours, like other tourist-centred walks, mass-marketed exercises in 'psychogeography'.[9] As with the numerous ghost walks of York and Edinburgh, the walker is seeking an appropriate feeling from the urban environment. The desire to have the places visited appear and feel just as they would have all those years ago is a strong one, sometimes leading to a sense of disappointment when that desire goes unfulfilled. Authors such as Iain Sinclair and Peter Ackroyd have used Jack the Ripper's London in their work, significantly so in the case of the former, whose novel *White Chappell: Scarlet Tracings*[10] repeatedly brings the reader on to the streets, digging up old associations and myths. Parts of the narrative recount the author's perambulations across Whitechapel and Spitalfields, and the names of the murder sites appear sporadically, sometimes repeated mantra-like, showing us that the legend of Jack is always part of that particular urban context.

The significance of sites where death has occurred is also another principle that must be considered, and J. F. Brewer's *The Curse upon Mitre Square* gave an early account of the importance of Catherine Eddowes's murder site as a place of ritual sacrifice, tainted by the blood of innocents across the centuries. From the grand scale of the battlefields of northern France, where millions fell during the First World War, to the more personal micro-memorials of flowers tied to lampposts signifying the scene of a fatal car crash, locations of sudden death maintain a power and mystique that the human psyche, for all the interference of the modern world, can still under-stand. To that effect, the Whitechapel murder sites have often been given improvised memorials, from stencilled graffiti renaming the location after its victim ('Mary Ann Nichols Row' and 'Mary Jane Kelly Court', for example) to small plaques recording the women by name, announcing that they 'died here'. These memorials are often removed or covered up soon after they appear mysteriously, and a more lasting monument to the victims of Jack the Ripper has long been sought by some.

By the mid-1990s that all-important urban milieu of the East End had begun to change significantly. Both Spitalfields market and the Truman Brewery had closed and were now being revamped as centres for leisure and the arts. These developments were now catering for tourists as well as a rapidly growing young crowd of artists and new-media professionals. To these new visitors and residents, Jack the Ripper was an anathema, and, annoyed by the regular tours outside their homes every night, they rose up in protest. The first complaint was lodged with the council in January 1996: one resident was quick to dispel the belief that visiting tourists injected much-needed money into the area:

The idea that the area will be regenerated by Jack the Ripper walking tours is pure rubbish. The people who go on these tours spend an hour walking the street being told in grisly detail about the murder of prostitutes, buy a pint in the sponsoring pub, then leave with the image of the East End as a seedy, dangerous red-light district firmly enforced in their minds.[11]

The crunch year was 1996. With so many groups of anything up to 200 people being led around the streets, the council felt that it might have to act. It was even thought at one point that the tours might be banned altogether. The *East London Advertiser* gave the new protesters a voice, and for several months during the spring and summer of 1996 the controversy over what to do with these disruptive tours was almost a constant feature on their pages. Even the national press picked up on the story when the *Sunday Telegraph* interviewed residents affected: 'It's a particularly nefarious and disgusting form of tourism. It wouldn't be tolerated at the scene of Fred West's crimes or in Dunblane: the fact that it's 100 years old doesn't make it quaint.'[12]

Nobody ever did say it was quaint, but the distinction was made, as Keith Baverstock did in 1971, between the Ripper crimes of 1888 and those perpetrated in living memory with the murderers identified and those affected by them still alive. It may well be significant that the rise of the Jack the Ripper tour began at a time when those directly affected by his crimes were no longer around to voice their dissent.

Eventually the situation reached bursting point when tour company owners met with Tower Hamlets council to thrash out a code of practice, promoting the use of sanctioned 'Blue Badge' guides to squeeze out the unofficial operators who were seen as being irresponsible and disruptive and ensuring that groups did not congregate outside private homes.[13] But such a code was difficult to enforce, because noise from the human voice did not constitute a statutory nuisance under the Environmental Protection Act, and it appears that no solution, or code, was forthcoming. By the new millennium, Ripper tours were even more numerous, and even the Ten Bells, once the Mecca for tour groups, felt compelled to put a sign up to the effect that it would not welcome tours of more than ten people without prior arrangement. By now, Spitalfields had become a burgeoning leisure area, with the eateries of the old market and the bars and curry houses of Brick Lane attracting visitors from far and wide. The Ten Bells, situated as it was in the middle and more popular than ever, no longer needed the extra clientele the Ripper tours so readily supplied in previous decades. Eventually, the pub would completely distance itself from its own dubious history. The tidal wave of guided walks which descended upon the area night after night presented a bizarre scenario on the streets of the East End, as documented by Jonathan Edwards in the *Daily Mail* in 2007:

An army walked up Bell Lane behind their tour guide. They were going north. It clashed with another army going east at Spitalfields. Then there was a coachload of Americans in Fournier Street. The Bell Lane mob were veered right by the guide and avoided them.

More coaches rolled in. A throng marched through from the Tower of London. Guides like generals shifted the routes of their people. 'We'll keep out of Hanbury Street since you can't move there,' one of the guides was saying.

Whole streets were choked with tour groups trying not to mingle and tripping on kerbsides hidden under a thousand pairs of feet. It was mayhem in Ripper country the other Friday night. Streets seething and more crowded than they had ever been in Jack's days.[14]

It did indeed seem like mayhem, proving that, despite the regular protests, there really was little anybody could do to quash interest in Jack the Ripper, whatever forms that interest took.

Presently, the Ripper walks continue to flourish, and there seems to be no stopping them. Thousands of people must attend these walks every week, and there are now many companies to choose from. Thanks to the internet, a company name is not a necessary requirement, and hardly a month goes by without some new individual appearing on the streets with a small, private group. There are tours in Spanish, French and Italian, coachloads of students from the European mainland and school groups getting an on-the-spot rundown of the murders to complement their GCSE history coursework. The strangest version of the Ripper tour is that which is conducted as a pub crawl: the office party with a difference or the hen-party for screaming girls, where everybody is essentially out for a night of serious drinking. They request to be taken around the East End, drinks in hand, only to get increasingly inebriated as the guide struggles to tell them a story of tragedy and brutality. For these people, Jack the Ripper never really existed; he is truly Jack the Myth, the figure from Victorian melodrama or the kitsch killer from a dozen tacky Hammer films. With similar lack of understanding of the true nature of these crimes, parents sometimes take small children on the tours, unaware that the guide will unavoidably have to speak of prostitution and the removal of sexual organs. Whether any of these people bring significant revenue to an area which is already bursting with bars, restaurants and flea markets is open for debate, but it does introduce some to a part of London they may never have traversed otherwise, one that has a rich history beyond the Ripper legend.

As for the guides themselves, they are multifarious in their approach. Undoubtedly there are some whose grasp of the basic facts takes a back seat to the job of entertaining; some have the knowledge through experience, others from learning a guide script. With so many in the streets at any one time, taking a group to a specific location can be difficult; the closure of Dorset Street for redevelopment in 2012 has created a focus for groups at the Crispin Street end, resulting in congestion; 'Ripper's Corner' in Mitre Square is often the scene of some mad dash to claim the all-important spot, made harder by ongoing redevelopment. On Halloween, the busiest night of the Ripper tour calendar, Mitre Square fills up to the point where there is literally nowhere to go. The push to be in the right place at the right time can cause some awkward moments and is part and parcel of some strange jockeying, where every Ripper tour guide would like to think they are more deserving of getting the exact spot, and there appears to be some unwritten hierarchy where guides assume they are delivering the ultimate experience and are thus better than the rest.

Perhaps the best method of measuring the way that Jack the Ripper, the reality and the myth, is perceived by the world at large is by observing the participants of these guided walks. Strangely enough, despite the previous protests about promoting violence towards women, it is women who seem to be most interested, and on pre-booked tours female names considerably outnumber male ones on the guest list. Some attendees appear genuinely shocked when told of the social conditions or the victims' injuries, as though their opinions on the Ripper have been fabricated from watching too many stylized horror movies (which is usually the case). A tour guide's ears will frequently ring with the question 'Wasn't he something to do with the Royal Family?' Other suspects get mentioned too, however. Occasionally one is asked about 'the American' or 'that bloke from Liverpool'; Montague Druitt becomes the 'guy that drowned himself', Kosminski is 'the one that the police thought it was', and the Duke of Clarence is usually rendered as 'the Prince of Wales or something'. The guide ends up filling in the blanks, but then after all that should be part of the job.

One final observation: the different walking tours, vying for business in an oversaturated market, stake their pitch with varying claims for prevalence in the field. Whether they are 'Blue Badge' guides, published authors or possessed of decades of experience, augmented by photographs, projectors, sound effects or costumes, most of these tour operators have one thing in common. No matter how they describe themselves, their marketing material usually depicts a foggy street, a solitary gas lamp or splash of blood; and in the middle walks the man with the top hat, cape, bag and glinting knife. It's that stalker in the dark again, the icon of fear – the mythical Jack that still haunts the shadows.

Afterword

London, June 2013

The peeling office blocks of this small City of London square, having lain empty for half a decade, stand shrouded in scaffolding and tarpaulins. At ground level, large metal containers lie stacked upon each other, and hoardings and makeshift fencing have blocked entrances and reduced the size of the square to the point of awkwardness. To the north-east, the service road at the rear of the Spitalfields Fruit and Wool Exchange is blocked off by similar metallic fencing, and the doors and windows of the Exchange building itself are boarded up with green panelling. Signs on the fencing tell us that guard dogs are in operation and a single security guard is seen strolling forgetfully across the lonely thoroughfare. Further east, behind Whitechapel Underground station, cranes and drills work feverishly in and around the narrow street. Metal hoardings hide great industry, and huge lorries struggle to back into the building sites from which emanates the sound of the construction of yet another 'grand project'.

This is Mitre Square, Duval Street (formerly Dorset Street) and Durward Street (Buck's Row) at the time of writing. By some strange coincidence, these three significant Ripper locations are about to be given drastic overhauls that will change their appearance for ever. The buildings of Mitre Square, deemed unsatisfactory, are to be demolished imminently, to be replaced by tall glass edifices, a clean piazza and a water feature. If the

279

planners' desires are successful, the former Dorset Street will soon no longer exist, covered as it will be by a large office and retail block, sanctioned by the Mayor of London, but rejected by practically everyone else. Durward Street features heavily in the new Crossrail developments and, if the developers' plans are anything to go by, will soon be invaded by parts of an extended Whitechapel station.

What is happening in the East End is no different from what happened in the grand sweep of redevelopment in the early 1970s, when it was felt that the London of Jack the Ripper was about to disappear for ever. Ultimately it did not, and the persistent walking tours continued regardless, as they will still do once this current wave of rebuilding has come to fruition. As long as the walls of buildings have those famous street names upon them, people will still go and see them in an attempt to capture some fleeting collective memory of the 'autumn of terror'. It will take more than a wrecking ball to extinguish that curiosity.

Meanwhile, bookshelves across the world heave with the continually growing writings of authors and researchers and new overviews, new suspects, reassessments and biographies place themselves into the canon of Ripper literature with predictable regularity. But will any of these contributions finally lead us to the elusive answer to that perennial question: 'Who was Jack the Ripper?'

Arguably not. One has to concede that even if, from the mists of obscurity, some definitive-looking official document appears naming the Whitechapel murderer, endorsed by relevant official signatures, there will be those who will question its provenance and authenticity, and thus the mystery will remain unsolved to everybody's satisfaction. And so the mystery will continue.

Had that mystery been solved before the end of the

nineteenth century, it would have been an entirely different matter. In some 'Ripperological' alternative time-line, we would probably see no more than a half-dozen obscure books on the subject, and it is possible that the guided walks industry would never have got any further than Frederick Gordon Brown's 1905 stroll. Madame Tussauds's Chamber of Horrors would no doubt feature 'Jack the Ripper', but under his real name, and we would, of course, know for certain whether the 'Dear Boss' letter that brought that name to the world was fake or not. There may be at least one movie version of the crimes, the odd documentary perhaps, as is the case for many true-crime cases, but probably no pop songs or video games, comics or plastic figurines. And there would, of course, have been no opportunity for Jack to metamorphose into the iconic 'super-villain' in his top hat and cape.

But it never happened that way and we are left with a powerful legacy that does not seem to fade with the passing of time. Jack the Ripper has become a concept, for some even a marketing strategy, and the fact that the very real murderer of vulnerable East End prostitutes has appeared on T-shirts, complete with 'Whitechapel Tour' dates, is testament to the reality that, in terms of celebrity, Jack is in the big league.

Only time will reveal how this legendary creature of the night will be perceived by future generations as interest continues in the young and old alike. It is notable that many who actively study and write about the Ripper were first attracted to the subject via the myth; the sense of dread, the well-defined melodrama, the 'romance' of dark deeds in high places courtesy of the royal conspiracy or high-profile re-enactments by stars like Michael Caine and Johnny Depp. And then, if the interest remains, reality begins to assert itself, and 'Ripperology' receives a fresh injection of new life.

Will it continue for ever? It probably will, for that is what myths and legends are: undying, eternal stories that resonate within generation after generation. Jack the Ripper, like Robin Hood, Dick Turpin, Sweeney Todd, King Arthur, Sherlock Holmes, Count Dracula and Batman, is malleable and responsive as a character, and whether or not any of these legendary figures existed or not, they give our creative consciousness an enormous amount of raw material to play with and inspire the imagination accordingly.

The dark side of human nature has always been with us and always will. The Ripper is a symbol of that nature writ large, rising up regularly to remind us that there is no Utopia, that danger lurks round every dark corner and in the shadows, and that we all have something to fear, whether we choose to admit it or not. Jack the Ripper has become an embodiment of fear, and, in the words of American President Franklin D. Roosevelt, 'the only thing we have to fear is fear itself'.

Useful Resources

Books and other media on the subject of Jack the Ripper are included in the footnotes.

Archives

The National Archives – www.nationalarchives.gov.uk
London Metropolitan Archives – www.cityoflondon.gov.uk/lma
Tower Hamlets Library and Archives – www.towerhamlets.gov.uk
Bishopsgate Institute Library – www.bishopsgate.org.uk
British Newspaper Archive – www.britishnewspaperarchive.co.uk
Evans Skinner Crime Archive – www. evansskinnercrimearchive .com/ripper

Websites

Casebook: Jack the Ripper – www.casebook.org
JTRForums – www.jtrforums.com
Ripper Wiki – http://wiki.casebook.org
'Ripperpedia' is a downloadable mobile app, featuring hundreds of articles and images relating to the people and places in the Ripper case including a GPS feature for locations. Available from the Apple app store.

Recommended Guided Walks

www.londonwalking.co.uk
www.londondiscoverytours.com
www.rippertour.com
www.walks.com

Publications

Ripperologist magazine – www.ripperologist.biz/
Journal of the Whitechapel Society 1888 – www.whitechapelsociety.com
Ripperana

Notes

Chapter 1: 'Wilful murder against some person unknown'

1 Police report dated 25 October 1888, MEPO 3/141 ff. 158–63 (National Archives).

2 *Morning Advertiser*, 9 April 1888.

3 *Lloyd's Weekly Newspaper*, 8 April 1888.

4 The report by Inspector Edmund Reid was transcribed by Ian Sharp during research for the BBC series *Jack the Ripper* in 1973. The material on this case went missing from the files prior to 1983.

5 Some newspapers claimed she was a widow, but in the London Hospital admission register she is described as 'married' and a 'charwoman'.

6 Register of Common Lodging Houses (London Metropolitan Archives).

7 Legislation under the Artizan's and Labourer's Dwellings Improvement Act 1875 (also known as the 'Cross Act').

8 *Walthamstow and Leyton Guardian*, 14 April 1888.

9 Inspector Reid's report has it that the incident happened on the footpath opposite 10 Brick Lane.

10 *People*, 15 April 1888.

11 Register of Common Lodging Houses (London Metropolitan Archives).

12 Philip Sugden, *The Complete History of Jack the Ripper* (London: Robinson, 2002; first published in 1994).

13 Report by Inspector Edmund Reid, 24 August 1888, MEPO 3/140, ff. 49–51 (National Archives).

14 *The Times*, 24 August 1888.

15 Ibid.

16 *East London Observer*, 25 August 1888.

17 Census return 1881, Whitechapel St Mary.

18 *The Times*, 24 August 1888.

19 *East London Observer*, 25 August 1888.

20 *Star*, 24 August 1888.

21 *Star*, 7 August 1888.

22 *East London Advertiser*, 24 August 1888.

23 *The Times*, 24 August 1888.

24 Ibid.

25 Ibid.

26 Renamed Gunthorpe Street in 1912.

27 Again, as a result of the 1875 Cross Act.

28 *East London Observer*, 11 August 1888.

29 *Eastern Post*, 18 August 1888.

30 Report by Chief Inspector Donald Swanson, September 1888, MEPO 3/140, ff. 36–42 (National Archives).

31 *The Times*, 10 August 1888.

32 Ibid.

33 *East London Observer*, 11 August 1888.

34 *The Times*, 9 August 1888.

35 *East London Advertiser*, 11 August 1888.

36 *East London Observer*, 11 August 1888.

37 Report by Inspector Edmund Reid, 16 August 1888, MEPO 3/140, ff. 44–8 (National Archives).

38 Report by Superintendent Charles Cutbush, 16 August 1888, MEPO 3/140, ff. 44–8 (National Archives).

39 *Daily News*, 24 August 1888 (and others).

40 Founded in 1865, the *Pall Mall Gazette* began as a paper for the 'higher circles of society', written 'by gentlemen for gentlemen'. By the time of William Thomas Stead's editorship (1883–9), the

paper had metamorphosed into a radical, free-thinking journal. Stead's exposé of child prostitution saw him imprisoned but also resulted in the age of consent for children being raised from twelve to sixteen in 1885.

41 *Pall Mall Gazette*, 24 August 1888.

42 *The Times*, 20 March 1886.

43 From a letter currently in a private collection.

Chapter 2: 'I forgive you for what you are, as you have been to me'

1 *The Times*, 18 September 1888.

2 Ibid.

3 Ibid.

4 Often referred to as 'Britten' or 'Brittain' in newspaper reports.

5 *Star*, 3 September 1888.

6 *Echo*, 6 September 1888.

7 *Evening News*, 1 September 1888.

8 Cross was actually born Charles Allen Lechmere. The surname 'Cross' comes from his stepfather after his mother remarried, but curiously the only time he used this name is during his association with the Nichols murder. All other records show him as 'Lechmere'. However, as he is recorded throughout the case files and press reports as 'Cross', that name is used here.

9 *The Times*, 18 September 1888.

10 *Daily Telegraph*, 4 September 1888.

11 Buck's Row, despite being in Whitechapel, fell under the jurisdiction of the newly formed J-division (Bethnal Green).

12 *The Times*, 4 September 1888.

13 Report by Inspector Spratling, 31 August 1888; MEPO 3/140, ff. 239–41 (National Archives).

14 *Daily Telegraph*, 3 September 1888.

15 *Daily News*, 3 September 1888.

16 She is referred to as 'Ellen' in the police reports; press reports say 'Emily', 'Nelly' and 'Jane Oram'.

17 *Evening Standard*, 3 September 1888 (and others).

18 *Daily Telegraph*, 4 September 1888.

19 *East London Observer*, 8 September 1888.

20 Report by Inspector Joseph Helson, 7 September 1888; MEPO 3/140 ff. 235–8 (National Archives).

21 *Daily News*, 1 September 1888.

22 *Morning Advertiser*, 24 September 1888.

23 Report by Inspector Joseph Helson, 7 September 1888; MEPO 3/140 ff. 235–8 (National Archives).

24 *The Times*, 1 September 1888.

25 *Morning Advertiser*, 24 September 1888.

26 American newspapers such as the *Atchison Daily Globe* (Kansas), *Austin Statesman* and *Galveston Daily News* (both Texas).

27 *Daily News*, 3 September 1888.

28 Letter formerly in the possession of the late Jim Swanson.

Chapter 3: 'A noiseless midnight terror'

1 HO 144/220/A49301B, f. 178 (National Archives).

2 HO 144/220/A49301B, f. 177 (National Archives).

3 *Sheffield and Rotherham Independent*, 1 September 1888.

4 *Star*, 5 September 1888.

5 *Pall Mall Gazette*, 8 September 1888.

6 *Austin Statesman*, 5 September 1888.

7 *Star*, 6 September 1888.

8 *Star*, 5 September 1888 (and others).

9 *Evening News*, 5 September 1888.

10 MEPO 3/140, ff. 235–8 (National Archives).
11 *Leytonstone Express and Independent*, 8 September 1888.
12 *Daily Telegraph*, 10 September 1888.
13 *Daily Telegraph*, 13 September 1888.
14 *The Times*, 14 September 1888.
15 *Daily Telegraph*, 14 September 1888.
16 Ibid.
17 Exact date found in Chapman family birthday book; information courtesy of Neal Shelden.
18 *The Times*, 11 September 1888.
19 *Echo*, 10 September 1888.
20 *Woodford Times*, 14 September 1888.
21 *Echo*, 14 September 1888.
22 *The Times*, 20 September 1888.
23 *Daily News*, 10 September 1888.
24 *East London Advertiser*, 22 September 1888.
25 *The Times*, 20 September 1888.
26 *Daily Telegraph*, 11 September 1888.
27 *Star*, 8 September 1888.
28 *The Times*, 11 September 1888.
29 Ibid.
30 *Daily Telegraph* and *Star*, 17 September 1888; *Echo*, 8 September 1888.
31 *Daily Telegraph*, 20 September 1888.
32 *The Times*, 14 September 1888.
33 *Lancet*, 29 September 1888.
34 *Daily Telegraph*, 20 September 1888.
35 *Daily Telegraph*, 13 September 1888.
36 *Morning Advertiser*, 13 September 1888.
37 *Daily Telegraph*, 20 September 1888.
38 *Echo*, 11 September 1888.
39 *East London Observer*, 15 September 1888.
40 *Daily Telegraph*, 13 September 1888.

41 *Pall Mall Gazette*, 10 September 1888; *East London Advertiser*, 15 September 1888.
42 MEPO 3/140, ff. 24–5 (National Archives).

Chapter 4: 'How can they catch me now?'

1 *Daily Telegraph*, 22 September 1888.
2 *East London Observer*, 27 October 1888.
3 William Fishman, *East End 1888* (London: Duckworth, 1988; Nottingham: Five Leaves, 2005).
4 Letter from 'A Ratepayer', *Daily Telegraph*, 21 September 1888.
5 Alan Palmer, *The East End* (London: John Murray, 1989).
6 *East London Observer*, 15 September 1888.
7 *Lloyd's Weekly News*, 9 September 1888.
8 Others being the *Pall Mall Gazette*, *Lloyd's Weekly News* and the *Illustrated Police News*.
9 *Star*, 13 September 1888.
10 *East London Advertiser*, 22 September 1888.
11 *Daily Telegraph*, 17 September 1888.
12 *Star*, 17 September 1888.
13 *Pall Mall Gazette*, 11 September 1888.
14 MEPO 3/142, docket 244, ff. 5–6 (National Archives).
15 MEPO 3/3183, ff. 2–4 (National Archives).
16 MEPO 3/3183, f. 1 (National Archives).

Chapter 5: 'No, not tonight, some other night'

1 Paul Begg, *Jack the Ripper: The Facts* (London: Robson, 2004).
2 Inquest testimony of Charles Preston and Michael Kidney; *The Times*, 4 October 1888.

3 Begg, *Jack the Ripper*, p. 138.

4 Census report 1881.

5 Much information about this period of Elizabeth's life can be gleaned from Neal Shelden, *The Victims of Jack the Ripper* (Knoxville: Inklings Press, 2007).

6 *The Times*, 4 October 1888.

7 'Payments to the Poor' book at the Swedish church. Found by Klaus Lithner.

8 *Daily Telegraph*, 4 October 1888.

9 *East London Advertiser*, 13 October 1888.

10 *Daily Telegraph*, 4 October 1888.

11 *Morning Advertiser*, 4 October 1888.

12 All reports and thus subsequent books refer to him as 'J. Best', living at 82 Lower Chapman Street. However, he was very likely John Bass, recorded there in numerous electoral registers until his death in 1889.

13 *London Evening News*, 1 October 1888.

14 *The Times*, 6 October 1888.

15 HO 144/221/A49301C, ff. 148–59 (National Archives).

16 *Evening News*, *Star*, 1 October 1888.

17 *The Times*, 2 October 1888.

18 *The Times*, 4 October 1888.

19 Report by Donald Swanson, 19 October 1888; HO 144/221/A49301C, ff. 148–59 (National Archives).

20 Report by Inspector Abberline, 1 November 1888; MEPO 3/140/221/A49301C, ff. 204–6 (National Archives).

21 *Star*, 1 October 1888.

22 *Evening News*, 1 October 1888.

23 *Morning Advertiser*, 3 October 1888.

24 *The Times*, 3 October 1888.

25 *Daily Telegraph*, 3 October 1888.

Chapter 6: 'Good night, old cock'

1 Coroner's Inquest (L), 1888, no. 135, Catherine Eddowes inquest 1888 (London Metropolitan Archives). The original signed statements by the inquest witnesses are still preserved and are used here unless otherwise indicated.

2 Transcriptions vary: the City Police version, taken by DC Halse, states: 'The *Juwes* are *not* the men that will be blamed for nothing.'

3 Report by Inspector McWilliam, 27 October 1888; HO 144/221/ A49301C, ff. 162–70 (National Archives).

4 Report by Superintendent Arnold, 6 November 1888; HO 144/221/A49301C, ff. 197–8 (National Archives).

5 Report by Sir Charles Warren, 6 November 1888, HO 144/221/ A49301C, ff. 173–81 (National Archives).

6 *Daily Chronicle*, 1 September 1908.

7 *Daily Telegraph*, 2 October 1888.

8 *Evening News*, 1 October 1888.

9 *The Times*, 3 October 1888.

10 *Echo*, 4 October 1888.

11 Neal Shelden, *The Victims of Jack the Ripper* (Knoxville: Inklings Press, 2007).

12 1881 census.

13 *Daily Telegraph*, 12 October 1888.

14 *Wolverhampton Chronicle*, 10 October 1888.

15 *Daily Telegraph*, 5 October 1888.

16 *Star*, 3 October 1888.

17 Today's Fournier Street.

18 *The Times*, 2 October 1888.

19 Report by Donald Swanson, 6 November 1888; HO 144/221/ A49301C, ff. 184–94 (National Archives).

20 *Star*, 1 October 1888.

21 *Evening News*. 1 October 1888.

22 *Daily Telegraph*, 12 October 1888.

23 *The Times*, 5 October 1888.

24 *Daily News*, 2 October 1888.

Chapter 7: 'O have you seen the devle?'

1 *Star*, 2 October 1888.

2 Official documents relating to the rewards debate can be found in HO 144/220/A49301B (National Archives).

3 *Pall Mall Gazette*, 8 October 1888.

4 Much official correspondence on the use of bloodhounds is to be found in HO 144/221/A49301E (National Archives).

5 Report by Donald Swanson, 19 October 1888; HO 144/221/A49301C, f. 147 (National Archives).

6 *Evening News*, 1 October 1888.

7 *Daily Telegraph*, 8 October 1888.

8 See Neil Bell, 'Defenceless Whitechapel', *Ripperologist* 95 (September 2008).

9 Report by Inspector James McWilliam, 27 October 1888; HO 144/221/A49301C, ff. 162–70 (National Archives).

10 *Evening News*, 19 October 1888.

11 Ibid.

12 *Star*, 19 October 1888.

13 Major Henry Smith, *From Constable to Commissioner: The Story of Sixty Years, Most of Them Misspent* (London: Chatto and Windus, 1910).

14 *Atlanta Constitution*, 5 October 1888; *East London Observer*, 20 October 1888; *Evening News*, 19 October 1888.

15 CLRO Police Box 3.16, no. 154 (London Metropolitan Archives).

16 Stewart P. Evans and Donald Rumbelow, *Jack the Ripper: Scotland Yard Investigates* (Stroud: Sutton, 2006).

Chapter 8: 'I hope I may never see such a sight again'

1 Unless otherwise stated, information pertaining to witnesses in the Mary Kelly case is taken from the surviving inquest papers (MJ/SPC, NE1888, Box 3, Case Paper 19) held at the London Metropolitan Archives.

2 *Star*, 10 November 1888.

3 Dr Thomas Bond's post-mortem report; MEPO 3/3153, ff. 10–18 (National Archives).

4 *The Times*, 10 November 1888.

5 *Daily Telegraph*, 10 November 1888.

6 *East London Observer, Illustrated Police News*, 17 November 1888; *Manchester Guardian, Daily Telegraph*, 10 November 1888.

7 Walter Dew, *I Caught Crippen: Memoirs of Ex-Chief Inspector Walter Dew* (London and Glasgow: Blackie and Son, 1938).

8 Sir Melville Macnaghten, *Days of My Years* (London: Edward Arnold, 1914).

9 Possibly Matilda *Buckey*, recorded at 1 George Street (later St George Street) in the 1881 census.

10 *Star*, 12 November 1888.

11 Most probably Mary *McCarthy* of 1 Breezer's Hill, as recorded in the 1891 census.

12 *Western Mail*, 12 November 1888.

13 Mrs Harvey had stayed with Mary on a couple of previous nights and claimed that she was present when Joseph Barnett arrived on the evening of 8 November, apparently at 6.55, which conflicts with Lizzie Allbrook's account and the claim by Elizabeth Foster that she had been drinking with Mary at the Ten Bells (*Evening News*, 12 November) or the Britannia (*Evening Express*, 12 November) the same evening until 7.05.

14 *Daily Telegraph*, 13 November 1888.

15 *The Times*, 10 November 1888.

16 Statement by George Hutchinson, 12 November 1888; MEPO 3/140, ff. 227–9 (National Archives).

17 Statements of Sarah Lewis and Elizabeth Prater from Kelly inquest papers, MJ/SPC, NE1888, Box 3, Case paper 19 (London Metropolitan Archives).

18 *The Times*, 10 November 1888; *Illustrated Police News*, 17 November 1888.

19 *Daily Telegraph*, 13 November 1888.

20 RA VIC/A67/19 (Royal Archives).

21 RA VIC/B40/82 (Royal Archives).

22 Dr Bond's report, 10 November 1888; HO 144/221/A49301C, ff. 220–23 (National Archives).

Chapter 9: 'Where have I been Dear Boss . . .'

1 *Daily News*, 20 November 1888.

2 The deleted expletive has never been ascertained.

3 *The Times*, 26 November 1888.

4 This correspondence can be found in HO 144/221/A49301H and MEPO 3/143 (National Archives).

5 Often referred to by that name in the press, it was owned by Thomas Tempany and consisted of a number of consecutive properties.

6 Report by Inspector Henry Moore, 17 July 1889; MEPO 3/140, ff. 294–7 (National Archives).

7 Report by Sergeant John McCarthy, 24 July 1889; MEPO 3/140, f. 278 (National Archives).

8 *The Times*, 18 July 1889.

9 Report by Detective Sergeant Albert Pearce; MEPO 3/140, f. 275 (National Archives).

10 Report by Dr Phillips, 22 July 1889; MEPO 3/140, ff. 263–71 (National Archives).
11 Report by Thomas Bond, 17 July 1889; MEPO 3/140, ff. 259–62 (National Archives).
12 Report by James Monro, 17 July 1889; HO 144/221/A49301I, ff. 5–6 (National Archives).
13 Sir Robert Anderson, *The Lighter Side of My Official Life* (London: Hodder and Stoughton 1910).
14 *The Times*, 16 February 1891.
15 Statement by James Sadler, 14 February 1891; MEPO 3/140, ff. 97–108 (National Archives).
16 MEPO 3/142, ff. 234–5 (National Archives).

Chapter 10: Murder and Motive

1 Sir Melville Macnaghten, *Days of My Years* (London: Edward Arnold, 1914).
2 T. G. Davey, MD, 'Lectures on Insanity, Delivered at the Bristol Medical School During the Summer Session of 1855', *Association Medical Journal*, 7 September 1855.
3 *Star*, 13 September 1888.
4 'The Whitechapel Murders', *British Medical Journal*, 8 December 1888.
5 *Evening News*, 7 December 1888.
6 HO 144/221/A49301C, f. 225 (National Archives).
7 *The Times*, 27 September 1888.
8 Report by Sir Charles Warren, 19 September 1888; HO 144/221/A49301C, ff. 90–92 (National Archives).
9 Unsigned report by Sergeant William Thick, 17 September 1888; MEPO 3/140, ff. 21–3 (National Archives).

10 Report by Inspector Frederick Abberline, 19 September 1888; MEPO 3/140, ff. 24–8 (National Archives).

11 *Echo*, 19 September 1888.

12 *The Times*, 19 September 1888.

13 Report by Sir Charles Warren, 7 November 1888; HO 144/221/A49301C, ff. 200–201 (National Archives).

14 *Evening News*, 31 August 1888.

15 Michael Macilwee, *The Gangs of Liverpool* (Wrea Green: Milo Books, 2006).

16 A. Davies, *The Gangs of Manchester* (Wrea Green: Milo Books, 2008).

17 *Freeman*, 16 November 1888.

18 Report by Edward Knight Larkins, received 11 January 1889; HO 144/221/A49301C, ff. 239–45 (National Archives).

19 Report by Robert Anderson, 22 January 1889; HO 144/221/A49301C, ff. 235–6 (National Archives).

20 Report by Donald Swanson, 10 October 1888, HO 144/221/A49301C, ff. 148–59 (National Archives).

21 *Daily Telegraph*, 19 September 1888.

22 *Star*, 4 October 1888.

23 *New York Times*, 6 October 1888.

24 Trevor Marriott, *Jack the Ripper: 21st Century Investigation* (London: John Blake, 2007).

25 CLRO Box 3.22 No. 358 (London Metropolitan Archives).

26 CLRO Box 3.18 No. 215 (London Metropolitan Archives).

27 HO 144/221/A449301, ff. 36, 46–7 (National Archives).

28 *The Times*, 2 October 1888.

29 Report by Sir Charles Warren, 25 October 1888; MEPO 3/141, ff. 158–9 (National Archives).

30 *Penny Illustrated Paper*, 3 August 1889; *Eastern Post*, 21 September 1889.

31 Report by Donald Swanson, 23 September 1889; photocopies of files missing since the 1970s.

32 Lyttleton Forbes Winslow, *Recollections of Forty Years* (London: John Ousley, 1910).

33 Stewart P. Evans and Keith Skinner, *Jack the Ripper: Letters From Hell* (Stroud: Sutton, 2001).

34 *Illustrated Police News*, 20 October 1888.

35 *People*, 14 October 1888.

36 *Mirror*, 29 July 1889.

37 Also *Williamsport Sunday Grit*, 12 May 1895.

38 *Pall Mall Gazette*, 1 December 1888.

39 Formed in 1903 by H. B. Irving and known unofficially as 'The Crimes Club'.

40 Samuel Ingleby Oddie, *Inquest* (London: Hutchinson & Co., 1941).

41 See Melvin Harris, *The True Face of Jack the Ripper* (London: Michael O'Mara Books, 1994).

42 O'Donnell wrote a manuscript for a book about Stephenson's candidacy as the Ripper based on the numerous stories he had heard and Stephenson's own writings. Never published, it can actually be found on JTRForums.com at http://www.jtrforums.com/forumdisplay.php?f=328.

43 Anon., 'Jack the Ripper by Aleister Crowley', n.p., article reprinted from *Sothis* magazine, vol. 1, no. 4, 1974 (Cambridge, 1988).

44 *The Times*, 18 September 1888.

45 CLRO Box 3.16 No. 150 (London Metropolitan Archives).

Chapter 11: Anecdote and Memory

1 *Sun*, 13–17 February 1894.

2 Report by Sir Melville Macnaghten; MEPO 3/140, ff. 177–83 (National Archives).

3 Druitt's mother Anne suffered from depression and paranoid delusions.

4 The fullest account can be found in the *Acton, Chiswick and Turnham Green Gazette*, 5 January 1889.

5 *Bristol Times and Mirror*, 11 February 1891.

6 *Western Mail*, 26 February 1892.

7 Major Arthur Griffiths, *Mysteries of Police and Crime* (London: Cassell, 1898).

8 *Referee*, 22 January 1899.

9 See Adam Wood, 'Copy Be Damned, That's the Original: A History of the Macnaghten Memoranda', *Ripperologist* 124 (February 2012), for a detailed analysis of the evolution and provenance of the memoranda.

10 Sir Robert Anderson, *Criminals and Crime: Some Facts and Suggestions* (London: Nisbet, 1907).

11 Alfred Aylmer, 'The Detective in Real Life,' *The Windsor Magazine*, vol. 1, no. 5 (May 1895).

12 Sir Robert Anderson, 'Punishing Crime', *The Nineteenth Century* (February 1901).

13 Sir Robert Anderson, *The Lighter Side of My Official Life* (London: Hodder and Stoughton,1910).

14 See Robert House, *Jack the Ripper and the Case for Scotland Yard's Prime Suspect* (Hoboken, N.J.: John Wiley & Son, 2011) for a most comprehensive overview of Aaron Kosminski's life.

15 Martin Fido, *The Crimes, Detection and Death of Jack the Ripper* (London: Weidenfeld & Nicolson, 1987).

16 *Pall Mall Gazette*, 24 March 1903.

17 *Pall Mall Gazette*, 31 March 1903.

18 Discovered in 1993, the 'Littlechild Letter' was purchased with other documents by Stewart Evans from antiquarian book dealer Eric Barton.

19 See Timothy B. Riordan, *Prince of Quacks* (Jefferson, N.C.: McFarland and Co., 2009).

20 A Special Branch file of Fenian activities and the Whitechapel

murders is known to exist but has not been publicly seen owing to the highly sensitive nature of the material; the file is closed indefinitely. This may include material relating to Tumblety which could shed new light on the man.

21 *New York World*, 29 January 1889.

Chapter 12: Naming Names

1 William Le Queux, *Things I Know about Kings, Celebrities and Crooks* (London: E. Nash & Grayson, 1923).

2 *People*, 26 December 1926.

3 Leonard Matters, *The Mystery of Jack the Ripper* (London: Hutchinson, 1929; W. H. Allen, 1948; Arrow, 1964).

4 *Salt Lake Herald*, 25 August 1901.

5 The manuscript was discovered in early 2008 among the effects of Sydney George Hulme-Beaman, creator of the hugely successful children's character Larry the Lamb and Toytown. See James Carnac, *The Autobiography of Jack the Ripper* (London: Transworld, 2011) for a transcript of the manuscript and analysis by Paul Begg.

6 See John Bennett, 'The Autobiography of James Carnac', *Ripperologist* 124 (February 2012) for further analysis on authorship and content.

7 *Ogden Standard Examiner*, 16 October 1888.

8 Edwin T. Woodhall, *Jack the Ripper: Or When London Walked in Terror* (London and Dublin: Mellifont Press, 1937; reprint London: P&D Riley, 1997).

9 Woodhall joined the Metropolitan Police in 1907 (warrant no. 94985). CID (Special Branch), 1910. Resigned, 1919.

10 In 1944, *Der Teufel von Whitechapel* by Graf Michael Alexander Soltikow was published in Germany. Although it dealt with

numerous other English criminal cases, it was ostensibly a piece
of anti-Semitic, anti-British propaganda.

11 Richard Whittington-Egan, *A Casebook on Jack the Ripper* (London: Wildy & Sons, 1975).

12 William Stewart, *Jack the Ripper: A New Theory* (London: Quality Press, 1939).

13 Sir Melville Macnaghten, *Days of My Years* (London: Edward Arnold, 1914).

14 Philip Sugden, *The Complete History of Jack the Ripper* (London: Robinson, 1994).

15 This report was sent anonymously to Scotland Yard along with other material – including the famous 'Dear Boss' letter – in 1987. It is in the file MEPO 3/3153 (National Archives).

16 Donald McCormick, *The Identity of Jack the Ripper* (London: Jarrold, 1959; Pan Books, 1962; Arrow, 1970).

17 Ripper episodes broadcast on 5 and 12 November 1959. These programmes have long been lost.

18 Tom Cullen, *Autumn of Terror* (London: Bodley Head, 1965; Fontana, 1966, 1973).

19 Robin Odell, *Jack the Ripper in Fact and Fiction* (London: Harrap, 1965; Mayflower-Dell, 1966; Oxford: Mandrake, 2008).

20 *London Evening Standard*, 8–12 August 1960.

21 The earliest known appearance of the term 'Ripperologist' comes in Wilson's introduction to Alexander Kelly, *Jack the Ripper: A Bibliography and Review of the Literature* (London: Association of Assistant Librarians, S.E.D., 1972).

22 Colin Wilson and Pat Pitman, *Encyclopaedia of Murder* (London: Pan Books, 1961).

23 Philippe Jullian, *Edouard VII* (Paris: Librairie Hachette, 1962); translated as *Edward and the Edwardians* (New York: Viking Press, 1962).

24 Wilson, introduction to Kelly, *Jack the Ripper*.

25 *Criminologist*, vol. 5, no. 18 (November 1970).

26 'Court Circular Clears Clarence', *The Times*, 4 November 1970.

27 UK broadcast 2 November 1970.

28 *The Times*, 9 November 1970.

29 *The Times*, 14 November 1970.

Chapter 13: Conspiracy

1 Michael Harrison, *Clarence: The Life of HRH the Duke of Clarence and Avondale (1864–1892)* (London: W. H. Allen, 1972), published in the US as *Clarence: Was He Jack the Ripper?* (New York: Drake Publishing, 1974).

2 As recorded in the *Listener*, 17 August 1972.

3 *Sunday Times*, 16 February 1975.

4 Daniel Farson, *Jack the Ripper* (London: Michael Joseph, 1972; Sphere, 1973).

5 The two detectives, played by Stratford Johns and Frank Windsor, appeared in *Z-Cars* and *Softly Softly*, which ran on the BBC from 1962 until 1978.

6 *Jack the Ripper*; BBC TV, UK broadcast 13 July–17 August 1973 (six episodes), Stratford Johns, Frank Windsor, producers: Paul Bonner, Leonard Lewis.

7 UK broadcast 17 August 1973.

8 *The Times*, 16 August 1973.

9 Donald Rumbelow, *The Complete Jack the Ripper* (London: W. H. Allen, 1975; Star Books, 1976/1981; W. H. Allen, 1987/8; Penguin, 2004; Virgin, 2013).

10 Richard Whittington-Egan, *A Casebook on Jack the Ripper* (London: Wildy & Sons, 1975).

11 Stephen Knight, *Jack the Ripper: The Final Solution* (London: Harrap, 1976).

12 Warren was made a Knight Templar in Freemasonry in 1863 and

founded the Quattuor Coronati Lodge, consecrated in 1886. It was the first Masonic lodge devoted to research into the history of Freemasonry.

13 *Sunday Times*, 18 June 1978.

14 Simon Wood's collected research material on the 'royal conspiracy theory' can be found at Tower Hamlets Local History Library and Archives.

15 Melvyn Fairclough, *The Ripper and the Royals* (London: Duckworth, 1991).

16 Fairclough suggests that the prince could have been the legendary 'Monster of Glamis', described traditionally as a horribly deformed member of the Bowes-Lyon family imprisoned in Glamis Castle.

17 *Evening Standard*, 5 December 1991.

18 *True Detective*, January 1989.

19 Peter Sutcliffe killed thirteen women, mostly prostitutes, in the north of England between 1975 and 1980. He was imprisoned for life at Broadmoor in 1981.

Chapter 14: A Crisis of Identity

1 'A New Theory on the Jack the Ripper Murders', *True Crime* (April 1982).

2 Mark Andrews, *The Return of Jack the Ripper* (New York: Leisure Books, 1977).

3 Bruce Paley, *Jack the Ripper: The Simple Truth* (London: Headline, 1995).

4 Paul Harrison, *Jack the Ripper: The Mystery Solved* (London: Robert Hale, 1991).

5 These include previously unseen mortuary photos of Nichols, Chapman and Stride and the long-missing 'Dear Boss' letter, which was returned anonymously.

6 *Weekend*, 6 August 1986.

7 James Tully, *The Secret of Prisoner 1167: Was This Man Jack the Ripper?* (London: Robinson, 1997).

8 James Kelly's criminal files in HO 144/10064 (National Archives); Broadmoor case file is in the Berkshire Record Office.

9 Melvin Harris, *Jack the Ripper: The Bloody Truth* (London: Columbus Books, 1987).

10 Paul Begg, *Jack the Ripper: The Uncensored Facts* (London: Robson, 1988), later expanded and republished as *Jack the Ripper: The Facts* (2004).

11 Adam Wood and Keith Skinner, 'Red Lines and Purple Pencil', *Ripperologist* 128 (October 2012), gives an exhaustive overview of the provenance of the book and marginalia.

12 'Has This Man Revealed the Real Jack the Ripper?', *Daily Telegraph*, 19 October 1987.

13 *Crime Monthly*; BBC TV, UK broadcast 10 August 1990.

14 *Hackney Gazette*, 10 October 1990.

15 US broadcast 1988.

16 Jean Overton Fuller, *Sickert and the Ripper Crimes* (Oxford: Mandrake, 1990, 2003).

17 Paul Begg, Martin Fido and Keith Skinner, *The Jack the Ripper A–Z* (London: Headline, 1991, 1994, 1996), updated as *The Complete Jack the Ripper A–Z* (London: John Blake, 2010).

18 Seth Linder, Keith Skinner and Caroline Morris, *Ripper Diary: Inside Story* (Stroud: Sutton, 2003).

19 Shirley Harrison, *The Diary of Jack the Ripper* (London: Smith Gryphon, 1993).

20 The Hitler Diaries were a collection of sixty notebooks allegedly containing memoirs written by Hitler between 1932 and 1945. They were proved to be forgeries, but *Stern* Magazine in Germany and *The Times* in the UK had already declared them genuine.

21 *Observer*, 25 April 1993.

22 A. P. Wolf, *Jack the Myth* (London: Robert Hale, 1993).

23 Philip Sugden, *The Complete History of Jack the Ripper* (London: Robinson, 2002).

24 Christopher Hudson, 'Playing Games with Murder Most Foul', *Evening Standard*, 25 September 1987.

25 Stewart P. Evans and Paul Gainey, *The Lodger: The Arrest and Escape of Jack the Ripper* (London: Century, 1996). Paul Gainey worked for the Suffolk Constabulary press office.

26 Bob Hinton, *From Hell . . .* (Abertillery: Old Bakehouse, 1998).

27 Paul H. Feldman, *Jack the Ripper: The Final Chapter* (London: Virgin, 1997).

28 Edited by Nick Warren and still extant.

29 Originally the *Newsletter of the Cloak and Dagger Club* (formed by Mark Galloway in 1994). The club has since been renamed the 'Whitechapel Society 1888' and publishes its own bi-monthly journal. *Ripperologist* has been an e-zine since 2006.

30 Originally edited by Christopher George. It has since been edited by Christoper-Michael DiGrazia (2001–4) and Dan Norder (2004–present).

31 Online at www.casebook.org.

32 See also 'JTRForums', hosted by Howard Brown, at www.jtrforums.com and 'Jack the Ripper Writers', Spiro Dimolanis's forum at www.ripperwriters.aforumfree.com.

33 Maxim Jakubowski and Nathan Braund (eds.), *The Mammoth Book of Jack the Ripper* (London: Robinson, 1999).

34 Stewart P. Evans and Keith Skinner, *The Ultimate Jack the Ripper Sourcebook* (London: Robinson, 2000), published in the USA as *The Ultimate Jack the Ripper Companion* (New York: Carroll and Graf, 2001).

Chapter 15: The Appliance of Science

1 Stephen P. Ryder, 'Patricia Cornwell and Walter Sickert – A Primer', www.casebook.org/dissertations/dst-pamandsickert.html, accessed 24 June 2013.

2 Matthew Sturgess, *Walter Sickert: A Life* (London: Harper Perennial, 2011).

3 Patricia Cornwell, *Portrait of a Killer: Jack the Ripper – Case Closed* (London: Little, Brown, 2002).

4 'Stalking the Ripper'; *Omnibus*, BBC TV, UK broadcast 30 October 2002.

5 *CSI: Crime Scene Investigation*; CBS, first US broadcast 6 October 2000.

6 *The X-Files*; Fox Network, US broadcast 1993–2001.

7 *Daily Mail*, 8 March 2004.

8 Marriott was a detective working for the Buckinghamshire constabulary. He joined the police in 1970.

9 Professor David Canter, *Mapping Murder: The Secrets of Geographical Profiling* (London: Virgin, 2007).

10 *Revealed – The Face of Jack the Ripper*; Channel 5, UK broadcast 21 November 2006.

11 *Daily Mail*, 20 November 2006.

12 Trow was the author of a series of books recounting the fictional exploits of Inspector Lestrade, a character originally created by Arthur Conan Doyle for his series of Sherlock Holmes stories.

13 M. J. Trow, *The Many Faces of Jack the Ripper* (Chichester: Summersdale, 1997).

14 In a conversation with the authors, Trow said that he had not intended to write a suspect-based Ripper book, but that his publishers suggested he do so.

15 M. J. Trow, *Jack the Ripper: Quest for a Killer* (Barnsley: Pen and Sword, 2009).

16 'Jack the Ripper: Killer Revealed'; Discovery Channel, broadcast 11 October 2009.

17 M. J. Trow, 'The Non-starter', *Ripperologist* 113 (April 2010).

18 *Jack the Ripper: The Definitive Story*; Channel 5, broadcast 11 and 20 January 2011.

19 Created by Jake Luukkanen.

20 Paul Begg and John Bennett, *Jack the Ripper: CSI Whitechapel* (London: André Deutsch, 2012).

21 Includes vanity publishing, print on demand and e-books. Popular outlets include Lulu, Blurb, Authorhouse and Amazon.

22 Gerry Nixon, 'Le Grand of the Strand', *Ripperologist* 16 (August 1998).

23 See Tom Wescott, 'Jack and the Grapestalk', *Ripper Notes* 25 (January 2006), and 'Le Grand: The New Prime Suspect', *Casebook Examiner* 2 (June 2010).

24 See Derek Osborne, *Ripperana* 37 (July 2001); John Carey, *Ripperana* 40 (April 2002); Michael Connor, 'Did the Ripper Work for Pickfords?', *Ripperologist* 72 (October, 2006).

25 Christer Holmgren, 'Two Murders in Buck's Row', *Ripperologist* 126 (June 2012).

26 This wartime tragedy saw the death of over 170 people during a panic-stricken rush down the stairs of Bethnal Green Underground station during an air-raid false alarm on 3 March 1943. Among the victims were Florence Lechmere (aged sixty-six); Thomas Allen Lechmere (aged sixty-six); Thomas Charles Lechmere (aged forty-three).

27 C. J. Morley, *Jack the Ripper: The Suspects* (self-published, 2011).

Chapter 16: Genesis of the Ripper

1 'The Ghost in the Ripper Machine', *Guardian*, 15 March 1988.
2 'Jack the Ripper is Back!', *East London Advertiser*, 2 May 1975.
3 There was a brief vogue for theming a pub around a particular concept, the best known being Irish-themed pubs. Closer to the Jack the Ripper is the Dr Jekyll and Mr Hyde in Edinburgh, one of four pubs with a ghoulish gothic theme run by the Eerie Pub Company, and Edinburgh also had a pub called the Burke and Hare. London boasts the Sherlock Holmes on Northumberland Avenue.
4 *East London Advertiser*, 23 October 1987.
5 Samuel E. Hudson, *Leather Apron or the Horrors of Whitechapel* (Town Printing House, 1888).
6 *Austin Statesman*, 5 September 1888.
7 *Star*, 5 September 1888.
8 See Paul Begg, 'The Conference Talks: Did Leather Apron Really Exist?', *Ripperologist* 109 (December 2009).
9 *Globe*, 10 September 1888.
10 *Star*, 11 December 1888.
11 *Irish Times*, 7 September 1888.
12 *Star*, 11 September 1888.
13 *Star*, 8 October 1888.
14 In 1884, a few doors along at 123 Whitechapel Road, Joseph Merrick, the 'Elephant Man', had been exhibited by his manager, Tom Norman.
15 *Irish Times*, 11 September 1888.
16 *Echo*, 11 September 1888.
17 *Daily Telegraph*, 29 November 1888.
18 See Mike Hawley, 'Whitechapel's Wax Chamber of Horrors, 1888', *Ripperologist* 130 (February 2013), for an examination of the exhibition and others like it.

19 *Daily News*, 1 October 1888.

20 *Birmingham Evening Mail*, 6 October 1888.

21 See Andrew Cook, *Jack the Ripper: Case Closed* (Stroud: Amberley, 2009).

22 Despite the popular image of gaslight and fog which permeates Ripper iconography today, none of the murders actually took place on a foggy night.

23 John Francis Brewer, *The Curse upon Mitre Square: A.D. 1530–1888* (Simpkin, Marshall and Co., 1888). Available as an e-book at www.hollywoodripper.com.

24 *Punch*, 29 September 1888.

25 *Evening News*, *Echo*, 11 October 1888 and others, where she is referred to as 'Mrs Sodeaux'.

26 Statement of George Hutchinson, 12 November 1888; MEPO 3/140, ff. 227–9 (National Archives).

27 *The Times*, 12 September 1888.

28 *Evening News*, 5 October 1888.

29 *Ottawa Free Press*, 21 November 1888.

30 Harold Furness (ed.), *Famous Crimes Past and Present* (London: Caxton House, 1903). The complete series on the Whitechapel murders was reprinted in one volume by Thomas Schachner in 2007, limited to fifty copies.

Chapter 17: The Lodger and Other Stories

1 *Ottawa Citizen*, 16 November 1888; *New York Herald*, 13 November 1888; *Pall Mall Gazette*, 28 November 1888; *East London Observer*, 1 December 1888; among others.

2 *Toronto Globe*, 15 November 1888.

3 Founded by Samuel McLure in 1893, it featured political and literary content, often publishing novels in serialized form as was

customary at the time. Before its demise in March 1929, it had published work by Rudyard Kipling, Robert Louis Stevenson, Jack London and Arthur Conan Doyle.

4 *Waxworks* or *Das Wachsfigurenkabinett* (Neptun-film 1924); Emil Jannings, Conrad Veidt, Werner Krauss; dir. Leo Birinsky/Paul Leni.

5 *The Lodger: A Story of the London Fog* (Gainsborough 1927); Ivor Novello, Marie Ault, 'June'; dir. Alfred Hitchcock.

6 *Pandora's Box* (Nero-film 1928); Louise Brooks, Fritz Kortner, Franz Lederer; dir. Georg Pabst.

7 *Jack the Ripper* (Paramount 1959); Ewen Solon, Eddie Byrne, Betty McDowall, dir. Robert S. Baker.

8 David 'Screaming' Lord Sutch, *Life as Sutch* (London: HarperCollins, 1991).

9 Both of which had depictions of the top-hatted Ripper emblazoned upon them.

10 *A Study in Terror* (Columbia Pictures 1966); John Neville, Donald Houston; dir. James Hill.

11 Jack the Ripper also made appearances in other popular TV series, notably *Cimarron City* (1968), *Get Smart* (1970), *Kolchak the Night Stalker* (1974), *Fantasy Island* (1980) and *Dr Who* (2011).

12 US broadcast, 22 December 1967.

13 The story was also televised in an episode of US series *Thriller*, broadcast 11 April 1961.

14 The Ripper crossed dimensions again in 1979's *Time after Time* where H. G. Wells pursues Jack to twentieth-century New York in his time machine.

15 *Dr Jekyll and Sister Hyde* (Hammer 1971); Ralph Bates, Martine Beswick, Gerald Sim; dir. Roy Ward Baker.

16 *Hands of the Ripper* (Hammer 1971); Eric Porter, Angharad Rees, dir. Peter Sasdy.

17 Originating from a one-off sketch in the TV series *Six Dates with*

Barker in 1971, the 'Phantom Raspberry Blower' serial was broadcast throughout 1976.

18 UK broadcast, 18, 25 October 1988.

19 *Murder by Decree* (Embassy 1979); Christopher Plummer, James Mason, Donald Sutherland; dir. Bob Clark.

20 Untitled news clipping, 27 October 1988 (Bishopsgate Institute Library).

21 *From Hell* (20th Century Fox 2001); Johnny Depp, Heather Graham, Ian Holm; dirs. Albert and Allen Hughes.

22 Alan Moore and Eddie Campbell, *From Hell* (1991–6); also *Dance of the Gull Catchers* (1998). Published in one volume by Knockabout Comics, 1999.

23 *The Lodger* (Stage 6 Films 2009); Alfred Molina, Hope Davis, Simon Baker, dir. David Ondaatje.

24 *Whitechapel*; ITV1, starring Rupert Penry-Jones, Phil Davis, Steve Pemberton, UK broadcast 2, 9 and 16 February 2009.

25 *The Times*, 10 February 2009.

26 *Guardian Online*, 30 December 2012.

27 Denis Miekle, *Jack the Ripper: The Murders and the Movies* (London: Reynolds and Hearn, 2002).

Chapter 18: A Question of Taste

1 Karl Berg, *The Sadist* (London: Heinemann, 1945).

2 In October 1975, Peter Samuel Cook was convicted of seven rapes and two woundings which had taken place in 1974–5, holding the city of Cambridge in a state of terror.

3 *Barbed Wire Dolls* told the story of 'prisoners in a barbaric camp of sadistic perversions' and *Violation of the Bitch* had the tag-line 'she asked for it'.

4 In 2005, it was discovered that John Humble was responsible for

the letters and tape; he was convicted of perverting the course of justice and sentenced to eight years' imprisonment.

5 *The Times*, 5 December 1980.

6 *Hackney Gazette*, 2 September 1986.

7 'Ripper Yarns Are Ripping Us Off', *Sunday Times*, 6 December 1987.

8 *City Limits*, 12–19 November 1987.

9 Described by Wayman as 'a Fagin's Den' in Paul Woods and Gavin Baddeley, *Saucy Jack: The Elusive Ripper* (Hersham: Ian Allen, 2009).

10 *East London Advertiser*, 2 May 1975.

11 *East London Advertiser*, 23 May 1975.

12 *Stage*, 19 May 1988.

13 *East London Advertiser*, 2–18 September 1988.

14 *East London Advertiser*, 23 September 1988.

15 *Hackney Gazette*, 23 September 1988.

16 *Hackney Gazette*, 30 September 1988.

17 *East London Advertiser*, undated articles (Tower Hamlets Library and Archives).

18 *East London Advertiser*, 9 December 1988.

19 *East London Advertiser*, 7 October 1988.

20 *Big Issue*, 20 July 1993.

21 Renamed the 'Whitechapel Society 1888' in 2005.

22 *Shadow of the Ripper*, broadcast on BBC2 on 7 September 1988, was an early, well-considered attempt by Sir Christopher Frayling to place the Ripper crimes in their historical and social context .

23 Finn Mackay, 'Another Jack the Ripper exhibition' (End Violence Against Women Blog, 5 June 2008).

24 Alex Werner (ed.), *Jack the Ripper and the East End* (London: Chatto and Windus, 2008).

25 Alexandra Warwick and Martin Willis (eds.), *Jack the Ripper: Media, Culture, Diversity* (Manchester: Manchester University Press, 2007).

Chapter 19: Murderland Revisited

1 *Pall Mall Budget*, 9 October 1890.
2 Record of Metropolitan Board of Works committee meetings, 1892 (London Metropolitan Archives).
3 *Toronto Daily Mail*, 27 February 1892.
4 As recorded in Samuel Ingleby Oddie, *Inquest* (London: Hutchinson & Co., 1941).
5 Tom Cullen, *Autumn of Terror* (London: Bodley Head, 1965; Fontana, 1966, 1973).
6 Philip Howard, 'In the Steps of Jack the Ripper', *The Times*, 17 August 1970.
7 'Expert in the Unusual', *The Times*, 25 January 1971.
8 *Daily Telegraph*, 27 August 1974.
9 Psychogeography is 'the study of the precise laws and specific effects of the geographical environment, consciously organized or not, on the emotions and behaviour of individuals' (Guy Debord, 'Critique of Urban Geography', *Les Lèvres Neuves*, September 1955).
10 Iain Sinclair, *White Chappell: Scarlet Tracings* (London: Goldmark, 1987).
11 *East London Advertiser*, 16 May 1996.
12 *Sunday Telegraph*, 12 May 1996.
13 *East London Advertiser*, 20 June 1996.
14 *Daily Mail*, 27 November 2007.

Index

He just wanted a decent book to read ...

Not too much to ask, is it? It was in 1935 when Allen Lane, Managing Director of Bodley Head Publishers, stood on a platform at Exeter railway station looking for something good to read on his journey back to London. His choice was limited to popular magazines and poor-quality paperbacks – the same choice faced every day by the vast majority of readers, few of whom could afford hardbacks. Lane's disappointment and subsequent anger at the range of books generally available led him to found a company – and change the world.

'We believed in the existence in this country of a vast reading public for intelligent books at a low price, and staked everything on it'
Sir Allen Lane, 1902–1970, founder of Penguin Books

The quality paperback had arrived – and not just in bookshops. Lane was adamant that his Penguins should appear in chain stores and tobacconists, and should cost no more than a packet of cigarettes.

Reading habits (and cigarette prices) have changed since 1935, but Penguin still believes in publishing the best books for everybody to enjoy. We still believe that good design costs no more than bad design, and we still believe that quality books published passionately and responsibly make the world a better place.

So wherever you see the little bird – whether it's on a piece of prize-winning literary fiction or a celebrity autobiography, political tour de force or historical masterpiece, a serial-killer thriller, reference book, world classic or a piece of pure escapism – you can bet that it represents the very best that the genre has to offer.

Whatever you like to read – trust Penguin.